GRIZZLY
Country

❧ ❧

GRIZZLY
Country

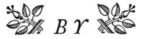 BY

ANDY RUSSELL

LYONS & BURFORD, PUBLISHERS

Lyons & Burford, Publishers
31 West 21 Street
New York, NY 10010

Cover design by Jane Treuhaft
Text photographs by Richard H. Russell and Charles Russell
Cover photograph © Kathy Dawson 1985

Published in Canada by Douglas & McIntyre Ltd.
Published by arrangement with Alfred A. Knopf, Inc.
Printed and bound in the United States of America

Library of Congress Cataloging-in-Publication Data

Russell, Andy, 1915–
Grizzly country.

Reprint. Originally published: New York: Knopf,
1967.
1. Grizzly bear.   I. Title.
QL737.C27R87   1986   599.74′446   86–57
ISBN 0-941130-12-6

10 9 8 7 6 5 4 3 2 1

TO KAY

with my love and

deep appreciation for

her great patience

Contents

Introduction to the 1986 Edition

The name of the grizzly evokes terror in many hearts; fear largely promoted by media accounts of maulings resulting in severe injury or death, when one of the big animals loses its temper for one reason or another. Books have been written about these incidents, chilling collections of stories not conducive to sound sleep in a wilderness camp in grizzly country. There are a thousand ways to get into trouble in the mountains, but few of them are as dramatic or as spectacular as a nose-to-nose confrontation with a grizzly, an animal of tremendous power and speed well armed with claws and teeth that can be terribly destructive. Strangely enough, the victim survives more often than being killed, which would seem to illustrate a desire more to drive away an intruder than to destroy him.

When my sons, Dick and Charlie, and I did the research preceding my writing of Grizzly Country and the production of the feature-length film of the same name back in 1961, '62, and '63, very little was really known of grizzly habits and character. The whole picture of the grizzly was rife with sheer myth and misinformation. My book opened a new horizon of thought and, since then, there have been uncounted scientific papers and books written following intensive field research backed up by thousands of man hours of observation and the employment of highly sophisticated equipment.

One might wonder if all this human contact and handling of bears has not had some bearing on the rash of maulings reported over the last few years, but to my knowledge no such incident has involved a bear wearing a radio collar with the exception of one, where a nuisance bear was transported by helicopter into the wilderness of Banff Park. As part of a film production, a sequence was being taken of the release by a cameraman assisted by a biologist. The bear was just recovering from being drugged and likely both men were concentrating on photography more than safety when the angry animal charged and killed the biologist.

Such men as Frank and John Craighead, Charles Jonkel, Stephen Herrero and Richard Russell along with many others have made an enormous contribution to the collection of scientific knowledge of the grizzly. It all points up to the fact that there have been some significant changes in bear-people relationships.

Perhaps the most important change is the enormously increased numbers of people using the back-country trails in our national parks. The odds of people and bears coming into contact in such places as Yellowstone National Park, Waterton-Glacier International Peace Park, Banff and Jasper, Kootenai and Yoho are greatly increased. Where there were once hundreds of people sharing the wilderness with bears, there are now millions.

Consequently, it is probable that the character of the grizzly is changing as a result, for in these confines of preserves they have largely enjoyed complete protection for generations. Through constant contact with humans, the big bears may be losing their inherent respect for man and some few may even be conditioned to look at people as possible prey.

But the learning of the bears is not all negative. Statistics still show that the odds against being hurt by a bear are well over a million to one. Recently my son, John, an experienced biologist, observed a mother grizzly with two cubs feeding on a timberline meadow in Waterton Park not far from a heavily used trail. As he watched from above on a steep mountain face, he could see a party of hikers coming up this trail toward the grizzly family. While they were still some distance away, the bear heard or smelled them, and calmly took the cubs into a small clump of scrub, where they stayed quiet in complete hiding. The hiking party walked past, within a few bounds of the bears, completely unaware of their presence. When they had disappeared around a bend of the trail, the mother and cubs went about their business with no sign of being disturbed. So in my opinion, the statistics hold good and bears are learning to accept inevitable human contact with equanimity.

If I were to rewrite *Grizzly Country*, I would not change it very much. The need for better understanding and management is still paramount. Under present regulations, hunters are the least of their problems. It is the destruction of vitally necessary wilderness habitat that is the greatest threat. Though people also need wilderness, too many are pushing to commercialize it and blindly plunder its resources. I hope that enough of us will wake up to the danger before it is too late.

Introduction

Who can say what generates the thought behind the birth of a book? For such an unlettered one as I, the conception is even more obscure. But this birth has been no less interesting in its development, even though at times it has been as acutely painful as the pangs that might be experienced by a cow moose giving birth to a sawhorse crosswise.

Certainly the choice of the grizzly bear for a subject was not difficult to come by; for ever since I first began to read sign, grizzlies have been a constant source of adventure, wonder, and entertainment. My association with them has been no fleeting thing enjoyed on special occasion; rather, grizzly country has been my country all my life—a vast reach of magnificent wilderness where the ashes of my campfires smoulder all the way from the edge of my home ranch here in southwest Alberta to the stark beauty of the mountains of central Alaska.

My early preoccupation with the thrills of hunting the occasional cattle killer and my twenty odd years experience as a professional big-game guide gave way to realization that here was a truly great and wonderful animal far different from what we supposed. I wanted to know him better. This desire was perhaps accelerated and developed by the knowledge that the days of the old-time wilderness pack-train operator with his long string of well-disciplined mountain horses was about finished. Wasteful and incredibly shortsighted exploitation of natural resources by industry was carving the wilderness into ragged ribbons. With its passing it was clearly evident that not only was the old-time mountain man almost nothing more than a character of history, but as I watched, the grizzly was being hard pressed to find the necessary environment for his continuance.

It was a sad thing to contemplate, especially for one who knew the freedom and the happiness of real mountain wilderness and had shown it to many people from all over the world; but tears of nostalgia do nothing for that being mourned. So I dropped the rifle and picked up the pen and the camera to see what could be done to save some of the fast-vanishing wilderness and thus to help, too, the grizzly that must have it to survive.

Along with my two oldest sons, Dick and Charlie, I organized and proceeded with several wilderness expeditions that took us through some twenty-five thousand miles of mountain country in western Canada and Alaska. Thus we conducted a comprehensive photographic and notebook research of the life of the grizzly bear and associated species. The photographic portion of the venture was particularly interesting. For sheer blood-stirring adventure rifle hunting couldn't hold a candle to this. At first we experienced considerable difficulty in establishing and maintaining contact with the grizzlies; but when we contrived to overcome this, we stepped through a door where the vista of possibility was purely fascinating. We were now meeting the grizzly bears on more or less equal footing and on their terms.

We filmed them as they really live, recorded their real character—tranquil almost to the point of outright laziness at times, and most certainly far different from the bloodletting and the confliction normally experienced by the hunter. Our film record was in fact so far from popular belief that it got us into some considerable difficulty, ending in forced abandonment through lack of funds. Among those viewers who saw the rough footage, hardly anyone commented on what was perhaps the most significant point made by it. This was the clearly illustrated fact that association without undue conflict is possible between men and grizzlies.

One critic connected with an organization that could have helped us tremendously, had they chosen, suggested that our pictures did not show enough real action and, in a written brief presented for our edification, that we should have filmed such things as "bears pursuing and killing young mountain goats and antelopes"! No doubt he was right, from the box-office vision of what wildlife movies should be. But how could we persuade a grizzly to kill a young goat—a thing I have never known one to do—or venture back into antelope country, where no grizzly had dared set foot for almost a hundred years? We had more trouble with men than bears!

Happily not all our efforts were so frustrating, for in the writing of this book our adventure broadened and bloomed into something very satisfying. My endeavor here is to show the true character of the grizzly and also the animal's association with humans. I do not condemn the hunter nor do I entirely condone him; I treat him as a natural predator using weapons of his own manufacture, sometimes not entirely innocent of great breaches of ethics but by no means the threat sometimes envisioned. I point out the real enemy of the grizzly as the spoiler and the waster, more interested in short range profit than long range wealth, who in his greed does more to ruin the environment so vitally necessary to the grizzly species, to say nothing of the development of our own culture and the continuance of real human happiness.

To be sure, no work such as this can be done alone. Many sympathetic people have helped tremendously in the necessary research, some directly, some indirectly. They have helped to cheer us along a difficult and rocky trail, where it sometimes seemed there was nothing to hope for, nothing but black despair to be found. To them our most grateful thanks.

To the following for material used in historical reference: *California Grizzly* by Tracey L. Storer and Lloyd P. Tevis, Jr., published by University of California Press.

Sand County Almanac by Aldo Leopold, published by Oxford University Press, Inc.

The *Journal* of Lewis and Clark.

To Dr. William A. Fuller and Mr. Keith R. D. Mundy for material gained from their paper on determination of the age of bears, *Journal of Wildlife Management.*

To Mr. Victor Cahalane and the New York Zoological Society for information gained from the paper on the population of the grizzly, cougar, and wolf.

Also my thanks to Mr. Frank Butler, retired director of the Fish and Wildlife Branch of the Government of British Columbia, and to his successor, Dr. James (Jim) Hatter, and his staff.

To Mr. J. B. (Fitz) Fitzgerald, director of the Fish and Wildlife Branch of the Yukon Territory, and to Mr. and Mrs. Joe Langevin of Dawson City.

Also a warm handshake of gratitude across the border into Alaska to the administrative staff and the Ranger Service of Mount McKinley National Park, who helped make our camera hunting there so successful.

Sincere thanks also to Canada's National Parks Branch in Ottawa and to the administration and Warden's Service of Glacier-Revelstoke National Park and Waterton Lakes National Park, where we have worked with no little enjoyment and success.

To the Glenbow Foundation and the Taplin Fund.

To my good friend Russell H. Bennett, who wrote *The Quest For Ore* (T. S. Denison and Company), from which material was gained; he also offered encouragement and cheer.

To another friend, Morris Tyler.

To my sons, Charlie and Dick, who shared the troubles and the fun and who took the illustrations used in this book with their ever-questing cameras.

My sincere gratitude to many others—some are mentioned in the book, some are not—all part of the fraternity of friends of grizzly bears.

1

GRIZZLY
Country

1. *What is* GRIZZLY *Country?*

*Man does not own the mountains
—they belong to the bear and the sheep and
all the rest—man is only a part of it.*
—BUCK DIXON

It was very early in the morning in mid-June. The stars were gone, except Venus, and night shadows lingered restively in the deeper folds among the hills and mountains. The air was cool and still, smelling of new grass, wild geraniums, and the golden blooms of Indian turnip, where the prairies sweep in close before soaring up to the saw-toothed eagle aeries along the sky.

The horse carried his head low, threading the winding trail at a fast running walk on a loose rein. Having bucked the kinks out of his frame and mine back at the corral gate a half hour earlier, he was now tending to business, his ears working to pick up the bells of the pack string scheduled to leave on the first trip of the season across the Rockies to the wilds of the Flathead River in British Columbia. He did no more than cock an ear at four big mule deer bucks, their stubs of new antlers sheathed in velvet, bounding up out of a draw in the long springy leaps so typical of their kind. When I reined him after them to the top of a lookout butte not far from Indian Springs, the red sun was just breaking over the rim of the plains to the east. On the crest the horse stopped of his own will. We stood motionless, facing the sun with only a light zephyr of wind fingering his mane and the fringes of my buckskin jacket, as we watched the new day being born.

This is something of nature's witchery, when the night goes and the day comes to the living world. Nothing matches the back of a good horse as a place to watch it. No other place but here at the foot of the Rockies, where the prairies and the mountains meet, can its awesome and beautiful display be seen and felt so well. Only on a June morning, between the last of spring and the first of summer, does it impart such a feeling of sudden-bursting life. Here the Rockies are its great backdrop, a timber-topped ridge winging it to the north and the sprawling peaks of the Great Lewis Overthrust walling it off to the south. Mountain meadows, lakes, and ageless stone couple into solid magnificence. It is a marriage of light and life, a promise and a fulfillment of that promise. While the mountains light up at first sun in deep rose, swiftly changing to gold, and all shot through with deep purple shadow, it is as though the whole universe pauses for a long, heart-stretching moment, locked in a spell of deep wonder.

Not a sound broke the stillness that morning. The horse and I stood waiting, breathless. Then he gave a long sigh; the saddle creaked under me, and a spur rowel jingled. A meadow lark burst into song and was joined by a white-crowned sparrow and a solitaire. The spell was broken. The day and the whole country jumped into wakefulness, vital and alive.

No wonder the old Plains Indians worshipped the sun, for it is the root of all life. They too were aware of this moment in the morning and made a ritual of viewing it from the brow of a hill. The sun was a simple explanation of their existence, their promise of tomorrow and their reassurance of today. For some reason wild animals also sometimes stand motionless at dawn, as though listening to the first soft music of the waking day— caught in the magic. It is a thing to ponder.

The horse lifted his head, pointing his ears at a ridge between us and the sun. Like a reincarnation of the past when black hordes covered the plains, a long line of buffalo broke from a hidden fold to feed along its crest. The big animals were shaggy in half-shed winter coats. To the south a half dozen cow elk, sleek and saddle brown in their new summer coats, came trotting out of a draw and fanned out to drink at a little lake. They were perfectly reflected in its mirror surface, until the calves suddenly went gamboling through the shallows, shattering their mothers' images. Above and farther to the right, high on the face of the mountain, white rump patches heliographed the presence of a bunch of feeding bighorn rams. Still higher a golden eagle suddenly dropped from the point of a pinnacle, plummeting down for a low level pass over the grasslands in search of a ground squirrel for breakfast.

The horse swung his head sharply to the north as a musical jingle of Swiss bells gave the other horses away. They were standing on a small bench watching something above them.

Out of a patch of aspens came a big she-grizzly with two small cubs at heel. The sun glinted on her bright silver ruff and shoulder mantle and bounced off the coats of the two small replicas bounding ecstatically behind her.

Here was the living symbol of the mountain wilderness, one giving an impression of power and royalty matched by no other. She seemed to go slowly with a certain massiveness; yet she moved with smooth grace, covering the ground with surprising speed. She stopped to investigate something, and through my glasses I saw the flash of ivory-white claws as she pawed up a bit of sod. One or the other of the cubs trailing her would discover something of fascinating interest, whereupon they would poke small inquisitive snouts into a clump of grass or flowers. Then they would gallop to catch up, carefree and happy, yet disciplined and careful not to lose sight of their big mother for a moment. Apparently she had no particular destination in mind, though she traveled steadily, angling up toward a saddle where the ridge butted into the mountain.

She had the bearing of a monarch. In the old days, when unbroken wilderness stretched from here to Lake Winnipeg and the Mississippi Valley, the grizzly's kingdom was as vast as that wilderness. The grizzly was then king of all animals across the thousands of miles of his range. The big bears ate berries and buffalo meat along the Saskatchewan, the Missouri, and the Yellowstone. They wandered the country drained by the Colorado and the Rio Grande. They fed on the pine nuts and oak mast in the sierras of Arizona, Nevada, New Mexico, old Mexico, and California. They caught salmon in the tributaries of the Snake and the Columbia. They ranged from the parched mountains of the south to the frozen, barren prairies of the arctic, from the Midwest to the beaches of the Pacific Ocean.

But when the white man came to plow the sod and kill the buffalo, this wilderness largely disappeared forever. The grizzly range shrank as the big animals were harried and decimated, running for the first time from any animal, the only one ever to challenge them successfully in their environment. More cautious and much less numerous, those that remained forted up in the mountain fastnesses of the west and north, never to venture far out onto the plains again.

This was the edge of the wilderness, where I sat my horse, comparatively untouched by man save for the fence built as a sort of repentant afterthought to enclose the buffalo. Because it is wilderness protected within the boundaries of Waterton Lakes National Park, this southwest corner of Alberta is still grizzly country, and always will be grizzly country if the principles of national parks are guarded well.

Watching the mother grizzly top out on the saddle, it was evident that the female knew where safe haven lay; for had she traveled as many minutes in the opposite direction, she would have been in ranching country. There she would not be welcome, and her appearance would likely spark someone to shoot first and ask questions afterward.

But there is plenty of grizzly country in the mountains—country that is high, wild, and rugged, a place where birds and streams and wind still blend in a song of the wilderness that lifts and falls in a cadence of freedom as sweet as life and as old as time among the proud gnarled trees and the rocky pinnacles.

That same wind blows across the plains to the east; the

same waters flow down the valleys there, and the birds still nest and sing in the coverts. But there the song of freedom is muted now. It is not grizzly country any more. It is man country. The grizzly I watched knew it, and she was teaching her cubs by following the sun back into the wild fastnesses among the peaks.

✿

It was mid-June and the middle of the morning high on a sprawling icefield among the Selkirk Mountains of British Columbia. The sun was clear and hot, lighting up a dazzling world among high peaks rearing their fangs like upturned teeth against a brilliant sky, above a rolling sea of mist filling the valley floors to treeline. This is a country where the scale of things is lost in the hugeness and the distance, seeming now like another planet, cut off from the world of men lost in the mist below.

It seemed lifeless too, but then out of a fold in the oceans of snow atop the millenniums of ice, there came a colossal bear—a great boar grizzly. Eight feet he must have been from nose to tail, and weighed perhaps eight hundred pounds. Four weeks out of den, he had burned away most of the left-over fat from the accumulation of the previous season, although he still carried a full winter coat of fur. It was glossy black on his legs and belly, with a bluish silver overcast on his back and flanks that lightened almost to white across his face. His roach was deep, curling forward under his jaw like a beard. His ruff was heavy and thick, almost hiding his dark-colored, rounded ears.

Like a king stalking arrogantly across the raised dais of an immense throne room, he moved in long strides as though he owned the place, which indeed he did; for it was locked away from all but the most venturesome of men. These few were intruders and knew it in their puny efforts to scale these cathedral spires. Like a king he came, made puny too among the towering peaks and glittering blue icefalls, where glaciers spill over cliffs; but he cared not. He was passing through, hungry and possessed of a driving urge. A full twenty miles over high snow he had come since dawn, crossing the range along this ancient bear road, which had no marks and showed no signs of passing except his big, long claw tracks on the slushy surface.

Then he came down across a vast, gently dipping incline to the rim of a great glacial cirque—a snowy bowl carved from solid rock by ages of ice, with one side missing where the valley ran out through a break in the mountains. He stood on the lip of the rim, where a huge snow cornice had broken off, looking down into the head of the Illacillowaet River. His nose was working the warm thermal draft lifting up the unbroken snow slopes—smells of budding spruces, tumbling waters, wet earth, and many things diluted by the distance smothered in the mist. His urge prodded him. He did not follow the dignity expected of such a one. He spurned the step by step descent, abandoned the role of king and reverted to that of clown: he sat on his broad rump and slid. Going at a speed close to a free fall on the almost perpendicular slope, he skidded sideways and lost his balance but did not care. He went with his tail leading his nose, the wind whistling between his ears. He somersaulted clean over, rolling one way and then the other like a drunken sailor on a greased chute, polishing his belly and then his back. He went on a wind-tearing, joyous plunge, daring catastrophe on the naked rocks below as carefree as a cub, until swallowed up in the mist. Even though the slope was easing, he was still going fifty miles an hour straight for a broken boulder field recently bared by melting snow. The distance to a shattering collision was closing fast, when he came up on his feet in one smooth easy-flowing motion to set his claws and skid to a stop scant feet from a giant boulder. Casually he stepped up on this, once more the regal presence.

Now the wind carried stronger messages for his keen nose to separate and pigeon-hole in their proper mental files. One of these electrified him, and he gave a long sniff that sounded like a wide silk sash being torn sharp and clean in two. He sprang off the boulder and galloped across the broken rock down past the frothing source of a cataract roaring from the bowels of the mountain. He skidded down across wet glacial clay flanking a terminal moraine to hit a faint trail at full speed. It led him down another thousand yards to where the first flower-strewn meadows lay along the mist-shrouded creek.

He paused in a timberline fringe to read the wind again. Out in the middle of a meadow, her magnificent wheat-blond coat glistening with drops of moisture, was a she-grizzly, belly-deep in glacier lilies. A weird, moaning call from him brought her up to a full stand on her hind feet as she peered in his direction. He came striding out toward her, and she came down on four feet again, making a dry coughing sound punctuated with sharp, jarring snaps of her teeth. Her scent excited him, tingling in his nose and roiling his blood; for she was coming into heat.

As he closed the distance, she gave a deep warning growl dripping with menace, which he ignored. He did not slack his stride or speed it up, but came on with all the inevitable purpose of an avalanche. She swung away, then paused, and pivoted into a flashing charge. With great casualness he stopped, standing alert like a bear carved from stone. At the last moment she skidded to a stop, and they sniffed noses with certain ceremony.

Whatever passed between them was of mutual favor; for when she swung away, he followed, and they began to feed across the meadow, gulping great mouthfuls of lilies—root, stem, leaves, and bloom. As the sun burned through the thinning mist, she led the way down over a patch of broken boulders past a fall.

There the she-grizzly almost stepped on a feeding marmot. It squealed in terror and dived for its hole. As quick as light she jumped to head it off, missed with a swinging paw that turned the little animal back straight into the jaws of the male. It was dead in one swift crunch. In almost unbroken motion he pinned it down with a front foot and tore it apart in one jerk. Rumbling a warning in his throat, he gulped hot flesh, intestines streaming from his jaws like ribbons. She squatted on her haunches and watched hungrily, not daring to challenge for a share.

The mating ritual of grizzlies is fraught with much footwork, the female always moving ahead and keeping well out of reach during the preliminary courtship. Such traveling may take them miles in a very short time at a walk, lope, or gallop; yet it may cover a comparatively small piece of country. Thus it was with this pair; for even as they fed, he was the enduring, implacable pursuer and she the constant desire that kept him on the move.

The mist was gone. The day was hot under a faultless sky. The streams rose with the hours, filling the mountains with their rushing roar as snow melted faster and faster to feed water into their channels. The grizzlies suffered in their heavy coats, but their restlessness drove them like a goad.

The female remained aloof. She would have liked to lie up in the deep cool shade, but the male was pressing. As yet not ready to accept him, she kept her distance. It was mid-afternoon when they came to a pocket full of water on top of an old moraine at the base of an avalanche track. She walked out into it belly deep to lie down, while the male sagged down with a great whoosh of expelled breath a few steps to the side. For a while they wallowed luxuriously, content in the soothing coolness. But when the male roused himself to move toward her, she swung a sharp blow against his shoulder. They reared briefly to trade haymakers like great, furry boxers, until he pushed her over and lunged to mawl her. With a gurgling roar of sudden fury she chopped a deep notch in one of his ears and broke away.

They prowled again, zigzagging all over the alder-strewn slope of the avalanche track. Time and again he pressed her closely, but she always moved away. Finally the heat drove them into the heavy timber at the side of the snow-swept strip, and they disappeared into the cool secret places beneath the towering spruces.

※

It was high noon in midsummer near the edge of a lake in the subarctic country among the Alsek Mountains of western Yukon Territory. We sat with our backs propped against our packboards, munching nuts and raisins, pondering the disadvantages of being our own pack horses, and resting our tired feet. We watched a couple of moose in some scrub willow and birch on the edge of a swamp across the lake. Both were cows, a big mature animal and a younger one, perhaps a two-year-old. As they fed on tender new growth on top of the bushes, their big ears worked back and forth constantly and their great flat noses swung.

Behind them my glasses picked up another movement. From the foot of a steep-pitched alder hell at the base of the mountain behind them a tawny-brown grizzly emerged, mooching along in the carefree way of a grizzly that lives undisturbed in a vast wilderness and has nothing more to do. He was bulging with berries; for huckleberries hung by the ton that season on bushes growing among the alders all over the country. He came threading down across the lazy loops of a little stream that embroidered the swamp, and suddenly the smell of moose came to his nose. He froze, digesting this news and obviously interested. He had been indolent. He was still indolent when he moved again—but now it was a mask, a study of deliberately misleading indifference.

Soft-footed in the deep spongy moss, he stalked the moose. He was devious and patient, making use of available cover and the wind. He made no more noise than a terrier walking across the deep pile of a Persian carpet. The moose, busy with their feeding and depending on ears and noses to warn them of any impending peril, were completely unaware of his presence. The grizzly reached a screening bush twenty yards from them, where he stopped to look them over. Both animals had their rumps to him and their heads down, completely vulnerable to attack.

Absolutely out of character with the impending drama, the grizzly suddenly sprang toward them, but stopped abruptly with a clatter in the midst of a clump of scrub birch. There he stood with head up and ears cocked, the picture of a bearish practical joker. The mooses' reaction was instantaneous and utterly satisfactory. They both leaped straightaway, looking back over their shoulders, and practically fell on their faces in the lake with a great splash. Another plunge put them in swimming depth heading for the opposite shore at top speed.

Meanwhile the grizzly proceeded sedately out onto the beach and took a drink, as though that was all he had had in

mind in the first place. Then he lay down and rolled luxuriously
on his back in the sand, wallowing and scrubbing from end to
end, waving his paws in the air. He jumped up and made a swift
circle, like a pup chasing its tail, and then hopped up on a big
driftwood log. The trunk led him on a gentle incline to the bone
white roots that propped it at the butt. Grasping a root with his
paws, he worried it aimlessly for a while. Suddenly he left off to
leap down onto the beach and plunge into the lake in the wake of
the vanishing moose.

On reaching the far side he emerged with a rush into a
scattering of spruces as though suddenly reminded of a pressing
engagement across the range for which he was two days late.
Appearing and disappearing among folds of ground and clumps
of scrub, he ran through and over and not around much of anything. With no apparent intent he again goosed the moose almost
out of their wits, but he paid them no heed. He was in a hurry.

He came to the foot of an almost perpendicular water-cut
gully on the lower face of the mountain. It swallowed him, only
to spit him out again at the top as though it could not stomach
his restlessness. Now he was up on the alpine tundra, climbing
at a lope across the multicolored carpet of arctic willow, moss,
and flowers where hundreds of parka squirrels played. They
reared ahead of him to bark shrilly and spring for their holes.
Behind him they poked up cautious heads to look and bark
again. But he lingered not.

When we last saw him, he was a distant dot high on a
saddle athwart the range between two domes of solid limestone.
He was skylined momentarily, still going at a long gallop, and
then he dropped from sight.

What motivated his exodus will forever remain a mystery.
We were the only humans within miles, and the wind had not
given us away. Perhaps the sudden memory of a berry patch on
the other side of the mountains moved him in its direction.
Maybe he was just a bear so saturated with a feeling of great joy
that he could not resist taking a run.

It was September dusk in the midst of the great rain forest on the bank of the Neschamps River at the foot of the high, incredibly rough coastal range of British Columbia. For the first time in three days and nights it was not raining. We stood hunched up around a smoky fire built against the huge trunk of a fallen spruce. Behind us our silk tent was pitched beneath the wide-spreading limbs of a giant spruce, which wept unrythmically on the roof. The river ran by a few steps beyond, fast and quiet, its flood aswim with driftwood. Across the river the mountain slope dropped steeply into the valley, wrapped in heavy timber and with its peaks lost in swirling wracks of rain and fog.

There was no sound apart from the eternal dripping, the occasional splash of broaching salmon, and the sullen hiss of our discouraged fire. Across the river I saw a drooping willow shake and shake again, as though some big thing stirred behind the wall of green. We moved quietly to the river bank to watch.

Out on a spit of sand almost awash in the flood stepped a grizzly, all brown and gold in the twilight. He paused with paw uplifted like a pointer dog on birds, then stepped out to the very end of the spit. Although no ripple gave its presence away and no part of it could be seen beneath the milky surface of the water, the bear casually thrust his head into the river and came up with a great spring salmon in his jaws. He walked back into his jungle, and for a while we heard occasional slurping noises of feeding.

Again the grizzly appeared on the spit. Again he paused as though reading the mysteries of the river. This time he turned to splash upstream beneath an overhanging canopy of willows and alders. Once again he reached down and clamped his teeth on a flapping salmon. The bear took this fish to a tiny gravel bar, put a foot on its head, and tore out its belly with one sweep of his jaws. He ate the piece with relish and then headed upstream once more to vanish into the forest, leaving the rest of the fish untouched.

The dripping stage of nature's theater was empty. We stood small and insignificant in this vast, savage place, where the death of fish is a thing to be seen and felt all day and all night—a drama inevitably accompanying the hordes of migrating salmon, a spectacle to make men wonder.

❦

It was dawn among the starkly beautiful mountains of Mount McKinley National Park, near the head of the Toklat River in central Alaska. Dawn, or what goes for dawn in a country never really dark in summer. Divided by wide flats of alluvial gravel, all flanked by the rich green roll of tundra, the tips of the high peaks draped in ice and snow were a deep rose. Above all others towered the regal, gold-capped frozen crown of Denali, or Mount McKinley, king of all the mountains of all the continent.

A limping caribou bull came along a steep slope flanking the river, for some reason spurning the easier going on the flats below. He was lame in a hind foot. Miles back along his trail fate had crossed him up while going over a mountain pass along the migration route. It had only been a minor slip, but his hind foot had encountered a sliver of stone imbedded in the ice, which cut away a dew claw like a knife. It hung now on a dirty flap of skin. Thus by a moment of mischance the bull was relegated from the mass of the robust to the cripples trailing behind the herd. As such he became a faster moving link in the wilderness chain of life.

Coming behind him, a bit above and downwind, was a lone gray timber wolf. The wolf was not pursuing in the true sense of the word; he was merely accompanying the unsuspecting bull, seemingly dallying with the life he planned to take. Perhaps he knew the country so well that he was just waiting for an opportune place to take his kill with ease.

A half mile of slope fell behind the caribou. Then he came to a steep defile where his path crossed a talus slope cut by the deep watercourse of a snarling stream. There were narrow trails crossing here at different levels, cut into the loose slide-rock by the passing hoofs of sheep and caribou. The bull followed a lower one out onto precarious footing. The wolf speeded up and took a higher one up behind a screening rock outcrop. He pulled up even with his quarry and suddenly cut down in long easy bounds. Before the bull caribou could more than start to make a jump, the wolf had him by the flank. The lurching, wild-eyed jump threw the caribou off its feet, and it rolled down into the stream in a great clattering cartwheel of antlers and legs among the jagged rocks. The bull landed hard on his back, trapped by his widespread, velvet-covered antlers twisted beneath his loin in the stones. With hardly a break in stride the wolf came after him, grimly ripping and tearing.

The wolf killed by simply eating the life away from his victim. A link in the natural food chain of the country had been joined, cruel and deadly, but nonetheless the fate of most living things in nature's pattern. When the wolf left off his feeding to swing away at a long trot across the tundra flats, his belly swayed with its load of meat.

Behind him hot blood still oozed from the torn carcass of the caribou, and a burly grizzly came following his nose upwind. His coat was faded to a pale yellow and hung in rags that gave him the look of a king burlesquing as a beggar. He came as surely as though led by a string to claim the dead bull as his own. The wolf did not know it yet, but he had just made a contribution to the tribe of ursus, and another link in the food chain had been forged.

The location of the kill in the confines of the gully did not suit the bear, so he picked up the carcass by the neck to half drag and half carry it up onto a small grassy bench jutting out above. Without preamble he began to eat, voraciously tearing off great mouthfuls of meat and gulping them down.

Two cheeky magpies sloped in to parade around him with beady-eyed interest, flirting their long jaunty tails. The grizzly fed on, oblivious of the birds. As though drawn by a magnet, three more magpies arrived in long swoops and added their saucy chatter. Occasionally one would hop close to grab a tidbit. The bear suddenly lunged at them, slapping with big paws at places recently empty of magpie and scattering them in much excited squawking. No sooner did he return to feed than they were back sharing his meal. The chain had grown by another link.

Finally, when completely sated, the grizzly lay down beside his hijacked booty like a great dog, his nose resting on his forepaws, loafing and guarding the kill before getting at the job of burying it, as is the way of grizzlies.

All this is grizzly country. It is as big as all the mountains; it is the wild outdoors; and it is full of beauty and drama. These vignettes so swiftly told are but a few of the moments of action in a great story seen in the signs and sight of animals across the wilds of Alberta, British Columbia, Yukon Territory, and Alaska in nearly forty years of wandering the wilderness as a hunter, professional guide, trapper and nature photographer. Like the grizzly following his nose through life from one interesting smell to another, I too have wandered foot-loose and fancy-free, my feet pointed only by curiosity to see what lay over the next hill and mountain ridge.

My original matter-of-fact acceptance has deepened into a greater appreciation of wilderness and those creatures that must have it to stay alive. Like the grizzly, with which I share a great and abiding need, I call it home. We have forted up together to try to hold a bit of it for our children to enjoy.

As surely as the sun rises tomorrow morning, grizzly country is wilderness country, and he cannot live without it. Man, through most of his recent evolution from primitive to present-day civilization, has chosen to fight the wilderness blindly, attempting to break nature to his needs, at war with it and sometimes mercilessly destroying the very things he needs the most. The grizzly can show us something of what it means to live in harmony with nature.

"Wilderness is the raw material out of which man has hammered the artifact called civilization," said Aldo Leopold. But now much of what is wilderness is gone, and there is no need to fight what is left. If we are to preserve a portion of the raw material from which we have gained so much, the time has come to recognize its many values as they stand. To come to some understanding of the grizzly is to know some of the aesthetic, scientific, recreational, and wildlife merits of wilderness—of the utmost importance to man.

2. *Portrait of a* GRIZZLY

Next to the apes and monkeys,
I regard bears as the most
demonstrative of all wild animals.
—WILLIAM T. HORNADAY

There are two major species of bears on mainland North America; the black bear and the grizzly. The black bear differs considerably from the several subspecies of grizzly. The fur is shorter and of more uniform length; the claws of the front feet are semi-retractable and about the same length as those of the hind feet; and there is some difference in tooth structure. Generally speaking, the black bear is smaller, although some individuals grow to a size equal to a medium-sized grizzly. The predominant feature of the grizzly is the shoulder hump, which makes it stand somewhat taller at the shoulder than does the black bear, which has a more pronounced forehead and a shorter muzzle than does the grizzly. A black bear's track in soft ground or wet snow shows claw indentions just ahead of the toe marks; while the forepaws of the grizzly leave sharp claw marks two and a half to four inches in front. The feet of the black bear are also smaller.

Since I first became interested in following the trails of a naturalist, I have read everything coming to hand in order to gather some formal knowledge of the animals found in our mountains. Back in the initial stages of my search I acquired a paper written by Dr. C. Hart Merriam, who was chief of the Bureau of Biological Survey, United States Department of Agriculture, for many years, and I almost gave up in despair. In his intensive and prolonged studies of grizzlies he had classified eighty-four species—my backyard grizzly had more kissing cousins than a Kentucky colonel!

Merriam was totally preoccupied with identification through variations of skull structure; so much so, it became evident that a grizzly mother with two cubs could represent three species in one family. What he failed to realize or to acknowledge was that most animals including man have definite variations of skull contour and size even among closely related individuals. If there are eighty-four species of grizzly, then there must be a host of species within the immediate families of goats, mountain sheep, caribou, elk, etc., found in North American ranges. Merriam persuaded himself by clinging to the belief that hybridization among animals is rare; he wrote: "One of the unlooked-for results of the critical study of American bears is the discovery that the big bears, like mice and other small mammals, split up into a large number of forms whose ranges in some cases overlap so that three or more species may be found in the same region." Like all who follow a trail of research, Dr. Merriam found himself handicapped by what can be done in one man's lifetime and became so wrapped up in his fascination of bears that he did not have the time to modify his conclusions, even if he had so wished. Being a dyed-in-the-wool scientist but also being subject to human frailty, he might have been understandably reluctant to abandon a theory of lifetime standing. Regardless, I was in a quandary clear over my head.

Then a discovery of some consolation was made. My discomfiture had undoubtedly been experienced by others of more notable achievement, for when H. E. Anthony prepared his *Field Book on North American Mammals*, he gave up trying to separate Merriam's classifications and settled for eleven species of grizzly and seven of Alaska brown bear—still bad enough for the struggling student, but a great deal better.

Grizzly bears mind their own business, and usually, as at top, they are as docile as grazing stock cattle. Indeed, in the top picture, the two bears are grazing tender grass shoots. When disturbed (below) the grizzly might look docile, but he could charge the next moment, as this one indeed did at point-blank camera range.

In the northern part of the range, grizzly country includes the caribou. They sometimes come in great migrating herds, here crossing the McKinley River bars.

Merriam was one of the cult known as "splitters," while Anthony led the revolt of the "lumpers"—two factions in biological classification that have been at war for many years. I am strongly in favor of the latter, for the sake of simplifying the textbooks if nothing else. Why deluge the student with a myriad hairsplitting classifications, many of which do not agree, when there are so many things of far greater importance to study? Let us recognize the Alaska brown bear, the mountain grizzly, and the small grizzly of southern arid regions as the three major subspecies formally known as Ursus arctos.

The Alaska brown bear, which even most "lumpers" agree to separate, is classified as Ursus middendorffi, an oversized product of a country with a shorter hibernating period due to milder climate and an abundance of excellent feed. Somewhere along their complicated way, the "splitters" failed to inform the big brown coastal bears that they are not supposed to interbreed with ordinary grizzlies. For when a boar Alaska brown bear meets a handsome lady of the latter extraction on the edge of his range, he does not pause to thumb through the social register before taking her for a mate. Coming from a country of much severer climate and harder living in the high mountains, she will be smaller, but she smells just as sweet. Resulting offspring will not be sterile and may come in large, medium, or small sizes according to the whims of chromosomes and genes, environment of her choice, and virtues of motherhood. Who can possibly identify them as one thing or another?

The Boone and Crockett Club, that venerable and much respected association that keeps the trophy records for North American sportsmen, has had a try at it. Somewhat dismayed by the fact that some outside skulls were showing up in grizzly competitions, they came to the conclusion that either some unscrupulous sportsmen and their publicity-conscious guides were smuggling brown bear skulls into grizzly ranges, or Alaska brown bears wandered a good deal farther inland than was originally supposed. So they set up an arbitrary line to be recognized in all future competitions.

According to Boone and Crockett Club regulation, all

bears east of the summit of the Alaska Range are true grizzlies, while all those west of the Range are Alaska brown bears. This puts a large part of what is mountain grizzly range into brown bear category, for the line is hundreds of miles inland in most places.

The sportsman hunting the top of the Alaska Range is treated to seeing the phenomenon of a so-called "brown bear" walking up a pass from the west and instantly being converted by the magic of topography into a common, ordinary grizzly. If the pass happens to be miles long and as flat as a billiard table, the sportsman is further confounded, for then the only person capable of identifying the bear is a graduate topographical surveyor. If they choose to take the bear for a trophy in such a place, certainly the sportsman and his guide are placed in the comic-opera roles of Kipling's Ethiopian and the leopard when they catch the giraffe in the dark of the darkest jungle. They do not know what they have got, and for that matter neither does the Boone and Crockett Club.

The same brand of nonsense occurs farther south, where Alaska brown bear range, according to the latest handbook and field guide on North American mammals, stops abruptly at the southern tip of the Alaska panhandle. There is ground for doubt that these bears wear a trademark reading "Made in Alaska, Patent Pending." At some risk of sending Alaska chambers of commerce into tizzies of consternation and discrediting excellent authority, I have seen bears on the British Columbia coast only 250 miles north of Vancouver that are classified by the experts—even the Boone and Crockett Club—as grizzlies, yet have every characteristic of Alaska brown bears. I have compared skulls side by side. To my unexpert eyes they look exactly alike, give or take a bit in average size. Why shouldn't they look alike? All these coastal grizzlies live in almost identical environment.

To conclude this confusion, it would appear that the separations of classification are merely the hocus-pocus inventions of men, so far as the grizzlies are concerned. As the old mountain man said, "It looks like so much smoke up the creek to me. A grizzly is a grizzly no matter if he comes from Alaska or Wyoming and it's a good bet they don't act much different in either place."

Grizzly range is much less than it was 150 years ago, but it still covers a fair portion of the continent. It reaches across the north from the Alaska coast to the east side of the MacKenzie River Basin in the Northwest Territories. To the south it takes in most of British Columbia and the western edge of Alberta. There is an isolated population in the Swan Hills region northwest of Edmonton, Alberta. Still farther south grizzly range tapers out through Idaho, Montana, and Wyoming to a final tiny pocket in Colorado. There is still a sprinkling of grizzlies in the remote fastnesses of the Cascade Range of Washington—probably wanderers from Canada. Far south in the Chihuahua country of Mexico there is a remnant of the small, desert, mountain-type grizzly.

A preliminary study of grizzly, cougar, and wolf populations of North America was carried out by Victor H. Cahalane beginning in spring 1962 with the assistance of the New York Zoological Society. Because of the scope and rugged nature of the territory, along with the characteristics of these animals, this could only be an estimate carried out systematically by questionnaires circulated among biologists attached to wildlife services in the United States, Canada, and Mexico. Many other reliable sources were also used. The resulting information was carefully analyzed and averaged. The subsequent report was published recently by the New York Zoological Society, and it is doubtless the most accurate and up-to-date of its kind.

In Canada grizzly population in the British Columbia-Yukon area, where they are believed to be distributed fairly equally, runs from 5,000 to 7,000 animals on each side of the separating boundary. Alberta and the Northwest Territories share the remainder about equally, with 850 to 1,000 animals in each. Total grizzly population in Canada is estimated variously at 11,000 "or more" up to 18,850 animals.

While at first glance it might appear that the grizzly population is adequate for safety over most of the range, the Cahalane report is based on somewhat slippery footing. Because of the size of the country involved and the extremely limited amount of comprehensive survey work carried out over it, especially in the north, much guesswork is involved.

For instance, in the two million odd square miles of grizzly country in the Northwest Territories there is rarely more than one or two biologists in continuous residence, and these are occupied with many things apart from grizzlies. It is very doubtful that there are more than 500 grizzlies in the MacKenzie River drainage, which means that an annual kill of 35 or 40 will, along with natural losses, put the tundra grizzly of this region in danger.

There are two full-time fish and wildlife officers residing in the Yukon Territory taking care of more than a quarter million square miles of mountainous game country. They have the help of a scattering of forestry officers and Royal Canadian Mounted Police on a part-time basis for law enforcement and whatever surveys are conducted.

In the huge Cassiar country of northern British Columbia there is even less official weight. In 1963, when we were last through that region, there was one game officer stationed at Fort Nelson. His territory reached from the Alberta border west to the Alaska panhandle.

Any surveys of game numbers in these areas have very likely been carried out largely from desk chairs.

Grizzly population is thought to be static in Alberta and British Columbia but decreasing in the Yukon. The tundra grizzly of the Northwest Territories was considered at the time of the survey to be increasing, with its range expanding over past years to a line running due south of Coronation Gulf.

This encouraging increase was without doubt due to the careful protection instituted by the Wildlife Branch of the federal government in Ottawa. But late in 1963, the Territorial Commission passed an order in council countermanding protection law. This was done in spite of strong recommendations to the contrary by officers of the Wildlife Branch. The excuse used was "to protect human life." With two million square miles of potential grizzly range in the territory, it is hard to understand how eight hundred to a thousand grizzlies could be threatening the safety of the sparse human population; but as almost always happens, the considerations of politics overrode common sense where wildlife conservation is concerned.

Grizzly numbers in the United States, excluding Alaska, are estimated between 500 and 1,000, with the former number more nearly correct. Most of these are in Yellowstone and Glacier National Parks, with 50 or less in Idaho, possibly 10 bears in Washington, and an equally minute number in Colorado.

Far to the south some 25 grizzlies still exist in Chihuahua, protected by the Republic of Mexico. The fate of these grizzlies is riding a thin edge, for poaching is well-nigh impossible to stop completely, and there are also possibilities of "accident" in modern land management. For instance, as reported by the U. S. Department of the Interior's Advisory Board on Wildlife Management on March 9, 1964, "some 1080 poison distributed by the Pan-American Sanitary Bureau (through a co-operative arranged with the [Fish and Wildlife Service]) for use in the northern states of Mexico is known to have killed several grizzly bears from the small surviving remnant in the Sierra del Nido, Chihuahua. These are the last surviving grizzlies in arid southwestern North America."

This occurred in spite of repeated assurances by those who recommend poison in predator control that 1080 mixed in sufficient quantity to kill wolves and coyotes will not kill a larger animal like a bear. It makes one wonder how many grizzlies have been destroyed by the use of this poison in wolf control campaigns carried out in Canada and Alaska over past years. Poison baits are dropped from aircraft on river and lake ice in winter, presumably as a safety measure to keep other animals from getting them. However in northern latitudes lake ice does not usually go out until after the bears come out of den. On May 21, 1959, I crossed Kluane Lake in western Yukon by dog team over ice three to four feet thick. Certainly no grizzly smelling such a bait, which they can do at considerable range, would hesitate to go to it. Furthermore poisoned wolves will sometimes go miles before 1080 kills them, and such carrion is readily eaten by grizzlies in the spring.

In Alaska the total grizzly population including brown bears is presently estimated to be 17,000 to 18,000 animals.

In the whole North American continent this places the total number at 28,525 to 37,525 animals.

This is a reasonably safe figure, and the grizzly is not in danger on most of its range. But the encroachment of industry proceeds everywhere. In critical portions of range there is not the slightest room for complacency or blundering, either political or otherwise. How Washington, Montana, and Wyoming can countenance an annual open season is beyond understanding. I cheer the memory of Aldo Leopold, who said: "There seems to be a tacit assumption that if grizzlies survive in Canada and Alaska, that is good enough. It is not good enough for me. Relegating grizzlies to Alaska is about like relegating happiness to heaven; one may never get there."

Grizzly cubs are born in the wintering den in January. The newborn young are surprisingly small and helpless to be offspring of such a large and vigorous animal. At birth they are blind and relatively hairless. I have seen the skin of one cub taken shortly after birth; it was about the size of a muskrat pelt and covered with very short, fine fur. Its mother was killed at the den in the Swan Hills region of Alberta by a trapper who took the cub home alive to show his family, and then killed it. This pelt is in the possession of Al Oeming, owner of the famous Alberta Game Farm.

By the time the cubs emerge with their mothers from den, they have grown prodigiously and weigh from twenty to twenty-five pounds. Their coats have also developed into thick glossy fur up to one and a half inches deep. I once weighed a cub killed in early May. Either it had become lost, or its mother had been killed, for it was in very poor condition. It tipped the beam at an even eighteen pounds.

The taking of this cub is worthy of mention, for it illustrates the inherent courage of the grizzly. We were sitting around the table enjoying a noonday meal on a visit to the ranch of my father and mother in spring 1946, when we were suddenly disturbed by an outburst of cackling from mother's pet bantam hen. Instantly assuming some predator was attacking her pet, which was nesting "wild" in some willows in a coulee not far from the kitchen door, mother flew to the rescue. Very promptly she came flying back through the door, exclaiming about a bear. My brother John and I grabbed rifles off a convenient rack and ran out to investigate. Jumping to the conclusion that only a black bear would be brash enough to wander up to a ranch house door in broad daylight at high noon, we ran down into the bottom of the coulee by a spring. At that moment the ranch collie dog ran past us into a tangle of willows and promptly came out again pursued by an absolutely furious little grizzly, bawling and wailing as only a grizzly cub can. We immediately expected the wrathful arrival of its mother coming to the rescue and were in a most undesirable spot to meet her. For several long moments we held our cocked rifles poised for a real gunsmoke mix-up at very short range, but no big grizzly showed up.

In the meantime the cub and the dog had tangled tooth and claw and were rolling end over end, biting, scratching, snarling and yowling in a most horrendous free-for-all in a washout by the spring. John grabbed the dog by the tail and hauled him out of the melee, but the cub, wild with rage, came right after him. At some expense of hide and clothes we managed to separate the battlers and lock the cub in a granary. Unfortunately the dog had torn the cub's throat, and the tiny warrior was slowly bleeding to death through a small perforation of the jugular vein. With regret and reluctance we killed him. Neither John nor I will ever forget the fire and spirit displayed by that small, half-starved grizzly.

Mother grizzlies keep their cubs with them until their second or third summer before breeding again. In the northern tundra country of Alaska, Dr. Adolph Murie is convinced that they rarely if ever breed before the third spring following their emergence from den with new cubs. If there was ever a man who could be considered thoroughly qualified to make such an observation, it is Adolph Murie, whose wide experience in the north plus many years as chief biologist of Mount McKinley National Park places him as the all-time authority on Alaskan grizzly bears. My observations there are much more limited, but they support his affirmations. So, while females will breed at an age of two and a half years in southern ranges and possibly reproduce every third year thereafter, in northern ranges this age limit is extended to three and a half years and new cubs are born four years apart. Hence grizzly reproduction in interior Alaska and similar climatic and geographical latitudes is considerably slower than has been previously supposed.

Twin cubs are likely born more often than singles, while three are not unknown. Several times I have seen sow grizzlies with triplets at heel. But four grizzly cubs following one mother is probably the result of a mix-up when two families met and one sow claimed all. Glen McLain, owner of a deluxe camera shop in Anchorage, Alaska, and an avid wildlife photographer, was filming brown bears fishing for salmon in the McNeal River one day and witnessed such an unusual event.

A large sow with three small cubs was fishing in a fast riffle, when a smaller female with two cubs came in on the same stretch of the river. While both mothers were engrossed with their fishing, all five cubs joined in a huge game, roughhousing, rolling and tumbling all over the gravel bar among smelly remnants of fish. When the mothers came out of the river, they got into a great row over which cubs belonged to which. Identification was no doubt difficult even for a keen-nosed mother grizzly, for by that time all the cubs very likely smelled alike. The larger bear claimed all five cubs, and both mothers fought furiously, roaring to heaven, for several minutes. In the excitement one small cub fell into the river and was rolled and tumbled downstream, until it finally clung to a projecting rock wailing its heart out. The smaller sow heard it crying, broke away from the fight and ran to the rescue. She fished the cub out of the river and left with it. Perhaps it was injured, or she killed it upon discovering it was not hers; for next time Glen saw her a couple of days later, she was alone.

Mother grizzlies are paragons of parental love and care.

They are forbearing and patient most of the time, but they can be very stern when bear etiquette is breached by their offspring. They insist on instant obedience, and when this is not forthcoming, punishment by way of a very ungentle paw applied to whatever portion of the cub is handiest is the order of the moment. Generally a mother grizzly will fight to the death to protect her cubs, and those who have witnessed such faithfulness have sometimes had more than good reason to be impressed.

One who has only observed the grizzly lolling in the lazy indolence of captivity may be misled into thinking this animal is ponderous and phlegmatic in its movements. But if that person takes a peanut, as I have done, and tosses it into some crack or cranny within its reach, the bear will quickly and delicately extricate the morsel with one claw and eat it. Despite the size of his front feet the grizzly can be extremely dexterous with them and often employs a claw as we would use a finger. Apart from that the grizzly is a highly coordinated acrobat, can move like lightning and strike a blow with either paw that will cave in the skull of a full-grown steer as if it were so much eggshell. Like nearly all animals, grizzlies are usually "right-handed"; but though they favor the right paw, they are far more ambidextrous than man.

The muscles, ligaments, and bone structure of bears are extremely powerful, elastic, and flexible. When flayed, the body of a bear looks startlingly like that of a man, a fact generating much superstition among primitive people. The bones are massive and dense, heavily socketed and hinged to make up a framework operating most efficiently from all positions. The plantigrade feet are heavily padded, the forefeet being armed with long, curved claws. The longest claw measured on a large male was five and a half inches around the outside curve. This grizzly was killed in the spring, before it had done any digging to wear its claws down. The well-armed front paws are both shovels and weapons.

The grizzly is wrapped in a coat of heavy hide covered by a pelage of soft, thick underfur overlaid with long guard hairs that give it a shaggy look. The coloration of pelage over the range

covered in my observations runs from pale cream through all
shades of brown and gray to almost jet black. While certain
colors predominate in certain parts of the range, color mutation
varies widely within a single family. I have seen a nondescript
brown mother with one cub colored like her and the other a
beautiful platinum blonde with deep chocolate feet, ears, muzzle, and belly and a round moon of the same color on the forward
slope of the hump. This distinctive and easily recognized bear
was born in January 1946, first seen in July of that year, and was
observed in following years until 1958, when it had become a
very large handsome animal still relatively unchanged in color.
The grizzlies of southeastern British Columbia and southern
Alberta have more dark silvertips among them than are seen
farther north. Four years ago in a high basin along the east side
of the Divide above the south fork of Castle River in Alberta my
son Charlie and Fred Sharp, Ducks Unlimited naturalist, and I
saw a very large male that was charcoal black with a mantle of
burnished silver over shoulders and flanks. We did not shoot him,
although we were big-game hunting at the time, for we were
more preoccupied with getting some winter meat. This was one
of the most outstanding specimens I have ever seen. Up in the
high country of the Selkirk Range in the Big Bend area of the
Columbia River drainage in British Columbia, the predominant
color is brown, with silvertip mantles pronounced on some individuals. The tundra bears of the north fade out to lighter
browns, straw yellow, and pale cream. Over on the west coast of
British Columbia, as previously described, grizzly bears are
mainly deep brown, with some individuals showing lighter
shades of golden bronze. Markings vary everywhere, some grizzlies wearing a distinct darker-colored line down the back with
another similar bar across the shoulders, like a cross fox. Some
have light-colored faces with dark muzzles and ears, others have
dark faces and ears with contrasting light jowls—there are many
combinations.

Color mutation also shows a marked difference in the
claws. Some grizzlies sport armament as ivory white as piano

keys, while the claws of others are amber, brown, and black. It has been said that the claws whiten with age, but this is questionable. I have seen young bears with white claws and very old ones with claws almost dead black.

The color of the coat changes somewhat with the season, fading out in the sun and weather until shed off in summer. At this time of molt, grizzlies take on the look of mountain hoboes—ragged, unkempt, and tattered—until again transformed by new, much darker coats. These robes reach their prime in late October, when the bears are well insulated by fur and fat for the long cold months ahead.

Anyone who has looked down the throat of an enraged grizzly is left with a lifelong, profoundly disturbing impression of heavy jaws and teeth. If that person has a photographic memory of detail, he will know that almost all taxidermists have been sustaining a lie. Almost invariably mounted trophies show the wrinkled, lip-curled mask of the grizzly showing most of its dental array in a fearsome snarl like that of a dog. In reality the tip of the nose lifts and lower frontal lip drops, while the lips at the side hang straight. There are only three or four lateral wrinkles across the bridge of the nose. Many old bear hunters will swear to the contrary, but the fact remains. Taxidermists will likely continue modeling grizzly trophies snarling like dogs, a time-honored though unrealistic picture of the living bear.

The skull of the grizzly is heavily constructed with large canine teeth and massive, distinctive molars. Two masses of muscle shaped like undersized, somewhat flattened rugby balls couch the ridged cranium on each side to power the jaws. These muscles lend massiveness to the head and give a biting power capable of crushing heavy bones. It is the skull that is measured in a combination of length and width for the trophy records—a somewhat misleading scoring system; for some mediocre grizzlies have very large skulls, and some large grizzlies have skulls that do not reach minimum requirement for trophy records. A mountain grizzly skull measuring approximately of 16 inches long and 8 inches wide after being cleaned of flesh will come high in the records. By comparison a large coastal brown bear skull will be 18 inches long and 11 inches wide. The largest black bear skulls will tape out at about 13 by 8 inches.

The weight of grizzlies is a physical attribute that has received more unreliable attention over the years than any other. One regularly hears of thousand-pound grizzlies, but these are so rare that they cannot be considered anything like a common category except among the large coastal bears. When it comes to the weight of grizzlies, the difference between an awful liar and a truthful man is a set of reliable beam scales honestly used. A grizzly shot at close range to settle a knock-down-and-drag-out argument automatically takes on five hundred pounds.

Al Oeming weighed several Swan Hills grizzlies alive and found the average weight of mature animals to be in the vicinity of 450 pounds with an odd large male reaching 900 pounds. These bears were captured in large box traps made from a section of 48-inch steel culvert. The big animals were then anesthetized with massive doses of ether, dragged out, tied up, and hung on a beam scale with block and tackle. Some bears required a great deal more anesthetic than others. Some "patients" woke up ahead of schedule, precipitating some fast action to apply more ether. Al's enthusiasm for the adventure of this kind of research was not completely reflected by his helpers, who migrated rapidly to other places on more than one occasion when one of the grizzlies regained consciousness while they were still involved with the data book.

The only bear I have ever seen that might have weighed somewhere between nine hundred and a thousand pounds was a very big male killed by my friend the late Jim Bennett on the crest of the McDonald Range west of the Flathead River in British Columbia. We had no means of weighing this bear, a huge, enormously fat animal. The skin, measured green and loose on the ground, was 9 feet 10 inches across the front paws and 9 feet 3 inches from nose to tail. The pads of the front paws were 9 inches across.

There have been others that looked as though they weighed a ton, but these I met under the most extenuating circumstances—at close range. The proud, arrogant bearing of the grizzly and his craggy profile make him look a good deal heavier than he is. For the most part the males are larger than the females.

It has been said that "the pine needle fell in the forest; the eagle saw it fall, the deer heard it, and the bear smelled it." A grizzly's eyes are mediocre, having thus evolved by his spending most of his time looking barely past the end of his nose at feed. Until the advent of the white man with his rifle the grizzly had no need of vision for defense. Many times I have approached grizzlies with no cover at all by simply moving ahead when the bear had its head down feeding. Like most animals, they see in shades of black and white and cannot distinguish a motionless form at anything but close range. Even against sharply contrasting background a grizzly has trouble identifying an object and sometimes walks or runs toward it for a better look. Many so-called "charges" are nothing but this. However, when the thing they are looking at chooses to run or to throw lead, then the curious approach can rapidly develop into a real charge.

Their ears are sharp—sufficiently keen to pick up sounds at considerable distance. The nose is superlative, probably as much better than a bloodhound's as a bloodhound's is better than a man's. Years ago I was out alone scouting for game up along the Continental Divide in southwest Alberta, when I saw something that illustrates well the grizzly's powerful nose.

It was a miserable day, drizzling and raw with about six inches of heavy wet snow on the ground. I had come up along an open valley across timberline alplands and climbed up into a mass of dense cloud shrouding a pass. As I reached the summit, the clouds lifted enough for me to use my glasses, and I sat down to look over the surrounding country. A moving object caught my eye away down my backtrail. It was a grizzly crossing the valley at right angle, striding along in a businesslike fashion toward my trail. I watched to see what would happen when it hit my tracks. About ten feet from my trail the bear suddenly slammed to a stop as though hitting a brick wall nose first; he half reared, spun away, and broke into a tearing gallop for parts unknown. Either I needed a bath worse than I thought, or that grizzly had experienced some painful contact with men. As far as I could see it, the big animal went as though lashed with a whip. He left me much impressed with his keenness of nose and fleetness of foot.

A bear can cover ground at astonishing speed for such a bulky animal. While I have never had the opportunity or the inclination to clock a grizzly, I once drove up close behind a black bear at dusk and pursued it for about a quarter mile, while it galloped in the beams of my headlights. For a way it ran at about twenty-eight miles an hour, and when crowded, it reached a speed of approximately thirty-two miles an hour over fairly level road. It did not maintain this pace for long before breaking off to the side, where it slipped on a skiff of snow on the road shoulder and turned clear over to skid on its back tail first into the jackpines.

Going downslope or for a short dash on level ground, grizzlies can likely attain an equal speed, although the black bear is thought to be the faster of the two. No doubt like dogs, horses, men, and most other animals, some bears are fleeter of foot than others.

The bear family has two traveling gaits and four speeds. The walk involves a long, rolling stride in which two legs on the same side move forward together, much the same way as a pacing horse. It can be slow when the bear is feeding, but when the grizzly is going somewhere, this gait likely takes him cross country at five or six miles an hour. Upon breaking from a walk, they either go at a slow, ground-eating lope or a tearing gallop. On one occasion I roughly measured the stride of a grizzly running wide open down a slope in loose snow. The running bounds averaged about seventeen feet in length. I have never seen a grizzly trot. Only trained bears walk on their hind feet, although I have seen them take one or two staggering steps when shifting position for a better look at something while standing upright. But they have always overbalanced and come down onto four feet.

The full upright stance of a bear is not commonly a

fighting position, as it is often portrayed, although they do stand up and box each other on occasion. The standing position at full height is used for advantage to see better. The fighting grizzly usually goes on four feet or lunges in a half crouch with both front paws swinging free. A grizzly standing up on his hind feet at full height is a most impressive sight, for a big one towers over a man. One feels small and insignificant standing a few yards away from a grizzly and looking up at his head. Just as long as they are in that position, there is nothing particularly threatening about them. A grizzly getting ready for war usually stands squarely on his four feet with head slung low, his ears set at half cock, and the hair of his ruff and back standing on end.

While grizzlies, being largely solitary animals, are relatively silent, they can and do use their voices to communicate with others and sometimes commiserate with themselves. A wounded or trapped grizzly can roar and bawl like nothing else on earth, a sound that echoes fearsomely off canyon walls and whose sheer savagery can be heard for miles on still air. The sound is not unlike the high-pitched bawling of an enraged bull. I have heard the big bears moan low to themselves when wounded, a most heart-rending sound. Their vocabulary runs through a whole series of explosive "whoofs," sniffs, snorts, and softer variations of these sounds. When suddenly running into an alarming scent, they sometimes give a long-drawn musical whistling sniff of soft pitch. The cubs sometimes complain with a sound not unlike the "mer-ow-wow" of a tomcat, but with flatter inflection. A mother grizzly warning her young of danger may give a short "koff-koffing" sound of which variations of volume and inflection can be a command to come, to go, and very likely other things beyond my translation. Cubs, when hurt, frightened, or fighting mad, give a whole variety of moans, cries, and wails on a wide scale of intonation and intensity. When excited or angry, both cubs and mature animals chop their jaws, sometimes causing a sharp clacking of teeth, that can be heard for half a mile. A startled or angry grizzly can lift a man's hair with the dripping menace of a deep growl.

I was driving home late one summer night after a shower

of rain, when my car slipped into a hole and stuck fast. Leaving it, I began to walk the last half mile up the hill along a narrow road wandering through aspens and cottonwoods all deeply shrouded in velvety darkness. I had no light and even with reasonably good night vision was almost feeling my way. Suddenly, at a bend of the road, I was brought up short in my tracks by a most eloquent growl a short distance to one side; there was no doubt about its origin. I stood perfectly still for several of the longest moments of my life, while a big grizzly let me know in no uncertain language just what he thought of my bumbling around unannounced in the dark. When the big animal finally ran out of invective and I heard it moving away, I could distinctly feel the hair on the back of my neck settling down to its normal repose. Next morning, upon returning to extricate my car, grizzly tracks were found exactly six paces from where I had been standing.

Once while hunting in the Grizzly Gulch country of British Columbia's Flathead region with my good friend Bill Farr, internationally known stockman of Greeley, Colorado, we were standing on a mountain lookout rimming a huge, steep-sided glacial bowl when a most unusual and startling sound came to us. It sounded exactly like a grievously injured man, half-delirious with pain and calling desperately for help. It echoed eerily off the cliffs that wall the basin on three sides, and the sheer agony of despair of the crying made us catch our breaths. At first we were fooled into looking too far for its source, but then we spotted a sow grizzly with two first-year cubs about seven hundred yards down at a lateral angle on the rim of a perpendicular sill of lava about two hundred feet high. As we watched, she repeatedly tried to find a way down over this cliff and just as often was brought to a halt with her tail over her ears in some impossibly sheer spot. Then she would stand and yell and moan, bitterly complaining about her bad luck while swinging her big snout out over the drop-off. Once her dead-end position was so bad that she was forced to back up the cliff, carefully reaching up and back with her hind feet, placing them one at a time, thus retracing her steps to a place where she could turn around. Meanwhile the cubs had scrambled back up to the rim, where she joined them. Again and again she climbed down over places that would give a goat pause, but always the cliff defeated her. Each time she moaned and bawled in self-sympathy. Finally she progressed around the rim almost directly under us, where she ran into our wind, and with a great whistling sniff she swiveled on her heels and stampeded away over the mountain ridge out of sight.

One would have to keep captive grizzlies—or better yet, tame ones running free, as did "Grizzly" Adams in the early days of California—to learn things more positive of their language. If a man could learn some of their terms, it would be possible to exchange signals with them and understand them much better. What would happen if some insult was accidentally uttered is anyone's guess.

To really enjoy some sympathetic understanding of these big animals and come to some acceptable strata of coexistence with them it is best to live with them for a prolonged period in a country containing a heavy population, which is open enough to allow some kind of continued contact. One must follow the role of an uninvited visitor—an intruder—rather than that of an aggressive hunter, and one should go unarmed to insure this attitude. Finally, when such an observer has learned enough of grizzly protocol and good manners, he begins to enjoy some fascinating glimpses into their private lives. When he reaches the point that he can think like a grizzly, he has a tremendous advantage over the casual observer, a position rarely attained by the hunter and unfortunately by too few scientists.

Certainly few subjects offer more of a challenge or greater variety of opportunities for study than the grizzly bear. The longer one associates with them, the more one realizes how little we really know, and they can teach us much. To see a mother grizzly ambling and loafing with her cubs across the broad, hospitable bosom of a flower-spangled mountain meadow is to see life in true wilderness at its best. The cubs love to play and are continually thrusting their furry, inquisitive snouts into every nook and cranny. They gambol and romp, roughhouse and quarrel with equal abandon—every waking moment in motion and only punctuating their carefree lives with nursing and sleeping. If I was asked to illustrate complete freedom and happiness with one picture, it would show a grizzly mother and her cubs wandering through their mountain wilderness on a summer day.

Nor is play confined to the cubs. For such large, formidable-looking creatures mature grizzlies are fond of play, and age has few limitations. Snowdrifts, especially those pitched steeply on a mountain slope, hold a particular fascination. Not only do they use these on occasion as a means of getting from top to bottom in a hurry, but often they take time off from feeding for repeated plunging slides, which obviously delight them. It is not uncommon to see such a big sloping drift with telltale marks on it of a grizzly that has enjoyed some whistling toboggan runs.

In May 1956 Clarence Tillenius, the famous Canadian wildlife artist, was my guest for a couple of weeks, while making study sketches of the bighorns near our ranch. We spent almost every day rambling the slopes of Pass Creek in the park. One morning we saw a big grizzly, presumably a male, feeding on glacier lilies at the foot of an avalanche track on the north slope of Black Bear Mountain. Clarence took the opportunity to do some study sketches and took up a position just across the creek from the bear, while I went farther up the valley to film some sheep. When I returned some time later, I found Clarence touching up a series of sketches that told a most interesting story.

He had been watching and sketching for some time, when the grizzly began climbing straight up a long snowdrift that filled the bottom of a draw. Clarence naturally thought the bear was leaving and watched him go with some regret; but when the bear was a considerable distance up the steep slope, he stopped and sat down as though to enjoy the view. Then the big animal launched himself in a high-speed slide back down the drift. Just short of bare rocks and snags at the bottom the grizzly came up onto its feet, set its claws, and came to a stop in a shower of slush. Again and again it climbed up to swoop down with all the joy and abandon of a child. It slid on its belly, back, and rump and sometimes rolled tail over teakettle for the sheer fun of it. Once the big bear sat down like a dog at the top of the slide as though he were lost in reverie. Absently a huge hind foot was elevated to scratch the back of an ear; then, with the paw still held up to its head, the grizzly took off in a plummet down to the bottom.

Mothers often join in a session of play with their cubs. A mother with a single cub seems more apt to frolic with her offspring. She seems to realize the lone grizzly child's need for play. Such play may take the form of aimless mouthing and wrestling, or it may become stylized games of considerable intelligence that apparently are invented on the spur of the moment.

One bright September day Bill Farr and I were seated squarely on the Alberta–British Columbia border on the ridge crest of the Continental Divide with our boot toes overhanging the two-thousand-foot drop on the eastern side. Away below us inside Waterton Lakes Park we saw a pretty silvertip sow grizzly with a single cub traveling along a small creek. The mother was walking the top of a low bank flanking the stream, while the cub was happily splashing up through the water. The she-grizzly came to a willow and reared against it, applying her weight till the top of the bush was sprung down into the water. The cub instantly leaped onto it to hold it down; but when the sow released her weight, the little tree sprang up and threw water in a shower. Again the sow pushed it down, and again the cub jumped on it with obvious delight. Once more the tree was released and tossed water in the air. There is no telling how long this game would have continued had the willow not broken off close to the ground.

During the heat of summer grizzlies often cool off by getting under a waterfall or plunging into a pool or lake for a swim. They suffer from heat and nearly always locate where water is readily available for drinking, wallowing, or swimming. I once saw a big grizzly come out of the timber along the shore of the lower of the Twin Lakes, walk out on a big stranded log projecting into the lake, and take a big belly-flopping dive off it into swimming water. It swam around in circles for a few minutes like a big beaver, and then it waded out on the gravel shingle of the beach, gave its head a gargantuan shake, and disappeared into the shady spruces.

Grizzlies love to wallow during the hot weather in the soft muck of a seep or spring, and often they appropriate an elk wallow for this ablution. One stifling hot day in June I was repairing fence on the ranch, when my thirst drove me to look for a drink. On this section of the ranch there is a spring bubbling up through a seam of sand in the midst of a growth of cottonwood and willow. Over the centuries the water has built up a mound several feet higher than the surrounding land. I approached the place against the breeze rustling in the leaves of the trees with my thoughts miles away. Through unconscious habit I came silently, along a little trail made by elk and horses. Upon pushing through the fringe of growth on the side of the mound I almost stepped on the tail of a big grizzly who was buried to the ears in the spring. There was an explosion of mud and water accompanied by a great WHOOSH as the bear took off—fortunately straightaway. Had the animal been facing me, or had there been a companion in the bathtub—this was mating season—results might have been catastrophic. At best it is not the safest thing in the world to walk up so close to a snoozing grizzly. There was some question as to who was the most startled, but it took me some time to get my circulation down to normal and proceed to find my drink elsewhere.

The June mating moon of grizzlies brings much traveling, ponderous and sometimes quarrelsome preliminaries, and long-winded, amorous culminations. When the female begins to come into heat, it is not long before the questing nose of a male picks up her cloying scent and he comes to pay court with the delicate finesse of an animated locomotive running on a one-way track. Charlie Russell, the famous cowboy artist, once remarked that it didn't matter much whether a man was headed for heaven or hell, there was always a small set of moccasin tracks ahead of him. With some modification of moccasin tracks, the same thing might be said for male grizzly bears in the mating season.

The first contact is likely brief in most cases, whereupon

the pair heads out single file with the female in the lead, never appearing to hurry unless pressed, always keeping just out of reach; thus they proceed around and around for miles and miles. If you doubt me, then let your curiosity try to keep you within sight of them. Rivers, interminable gravel bars, boulders, brush and tangles of fallen logs are bypassed with utter disregard. If two or three mountains chance to get in the way, they are trod under foot with no slackening of pace, completely unnoticed. It is the monument of all monuments to commemorate the power of the female over the male in the age-old quest.

When the courtship begins to ripen, she will on occasion allow her suitor within reaching distance, and they will trade nips and paw each other among grunts, snorts, and other bearish terms of endearment. Such preliminaries can go on for days and can degenerate betimes into lusty quarrels laced with profanity, real biting, and pounding paws.

When another male interferes, sometimes dramatic fights occur. My friend Jack Christiansen, of the National Parks Wardens Service, saw two males tangle over a female up on the gravel bars of the North Saskatchewan River in Jasper Park. Both were big animals. They threw haymakers that would have decapitated any lesser animal as they roared, bawled, and bit. They rolled and tumbled, knocking hair out of each other in wads. All the while the female stood aloof and unconcerned. When one male finally drove the other away, she led out once more with the weary victor trailing along behind.

Another incident was observed in Alaska's McKinley Park by some of the park's personnel. When a precocious three-year-old male approached a mating pair, the old boar suddenly charged the young one, which took to its heels up a slope above the river bars and onto the road a short distance ahead of the truck in which the men were riding. The big bear drove the smaller one down the road, and when it dodged down into a draw, there was a brief collision. With one swipe of his paw the big boar killed and almost disemboweled the other.

When a female is ready to accept her mate, the copulation lasts for twenty to thirty minutes and may be repeated several times. Then the pair splits up to go their separate ways. At no time during the rest of the summer or when she is nursing cubs will the female tolerate the proximity of a male.

When two grizzlies of opposite sex are confined together, there can be some exception. The female and the male presently in captivity in the Winnipeg Zoo are enclosed in a large, attractive moated pen. They are together all year round, and probably because of an abundance of rich feed, easy living, and boredom they breed promiscuously at any time. However the female only conceives during regular breeding season. The cubs are taken from her shortly after birth and raised artificially. Consequently she regularly has cubs every second year and at one time in her life had three sets of cubs in three years.

After conception the development of the embryo begins, but then its growth is suspended for a time to be resumed later. This is a peculiar physical attribute of bears that is called delayed implantation in technical biological terminology. It means that the embryo floats about freely in the uterus for several months before it becomes implanted and proceeds to grow. This is why pregnant females are never reported by hunters. The early stages of development are so minute that only the trained biologist with access to laboratory facilities can detect it.

During breeding season and at all times outside of den grizzlies indulge in leaving scratch and tooth marks on trees in various portions of their range. These "rubbing posts" seem to be used by both males and females. The bears rear against the tree to rub and scratch themselves; sometimes they exercise their claws on the trunk and occasionally culminate the ritual by reaching to full height and nipping out a sliver of wood. Always they approach the tree in the exact tracks of preceding bears, and on favorable ground the worn imprints of the foot marks are very noticeable. Many observers credit the habit to breeding ritual or suggest that it is a means of identification, a sort of "post office" where individual bears leave their calling cards of scent and pull out a sliver of wood to show how big they are. In my opinion there is no special significance to this procedure; the bears simply enjoy scratching itchy places and perhaps testing their teeth and claws on unyielding wood. Only once have I seen a grizzly rubbing on such a tree, although I have seen countless rubbing posts all over their range. Both black bears and grizzlies indulge in the habit. If there is any special significance, then only the bears know about it and so far it is a well-kept secret.

Like most animals, grizzlies make and use trails leading from one portion of their range to another. In places where the ground is soft and the population heavy these "bear roads" are very noticeable. They are easily recognizable, being double-indented ruts with a ridge between. Sometimes such a trail is worn in distinct steps, where each bear places its feet in the tracks of preceding ones.

They regularly use trails made by other game and domestic stock. All natural and man-made trails in grizzly country are the thoroughfares of bears—even superhighways on occasion. A motorist coming downslope one night on the Trans-Canada Highway west of Banff saw a grizzly loafing along in the bright moonlight ahead. He shut off his motor and lights and coasted silently up close behind the bear and gave a great blast on his horn. The bear might have been half asleep, but its reaction was instantaneous. He went straight up, swapped ends in the air, and came down on the hood of the car with smashing blows of his paws, then left hurriedly for his mountain. The motorist was left stranded with a car that could not be moved and a lasting lesson on the folly of goosing grizzlies.

On the west coast in the rain forest jungles the grizzlies make trails along the banks of the rivers between fishing locations that are virtually tunnels through the almost solid greenery of willow, alder, devil's club, and other shrubbery.

Normally a grizzly's range is not extensive over a given season unless some unusual disturbance causes a move to another portion of the country. In wilderness country many grizzlies probably live out their lives within a twenty-mile radius of where they are born. However there is no doubt some individuals, especially males in breeding season, may go much farther than this.

In comparison with most animals the grizzly is long lived.

The known ages of bears have not been recorded until quite recently by zoo officials dealing with captive animals. Zoo-kept grizzlies have been known to live thirty years. Old Dynamite, a venerable and irascible grizzly kept by the Calgary Zoo in Alberta was twenty-eight years old in January 1965. This ripe old age has been reached in spite of the fact that her tongue was torn out years ago when she stuck it out at a polar bear between the bars separating their cages and that annoyed animal grabbed it.

Quite recently a new scientific method has been discovered to determine the age of bears. This has to do with the microscopic readings of cross-sectioned teeth. The cementum (outer layer) grows in alternately opaque and translucent rings like the annular rings of a tree, with two rings—one of each color—for each year of the bear's life. The first ring does not appear till the bear is one year old. From readings taken to date on twenty-five collected skulls it has been found that grizzlies living in the wild have reached ages of from twenty to twenty-five years. Unlike the scales of fish, where the annular rings show the number of times the individual has spawned, the teeth of bears do not indicate the breeding schedule.

While the method of this scientific investigation is new, the idea is not. Amazingly enough, way back in 1860 "Grizzly" Adams was reported to have said: "Every year a ring is added to its tusks—the first being for the second year—and as the animal sometimes reaches the age of fifteen or sixteen years, a corresponding number of rings are found." Such a remark illustrates the tremendous power of observation of this man who was much more hunter than scientist, although he was undoubtedly a keen naturalist. Probably because he used his eye unaided or at best with the help of a hand magnifying glass, the two-color rings appeared as one.

When summer days shorten into autumn and grizzly country begins to tighten up under the first tentative strokes of winter, the big bears head up onto the high slopes to dig their dens. Usually a bear digs a new den every year, although some ideal locations may be used again and again. My father-in-law,

Bert Riggall, found one such den in the rugged country of northern Glacier Park, Montana, years ago. It had been dug beneath a huge boulder that had originally come down off a cliff and half-buried itself in the soil of the lower slope. It was supported below by two smaller boulders. Sometime ages ago a grizzly had dug out a den chamber under the monster boulder with its portal between the two lesser ones as natural doorposts on either side. Because it was so well supported and did not cave in following its initial usage, this den had been used by so many grizzlies over the centuries that the exposed rock on either side of the entrance tunnel was polished by the going and coming.

A grizzly usually chooses its den site near or above timber-line on a northeast or east face, where snow will drift over it in winter. The entrance is three or four feet in diameter and leads from eight to twelve feet horizontally or dipping down slightly into the mountainside. There a chamber from six to nine feet in diameter and three or four feet high is dug out. This is finally floored with a mattress of dry grass, forbes (broad-leafed plants), and brush to a depth of several inches.

In October 1937 Bert Riggall, Frank Marr, and I watched a grizzly digging its den for over an hour on the east side of the Divide high above the head of the Oldman River, an operation carried out with great industry and purpose. And on that same trip the three of us were scouting along the top of a high mountain ridge farther north on the head of Cataract Creek, a tributary of the Highwood River in Alberta, when we spotted a big, freshly dug hole in a snowy bench below us. Big dirty tracks radiated in every direction from the mound of dirt thrown out of the hole. We thought the grizzly was home, but when several rocks tossed into the hole failed to rouse the bear, we proceeded to investigate the place. Bert had a flashlight in his rucksack, which I took to light my way down into the den. The entrance tunnel sloped down for perhaps eight feet at about a twenty-five-degree angle, and then it turned laterally along a sunken rock ledge for another six feet before opening up into a chamber approximately eight feet wide and three and a half feet high. The floor was packed with dry herbage to a depth of about eight inches. It was a cozy hole, and if the size of the nesting chamber and the tracks were any indication, it was to be the wintering den of a large grizzly.

Grizzlies do not hibernate in the true sense of the word. They can better be called semi-hibernators; for they do not go into the cold-blooded coma of ground squirrels, when heart beats slow down to four or five pulsations a minute and breathing is almost imperceptible. Theirs is not such a state of suspended life, and they wake readily if disturbed. Undoubtedly they move around to some extent in den, especially females giving birth to cubs. Sometimes if a bear goes into den in poor condition, it will emerge in winter for short forays.

Here in the south Canada Rockies the denning period usually begins around the end of October and continues till early May, although some individuals will occasionally appear in late April. On the British Columbia coast and along coastal Alaska the hibernating period is considerably shorter. In the subarctic and arctic regions they den up about the first of October and emerge in May.

During winters of severe cold and little snow it is thought that considerable mortality sometimes occurs. Enos Mills records finding a young grizzly in excellant condition frozen to death in its den. Normally the big animals winter comfortably and use up only a fraction of their accumulated fat. I have examined several grizzlies killed shortly after emerging from den that carried a great quantity of body fat.

Only once over the years of wandering in grizzly country have I found possible evidence of a grizzly that died a peaceful death. This was the skull of a large old animal picked up on a gravel bar along the head of a wilderness stream not far from timberline; it was likely washed out of an old den by spring freshets.

When the end of the trail comes peacefully to an old grizzly or some kind of sickness attacks an individual, understandably enough death almost invariably occurs in the den. The prolonged winter sleep drifts gently into eternity, and the remains are hidden from prying eyes forever in a self-made grave.

3. *GRIZZLY Feeding Habits*

*His stomach is his
passport to paradise.*
—ANDY RUSSELL

If we ask the experts to classify the grizzly in his proper biological pigeonhole, we will likely be told the big bear is a carnivorous predator. Having the proper dental equipment and being a bit of an opportunist where meat is concerned, this description is scientifically justified, even if it does stretch a couple of points far too far.

The grizzly joins man, the hog, and the common rat in being the four outstanding omnivores on earth. Like them, he will eat almost anything when hungry and a great variety of things most of the time. It would be much easier to list the things the grizzly does not eat than those he does. Because of the very complexity of his choice of food his habits are vastly more colorful and interesting to observe. His appetite fits his huge frame, which requires a tremendous amount of fuel; this probably accounts for the wide choice of food he takes during his spring, summer, and fall outside the wintering den. His voracious feeding causes him to put on a great store of fat that sustains him over the cold six months spent in den.

Contrary to popular belief, the grizzly's main diet is vegetable. In early May, when the glacier lilies burst into bloom here at our ranch at an altitude of 4,700 feet above sea level, we know that we will soon see the first grizzly track of the season. The bears seem to prefer breaking their long winter fast with feeds of lush vegetation, and the glacier lily is a favorite choice. They strip the plants from the ground—root, stem, leaves, and bloom—and when the lilies follow the season to higher altitudes, where they bloom profusely in the timberline basins in July, the grizzlies follow after them. In the high country where the lilies grow in thin sod overlaying solid pan rock, the grizzlies dig for the bulbs. In such a place the small, onionlike bulbs lie against the rock, so the bear only has to turn the sod over and pick them off. Sometimes hundreds of square yards of earth are thus plowed by the big animals.

Their diet in spring and early summer also includes a host of other plants and succulent roots. Where grizzlies come out of den before the new growth comes up in spring, such as in the mountains of the subarctic regions of their range, they concentrate on digging roots. In the Yukon and the Mount McKinley region of central Alaska we have often seen places that look as though some wilderness gardener were preparing a spot for cultivation. Every inch of sod for many yards will have been completely turned over by grizzlies searching for the roots of wild dock, pea vine, and other plants. At such time their scats reveal almost total vegetarian diet.

When the frost recedes from the ground under the hot sun and grass and forbes come up in lush new growth, grizzlies spend a great portion of their time grazing, exactly like cattle or horses. It is hard to picture them as predators at all when one sees them grazing hour after hour and day after day, alternating periods of filling themselves with food and periods of loafing and sleeping.

Our observations, reaching from the forty-ninth parallel on the northern rim of Montana through Alberta and British Columbia into the Yukon and central Alaska and extending over several seasons of concentrated film work among them, have convinced us that the grizzly diet is 80 per cent vegetable over their entire range. In such country as the Selkirk Mountains of interior British Columbia, where annual snowfall may exceed five hundred inches and few large animals except mountain goats and bears can exist, the grizzly diet is probably 90 per cent vegetable. Again in the high tundra country of the central ranges of Alaska and the mountains of the Yukon Territory this holds true, even though bears share this range with numerous other species. If grizzlies had to live on the meat they could catch in such country, they would have been extinct long ago. They are just too big and too conspicuous to be very successful at gumshoeing through the scanty cover and snatching their food from among herds of caribou and sheep and moose. However they do not pass up the good chances that fortune may throw their way, for grizzlies are very fond of meat. Adolph Murie recounts some interesting observations of the relationship between grizzlies and other big animals.

Not very far from his cabin on Igloo Creek in Mount McKinley Park the caribou use a calving ground on the flats of the Teklanika River. Caribou calves, like those of all deer species, are wobbly-legged and comparatively helpless during the early postnatal weeks of their lives. Adolph has observed grizzlies killing and eating young caribou calves left cached by their mothers during this time. When the calves gain strength and find their legs, the bears still try to catch them for two or three weeks, and it is not uncommon to see the big animals engaged in spirited foot races across the alluvial gravel bars along the river. This generally yields the pursuer little more than sore feet. After several fruitless runs the caribou calf hunters are persuaded of their folly and hardly look at caribou for the rest of the season. Mature caribou are very rarely attacked. It is my firm belief that many grizzlies never learn to kill anything but small game. In the North, when a grizzly is seen eating a full-grown caribou, it is usually a kill the bear has hijacked from wolves or one that has had an accident along the very precipitous trails in parts of the caribou migration routes.

Although grizzlies rarely have an opportunity to kill a

mountain sheep, Adolph Murie told us of such an incident while we were observing grizzlies in the Mount McKinley area in 1963. He was photographing a band of dall sheep on the slopes of Cathedral Peak. The sheep were feeding across a draw, when he saw a grizzly coming toward them. The big animal came out on a rise of ground above the sheep and suddenly charged down through them directly at Adolph. The sheep scattered wildly in all directions, and Adolph, his position not being the best in which to meet a charging bear, also retreated to more favorable ground. When he turned to look back, it was just in time to see the grizzly tear up a lamb and eat it.

The calves of moose, elk, and deer come in for a certain amount of attention in other portions of grizzly range, but nowhere is such depredation heavy enough to show any appreciable difference in the general population of other animals.

Almost anyone who has traveled grizzly country will have noticed excavations where the bears have dug for ground squirrels and marmots after these small animals have gone into hibernation in the fall. While many consider that this activity yields a good portion of their diet, I very much doubt if it makes up more than a very small percentage. Certainly the energy expended in moving large quantities of earth and rocks in such excavations must be largely overbalanced in proportion to the food obtained. Ground squirrels provide the greatest part of such food; but they are small animals, and even though they hibernate in family groups of four to six in a den, the total amount dug up in one day by a grizzly cannot amount to very much poundage.

Marmots are a larger and much desired delicacy, but they usually choose a den site under some house-sized boulder and locate their nesting pocket in among heavy subterranean rocks or in a niche in the solid bedrock. I have seen marmot dens that grizzlies had enlarged into small cellars—with no reward for their labors.

Once while hunting high up on the headwaters of the Highwood River in early fall, I found a place where a grizzly had had a most frustrating time trying to dig out a marmot. The marmot had chosen his homestead in coarse talus slide-rock on a high saddle. Almost as fast as the grizzly dug away at the loose stuff, more fell into the hole. A skiff of new snow told a story of real wilderness comedy.

At first the bear had dug with boundless energy, working up a great head of steam as he threw rocks in every direction. Finally a wide, saucer-shaped depression was cleaned out down to bedrock. But the marmot had withdrawn into a crack in the solid bosom of the mountain, and although the bear could almost thrust his big snout into its fur, the marmot was just barely out of reach. For some time the grizzly heaved, scratched, grunted— and undoubtedly swore—as it tried to enlarge the niche sheltering the marmot; but the solid rock was unyielding. Finally the grizzly's temper snapped. There was evidence of the bear leaping, stomping, and cavorting in a paroxysm of rage and then leaving at a gallop over the top of the mountains. Apparently the marmot was not yet in the winter coma of hibernation, for when I arrived, its tracks led away toward more sympathetic surroundings.

Another time I watched a big old grizzly trying to dislodge a pine squirrel from under the tough, gnarled roots of a wind-tortured white pine at timberline not far from our ranch. Try as he might, the bear could do little more than thrust his nose into a crack between two roots growing on solid rock and sniff of the tiny snack hidden beneath. No amount of tearing and heaving did any good, although he could almost inhale the terrified squirrel. Finally the squirrel's nerves apparently cracked, for it suddenly shot out under the bear's belly and away between his hind legs. The grizzly whirled like a flash to pounce on his small quarry, but the squirrel dodged up a tree out of reach, chattering and barking with fright. To see the tiny one outwit the giant was salutary.

Probably every grizzly that walks the mountains has at one time or another experienced a most painful introduction to a porcupine. More than likely one lesson is enough for most grizzlies, but undoubtedly some individuals work out a technique for taking porcupines.

Bert Riggall and I were scouting for sheep over a high

shoulder up on the main range near the head of the Oldman River one bright September morning, when we came on an interesting story written in new snow. We were following fresh grizzly tracks and found where they met those of a porcupine. Once, twice, or three times the grizzly had circled the quilly, which had undoubtedly swiveled around presenting a well-armed back and tail. The bear had suddenly jumped clear over the porky in order to spin and scoop a paw under its vulnerable head and toss it several feet. Before it could move, the grizzly clamped down on its belly with heavy jaws. We found the perfectly skinned out hide with tail attached and some blood smears on the snow. Nothing else remained.

Very few grizzlies ever develop a technique for habitual killing of big game, as they sometimes do with cattle and sheep. Only twice in my entire experience have I seen places where grizzlies have made such kills.

On April 7, 1961, our third son, John, an eighteen-year-old with a penchant for wandering wild country, was coming down through the Horseshoe Canyon, two or three miles west of the ranch, when he cut the tracks of a large black bear and a small grizzly. Realizing this was a rare occurrence so early in the season, John began unraveling the clear, interwoven tracks in the snow to see if he could find the bears. In a little draw among some scrubby poplars he jumped the grizzly, where it had been lying asleep on top of a pile of dirt and debris covering the body of the black bear. There was evidence of a fight all around.

When John reported the kill to me, I went with Frank Camp, chief warden of the Park, and together we examined the place carefully and reconstructed the incident from the signs. The black bear had apparently been feeding on roots along a bare, exposed bank where the sun had melted the snow. While the bear was thus occupied, the grizzly had approached the location against the wind and, unnoticed, charged. The black bear, a big male, had probably fought successful battles with his own kind, and he may have stood his ground instead of running; maybe the grizzly gave him no choice. The fight had been short and fatal for the black: his nose was broken just forward of the

*G*rizzlies are great
travelers; porcupines mostly
homebodies. This prickly
customer, shown below the
grizzly sow and cub,
was crossing an untimbered
shoulder en route to
another area.

*T*he bighorn sheep is a resident in grizzly country. Except during the mating season, rams (below) stay to themselves, away from the ewes and lambs and even from the "junior" rams (left). They feed in the alpine pastures, but usually close to the rocky outcrops where they are safe from wolves, a. the Dall ram (above, right) was no eyes, both ears were torn out by the roots, and there were numerous other signs of violence all over him. The grizzly had buried his victim without taking a feed, but when we revisited the place a week later, the entire carcass had been eaten.

Bert Riggall reported a similar incident near the head of the North Thomson River in British Columbia in 1911. He and his partner, Cyril Watmough, were traveling through that area by pack train, and they spotted a black bear coming around a ledge under the rim of a flat-topped mountain. At the same time a grizzly was coming across the top of the plateau at a fast walk with his head up and his nose swinging alertly into the wind. With a certain purposefulness the grizzly came to the edge of the drop-off ahead of and above the ledge the black bear was traveling on, and he flattened out to wait. When the black bear reached a spot almost directly beneath, the grizzly leaped down on him. A bulge of rock hid the fight, but when Riggall and Watmough climbed across the canyon to investigate, they found what was left of the black bear. The grizzly had taken him with all the dispatch of a hound killing a rabbit; he had eaten a portion and then left.

In early July 1961, while on a pack train filming grizzlies in southeast British Columbia, my sons and I found a place where a grizzly had ambushed several animals. Apparently the bear had hidden along a trail beaten through deep snow from the high slopes down through timber to a salt lick near the bottom of a valley. It had killed the animals singly over a period of time and had carried them into some thick stuff on the downwind side of the trail. When we found the spot, the latest kill was at least six weeks old and the bear's cache was a heterogeneous mixture of hair, hide, and bones. It was difficult to be sure how many animals had been killed, but we did find parts of two goat skulls and a ragged remnant of sheep hide.

Grizzly bears have a great fondness for well-ripened meat, the higher the better; and any bear that locates a dead animal takes possession with the happy abandon of a hobo confronted with a platter of T-bone steak. Grizzlies are the clean-up squad of the wilds—they fulfill the function of the vulture in more southerly latitudes. Any animal dead from the hard weather of winter that has missed the attention of coyotes or foxes is feed for the bears upon their emergence from wintering den. Cattle killed by some accident or dead from disease are claimed with the same enthusiasm; and many an innocent grizzly has been blamed for such killing, when the animal was dead for days when the grizzly found it. After a grizzly has torn up a carcass and buried it, only the most experienced observer can tell the difference.

I once found a cow that had been killed by lightning in the middle of a wet seep on summer range used by stockmen near the edge of the mountains. Upon passing the place a few days later, I found that a grizzly had located the carcass and dragged it to higher ground close by. A good portion had been eaten, and the remainder was buried in typical fashion under a mound of sod and forest debris. Two weeks later I again rode past this place and found that the stockrider employed to look after the cattle had set a trap and caught and killed the grizzly. No doubt he blamed the death of the cow on the bear. As Henry David Thoreau profoundly stated, "Some circumstantial evidence is very strong, as when you find a trout in milk"; but even the strongest of such evidence is not always completely conclusive.

Sometimes during late winter and early spring, avalanches take their toll of big game. To be caught in such a thundering fall of thousands of tons of snow is fatal, and the bodies of those unfortunate animals are placed in a sort of natural deep freeze. But when the snow melts in early summer, the meat is exposed, and the bears enjoy it. The location of such a tragedy has been called to my attention more than once by feeding grizzlies and ravens.

When, through constant exposure to cattle, certain grizzlies acquire a technique for killing and a taste for beef, they can develop into avid predators and do great damage among the herds. However, even where hundreds of cattle intrude into grizzly country, comparatively few individuals learn to kill domestic stock. The worst of these are those that acquire great cunning by escaping from traps and dodging men. These can be very difficult to destroy. Such a grizzly has been known to do thousands of dollars worth of damage, and unfortunately he gives the whole species a bad name.

One such killer bear set up his own private butcher shop one year on the Castle River range about thirty miles from my home, and he was responsible for the trapping and shooting of thirty-five other bears before he, the real culprit, was finally taken. Fortunately such indiscriminate destruction is no longer allowed, but until only a few years ago bears in general were regarded solely as predators in this part of their range and were destroyed on sight.

If grizzlies were true predators and natural killers of domestic stock, it would have been impossible to establish the cattle business without first killing every bear. Since the contrary is true, it demonstrates the grizzly's natural desire to live in peace if given a fair chance; for even when surrounded by easy pickings among domestic livestock, most grizzlies feed in their usual fashion, largely on herbage, and give very little disturbance.

Perhaps the most outstanding example of such accommodations in the face of what might be considered temptation is Jim Stanton's unusual experience with pigs and grizzlies. Stanton, a trapper, big-game guide, and naturalist of no mean accomplishment, has spent most of his life in some of the finest grizzly country in the world, on the head of Knight's Inlet on the British Columbia coast, where the Kleena Kleene River empties into the Pacific.

One summer Jim and his wife, Yvette, were visited by a millionaire British sportsman, on a world cruise aboard his private yacht, who gave them a pig from the South Sea islands. The pig had been a present to him from a Polynesian queen. It was a young sow pig and quickly became a much-loved pet in the Stanton ménage. She had the run of the place, and fortunately was accepted by the grizzlies wandering the grass flats round about. But something was missing from the lady pig's life, which Jim undertook to remedy. The introduction of a boar promptly caused the pig population to increase greatly, and it was not long before the Stantons had forty pet pigs instead of one.

The Stantons thought so much of their pigs that they never considered eating home-cured pork, but rather they allowed them to run free with the grizzlies. The bears and pigs mingled as they dug for roots and foraged, and for the most part they got along amazingly well together. Only once did a grizzly take exception to a pig to the point of doing it harm. His decision to make pork a part of grizzly diet came to a sudden stop when Jim shot the offender. In Jim's opinion there is only one thing to do when a bear gets a taste of pork, and he acted accordingly. The experiment worked out very well, and the Stantons kept their pigs for several years before finally giving them away.

More recently there is a contrasting incident concerning hogs and grizzlies in the Yukon. A dry-land farmer from Saskatchewan migrated from his home province to the Yukon Territory, where he sought his fortune by raising hogs on a homestead along the Alaska Highway not far from Whitehorse. The hogs did well enough, but these were enclosed in pens and fed from troughs. The smell of soured feed and rotting manure around the yard attracted grizzlies, and they invaded the place. They tore down fences, overturned troughs, and altogether created a considerable disturbance, although hog mortality was practically nil. Over a comparatively short period the hog rancher shot forty-three grizzlies before he decided to go out of the hog business—not because the bears were taking his profits but because of the high cost of feed that had to be trucked hundreds of miles from grain country farther east and south.

Most of the time the grizzly follows his nose through life, wandering from one smell to another, always seeking, nearly always hungry, but as carefree and happy as an animal can get. He makes use of his natural endowments to the fullest, fitting his way to conditions as they are found. Probably a grizzly bear's idea of pure heaven is a mountain slope glistening with the blue-black shine of huckleberries hanging thickly on the bushes, the brilliant glow of buffalo berries, or the luscious smell of acres of wild raspberries, strawberries, and saskatoons.

Nothing ever invented by man can possibly equal the berry-picking equipment of the bear. To see grizzlies feeding in a heavy crop of wild fruit is observing this equipment—lips and teeth—being used with marvelous efficiency. They are compulsive eaters of berries and run them through their digestive mills in an almost unbroken stream. Although they enjoy all kinds of wild fruit, I think that most likely the abundant, juicy, sweet huckleberry of the western mountains and high tundra of the subarctic wilderness is their favorite forage.

Where grizzly population is heavy, it is not unusual to see several bears feeding in the same general locality in certain particularly choice regions; but each animal or family group has its own special claim that is treated as private property while they are using it. Intrusion by another bear invites a short, terse request to leave by the nearest exit. They largely honor each other's preserves, and such arguments rarely go beyond the verbal stage.

Grizzlies seem to have mental maps in their heads of all the choice spots in their territory and inside information on the abundance and ripeness of the crop. With no preamble or apparent reason they will leave one patch to journey some distance to another one. Like people, they seem to enjoy a change of scenery and perhaps delude themselves that the grass beyond the mountain is greener or the berries riper and sweeter.

I was busy with my binoculars one day up on the head of a wild fork of Kishaneena Creek when I saw a curious facet of grizzly behavior. From my position at the foot of a big avalanche track near the bottom of the narrow valley I spotted a sow grizzly with a yearling cub coming at a high run across the top of an eight-thousand-foot open dome about a mile above me. She acted as though she had been very throughly spooked by something and was putting distance between her and the cause of the disturbance. It was puzzling, for there was no one else in the area and I knew she had not smelled me.

Running as though pursued by devils, she poured down

over ledges and rough ground into scattered timberline parks. The cub was hard pressed to keep her in sight, but she paid it no heed. Over rocks and dead logs she bounded in a line as string straight as a compass course until she finally plunged through the creek a quarter mile above me. Without pause or a look back at the trailing cub she shot up onto an open knoll and skidded to a stop to begin feeding furiously on heavy-laden huckleberry bushes. The cub stopped wearily in the creek for a much-needed drink and then looked up at its mother as if to say: "What the heck was the big rush all about?" The cub's obvious disgust was understandable, for the mother had led the way at a tearing run for at least a mile in my sight and how much farther before that I could only guess.

Nothing can compare to grizzly country in Indian summer, when foliage is in brilliant color and juicy wild fruit hangs weightily on the bushes. Working their lips and jaws like machines, the bears have an orgy of feeding, stripping leaves, twigs, and berries without discrimination in a joyous stuffing before the long fast in the wintering den.

Even the big trees contribute to the capacious maws of grizzly bears. White pines and firs provide feed, and in the old grizzly ranges of California wild oak mast was a favorite food. Anyone who has spent much time in the high forests of the Rockies will have noticed white pines and alpine fir trees with great jagged blazes on their trunks, blazes sometimes so extensive that the tree is girdled and killed. These are made by both grizzly and black bears in the spring. When the sap begins to run, the bears tear off great slabs of bark with their claws and teeth to expose the white cambium layer beneath; they then lick off the sweet sap. Sometimes a bear will thus mark a whole line of trees and for several days will go back around this string of blazes to get the sap bleeding copiously from such wounds. This marking of trees is in no way connected with the "rubbing trees" described elsewhere but is strictly an early spring feeding procedure.

The white pines that grow in grizzly country periodically yield heavy crops of nut-laden cones, and these oily, fine-flavored seeds are a favorite feed of the bears. Such a crop is never universal all over the country. Widely scattered groves produce a heavy seed crop every five to seven years. The nut-bearing cones are on top of the trees, well out of reach of the bears, but they have developed a most ingenious method of harvest.

When a mountain basin, however secluded, produces a crop of cones, somehow the news spreads by whisker-and-paw telegraph and calls pine squirrels by the hundreds. The same telegraph informs the grizzlies and Clark's nutcrackers, which also converge in heavy concentration. I have seen seven grizzlies within a thousand yards in one small basin, a most unusual circumstance that is comparable to an equal number of people somehow seating themselves on four stools at a coffee bar.

From daylight to dark, while the nutcrackers compete, the squirrels busily cut down cones, collect the nuts in their cheek pouches, and bury them in small caches all over the forest floor. They harvest in the midst of plenty and at the same time stare privation in the face, for the arrangement is made to order for the grizzlies. Just as busily the big animals dig up the caches to stuff themselves with the rich nuts, until sometimes the ground beneath the trees looks as though acres of it had been plowed. The bears most likely miss enough nuts to provide some fare for the squirrels during the following winter, but in view of the changes in topography, finding their caches must be a hit or miss business for the squirrels.

Perhaps the most notable specialization of grizzly feeding habits is foraging for fish, where they range within the migration routes of the several species of Pacific salmon. Grizzlies cannot be called anglers, nor can they be correctly designated as fishermen; but most certainly they are enthusiastic catchers of fish.

When the coastal streams of British Columbia and Alaska teem with the annual hordes of migrating fish, the bears gather on the bars and along the riffles to feed voraciously on this mighty source of provender. Sometimes twenty or thirty bears will congregate in one particularly choice section of stream, and then you can see a sight akin to a three-ring circus, with the sky

for a tent roof and somber rocks and towering green timber for
the walls.

Nor are the bears alone, for mixed with the grouchy roaring of grizzlies complaining about being crowded in their choice
fishing spots are the whimpering cries of hundreds of gulls and
the screams of bald eagles. Occasionally the surface of the river
is broken by the sleek heads of seals, otters, or mink. Great blue
herons stalk the shallows on their stilt legs, picking at spent fish.
Above it all is the muted roar of the river.

It is movement and life, drama and color, and inevitable
tragedy, the destiny of fish driven by the urge to procreate from
the broad, free water-pastures of the ocean, urgently seeking the
river bars far inland where they themselves were hatched. There
they must lay their eggs, as their parents before them, in redds
dug in the gravel of the home riffles. The eggs are cast and
fertilized, and the spent fish, ravaged by abrasive snags and
rocks and covered with cancerous-looking fungus growths, inevitably falter in the current and die to the last one. There is a
rotting stench of fish in the damp air. Through it all, the bears
and other fisheaters move, taking their fill from unbelievable
abundance. At this time the salmon streams are one of nature's
fastest moving food chains.

Contrary to popular belief, the bears do not enter the water
to swat fish out onto the bank with their paws, although this
technique has reportedly been used by one individual grizzly.
They wade into the riffles, watch their chance, and thrust their
heads down into the water to grasp the passing fish in their
jaws. Sometimes a salmon is pinned to the bottom with a paw
and then taken in the mouth. In smaller streams it is not uncommon to see a grizzly sitting or standing in the water among
crisscrossed logs waiting for fish to come within reach. There
they have little difficulty making their catches. In larger streams
with heavy current the techniques vary somewhat as each bear
develops its own particular variations of style. Some bears, like
some people, are masters of the craft; while others seem destined
to remain mediocre, and they experience considerable frustration
in taking fish.

Upon catching a salmon, the grizzly takes it to the flanking gravel bar and usually eats it in a secluded spot hidden by alders and willows. One pictures such a big burly animal gulping his catch in great crunching bites—bones, guts, and all—but they are surprisingly fastidious feeders. Using teeth and claws, they strip off the flesh with astonishing delicacy and skill, often leaving the skeleton intact, the gills still attached to the skull and the viscera largely undisturbed inside the rib cage. Like human gourmets, grizzlies seem to prefer the belly and cheek muscles of the salmon, and sometimes, when the animal's appetite is flagging, this is all that will be taken from a fish. They never seem to eat the viscera or gills. No matter how many fish are readily available, grizzlies do not feed exclusively on them. Examination of scats shows a certain proportion of vegetation, even when the streams are running full of fish from bank to bank.

The diet of the grizzly prior to denning up for the winter seems to vary considerably, according to somewhat sketchy observations made by various people. Bert Riggall and other mountain men have told of seeing grizzlies eating heavily on mountain ash berries as a sort of bedtime snack. Once while following the tracks of a grizzly through snow in a late October blizzard in the southeastern British Columbia Rockies, I saw where the bear had fed heavily on these. Earlier in berry season they apparently do not take these berries as food. Some people think the tough, woody, astringent fruit puckers and shrinks the digestive tract for the long winter fast ahead.

Another time I had the opportunity to conduct an autopsy on a grizzly at this season, and I found it crammed with recently frozen alder leaves. Frost seems to release some kind of acid from these leaves, an acid so powerful that on one particular occasion water dripping through them lifted the bluing off a good rifle barrel after only a few hours' exposure. What this acid does to the digestive tract of a grizzly can only be guessed, but it poses a very interesting question. Quite possibly it is one kind of necessary pre-denning period feed required to prepare the animal for the months of digestive inactivity.

Few things of an edible nature escape the attention of the

grizzly, and nothing is too small to be unworthy of notice as possible food. Sometimes the bear's tastes seem ludicrous in proportion to its size.

The mountain ridges adjacent to my home are liberally covered with loose flagstones lying in broken shards everywhere. Tiny ladybugs hibernate beneath these, and in spring when the warm sun and winds lift the frost from the ground, thousands of these insects are swarming beneath these rocks. Many is the time I have seen both grizzly and black bears busily turning over rocks by the hour and feeding on ladybugs by the gallon. They get them during the short time before the insects take wing to scatter far and wide over the country, and they concentrate on them so completely that their scats are almost solid with the body husks and wing covers of the little beetles.

There are few things a bear enjoys more than a feed of ants. Apparently the tart flavor of the formic acid in the ant bodies makes these insects a real delicacy to grizzlies, and some bears seem to develop a taste for them particular to the point of compulsive searching.

Years ago a three-year-old grizzly made himself at home on the ranch one summer and mingled about with cattle and our small sons. Had our neighbors known we were entertaining such a guest, they would have thought us out of our minds. However the bear had not been around very long before we noticed that every anthill and rotten stump was being searched attentively for ants. The bear paid no attention to the cattle, and we were not much concerned for the boys' safety; for when grizzlies and boys are used to ranging together, they get along very well and exercise a sort of mutual diplomacy. Certainly this bear was so preoccupied with ants that he paid attention to little else.

Another time my wife, Kay, observed a big grizzly busily licking out the case of a car battery that had been smashed in a stalled vehicle by frost the previous winter and discarded beside our road. The bear was lying on his back and holding the battery box in his paws, completely engrossed with licking out the inside of it. Sulphuric acid probably tastes something like formic acid, and perhaps he thought his find was some kind of newfangled ant's nest.

Ants are not bad food, as we once found out when my brother and I were small boys wandering the wilderness like Seton's "two little savages." We were exploring new country clear over a mountain range, when we lost our horses and were left afoot with no choice but to walk out. We had nothing to eat and were still miles from home, when we were brought to a reluctant halt by sheer hunger and exhaustion.

We found a big cottonwood stump swarming with huge wood ants. The bears ate them, we knew, and why not us? We tried them and found them delicious—something like gooseberries in flavor—if one shuts his eyes and chews swiftly. A good feed of ants put us on our feet again, and we reached home none the worse for our adventure.

As I said earlier, grizzlies can teach us much. Quite likely the wilderness traveler walks past a great variety of nourishing food every day without recognizing it. It might not be a bad idea for the man caught in the wilds without food to find out what the bears are eating and follow suit. Short of carrion, most bear food is fairly acceptable to man, and the big animals could probably point the way toward emergency rations and a means of survival.

4. *Are* GRIZZLIES *Man-Killers?*

A man is not a criminal for fighting
in self-defense; neither is a grizzly—
apparently the self-defense of the
grizzly is responsible for his
criminal reputation.
—ENOS A. MILLS

Men, being largely of a mind to shoot grizzlies full of holes on sight and too often being sloppy enough about it to get themselves into trouble, are inclined to paint the big bear as an uncompromising, fierce, and ferocious killer. If the grizzly bear were half as bad as commonly portrayed, such explorers as Kelsey and Lewis and Clark would not have gotten far across the prairies, and the opening of the West would in all likelihood have been delayed until the advent of repeating rifles.

The big trouble is, men and bears have never been able to get together and work out what constitutes an attack on the part of the bear. Man, being civilized and having highly cultivated ethics, not to say the last word in principles, has always had difficulty recognizing the ethics of others. Grizzlies also have ethics and very definite ideas of proper protocol, wherein lies the crux of the dispute. Consequently the history of their meetings is made infinitely more interesting and colorful; but unfortunately man has still not developed much sympathy for the bear, and grizzlies have largely concluded that the farther they can get from men, the better.

A grizzly is a big animal—one of the biggest carnivores in the world—and he has a stern countenance. Even when just moving along in a very carefree fashion, he looks like a charge of dynamite wrapped up in hide and fur with a short fuse smouldering. Rare and intrepid is the man who would think for a moment of keeping one as a house pet. Upon meeting the bear suddenly at close range, most men either reach for their weapons or come apart at the seams and fall into character by rushing into panic. Either way they smell bad to the sensitive nose of the bear, and that animal reacts according to its nature. Consequently all hell has been known to break loose, and no matter what the result, the case for the true defendant has most often been influenced by a biased jury.

Too often the grizzly bear has been maligned through no fault but being present. Like men, individual bears react differently to intrusion upon their privacy, and the variation of behavior covers some considerable range. Shy individuals will move out to new territory when men intrude. Some will adjust partially, sometimes even going so far as to show little alarm upon contact with man-smell, sometimes perhaps growing contemptuous to the point of raiding grub caches and garbage dumps. Others will tolerate the presence of humans but remain furtive, nervous, and suspicious. These are subject to what psychologists label "negative conditioning," a polite way of saying, "I know all about it and am damned well fed up with it!" In these latter cases something one day occurs to tip the delicate balance of temper, and then things most unpleasant can happen.

My good friend the late Levi Ashman, well-known British Columbia trapper of many years' experience in the wilderness, once told of a somewhat laughable adventure with a grizzly. Levi was cutting trail along a mountain slope in the midst of his

wilderness territory one hot day in June. He was suffering from
thirst and climbed down into a wooded canyon for a drink. He
was accompanied by a dog, a crossbred husky-German shepherd
someone had given him. While Levi lay flat drinking from the
stream, the dog let out a great roar and took after something in
the timber across the creek. Before Levi could do more than lift
his head, a returning procession split the creek in a cloud of
spray, the dog leading with a large and very angry grizzly
bringing up the rear.

Levi was not a young man any more, but this did not slow
his enthusiastic squirreling up a tree. There he clung to the slim
bole of a lodgepole pine, while the dog and the bear played
ring-around-a-rosy at its base. The bear eventually wearied of
chasing the dog in the hot sun and left, whereupon Levi slid
down to terra firma.

The dog greeted this belated arrival of reinforcement with
great joy and, emitting another enthusiastic roar, promptly took
off after the grizzly again. Following Levi's profane instructions,
the dog came back even faster, again closely pursued by the irate
bear. Once more Levi went up the tree.

"By the time that damfool dog got it into his thick head, I
wasn't about to come down and help him fight that grizzly and
the grizzly decided to leave for good, I was sure getting tired of
camping in that tree," Levi said, by way of winding up his story.
"It didn't have a branch for forty feet and was slippery as a
barber's pole!"

"I'll bet you tied the dog up in camp after that," I remarked.

"Hell no!" Levi snorted. "I shot the son-of-a-bitch! Dog
like that can get a man killed. Didn't know how to mind his own
business."

However sudden and final for the dog, Levi was a man who
put the blame where blame was due. When a grizzly decides to
show his independence and assert his claim to his country, he
can be a most impressive animal.

Another good friend, Russell Bennett, a mining engineer
and author of note, tells of an interesting incident illustrating

the grizzly's inborn streak of fearless independence. Russell was surveying some mining claims in the mountains of southeast British Columbia and was hiking up a well-used trail one day with a strong breeze at his back. A couple of hundred yards ahead, he spotted a big grizzly coming down the trail toward him. Obviously the bear had his scent, but the big animal did not hesitate. It was apparent he meant to use this trail regardless of the man.

Russell was carrying his rifle, but he had no intention to use it unless the bear chose to press an attack. Wondering what the grizzly had in mind, he climbed a few feet up onto a ledge above the trail and sat down to wait. The bear came on at a fast walk, and upon reaching a spot only a few yards away, he stopped to look squarely at the man. For several long moments the bear stood his ground. His attitude spoke plainer than words: "This is my trail. Keep that in mind!" Suddenly he moved to pass below and disappeared down the canyon.

Stories about grizzlies are legion. Some are true, and some are so distorted by passage from one campfire to another that true grizzly character becomes so well hidden as to be hardly recognizable. The historian is hard pressed to separate the wheat from the chaff, a necessity not particularly helped by the great individual variations of character inherent to the grizzly bear. The longer I live, the more I hesitate to state firmly that grizzlies do or do not do certain things; for as surely as one does, some grizzly comes along and proceeds to upset the applecart of profound wisdom.

There are eminent authorities who will unhesitatingly claim, for instance, that grizzlies will not eat human flesh. I go along with this assertion, for I know the smell of man in a grizzly's nose is disgusting almost to the point of nausea; but there might be extenuating circumstances. Certainly the grizzly of the wilderness frontier was not afraid of man. Fear came with the white man and his powerful rifle.

Perhaps the strangest story ever circulated in our mountains was told by an old Indian chief many years ago to my father-in-law, Bert Riggall, one of the pioneer outfitters and

guides in the Alberta Rockies, a recognized naturalist and botanist. When Bert Riggall first came to this section of the country
with a survey party in 1903, a big party of Stonie Indians were
camped on Cottonwood Creek about a mile north of our present
home. These Indians were an offshoot of the Assiniboin tribe of
the Assiniboine Mountains in Manitoba. They were excellent
mountain hunters, who made their climbing moccasins from the
thick, spongy hides of mountain goats and ranged up among the
peaks above the hunting grounds of the Blackfeet.

The Stonies were methodical, well-organized hunters, who
perfected a most effective system of driving in pursuit of mountain game. While the squaws, youngsters, and old people went
into the valleys with numerous dogs, the braves deployed along
high trails crossing the ridges and passes. Sometimes they used
natural cover for a hide, but if such was not suitably located,
they built blinds of loose stones close to the game trails. At a
signal a great din was set up by the drivers and their dogs that
was sufficient to send the game animals scampering for the
heights. There they ran into the ambushes and were sometimes
slaughtered in piles along narrow defiles. Bert Riggall recorded
that the party on the Cottonwood packed out forty pack-horse
loads of dried jerky and buckskin when they left. This repre-
sents a considerable number of animals the size of deer and
sheep; for there was practically no bigger game left in the
country at that time. Consequently, when Bert took up his homestead on the Cottonwood shortly after, he found lean hunting.
One valley, Yarrow Creek canyon, was an exception. No Indian
trails penetrated its thickly wooded bottom, and it teemed with
bighorns and mule deer.

Bert was friendly with the senior Stonie chief, King Bear's
Paw, and when the old man heard he was hunting the Yarrow
country, he made a long ride to warn Bert of a peril. Yarrow
Creek valley was taboo to the Indians. The old chief told a tragic
story of the origin of the taboo.

About 1860 most of the Stonie tribe was gathered in a great
wintering camp on the edge of the mountains along the Bow
River, just east of where Banff National Park is now located.

Their lodges were pitched on ground later to become their reservation. During the winter they were stricken with smallpox, the dread disease introduced by white men. Having no resistance to it and understanding nothing of its treatment, the Indians died like flies. Very early in the spring a party of still healthy survivors packed their travois and fled south, trying to escape the scourge. They set up their teepees on the flat where Yarrow Creek debouches from the mountains.

But they carried the infection with them, and this camp was soon paralyzed with sickness. The Indians became so demoralized and helpless that they could not even dispose of their dead in the usual fashion, but they just dragged the bodies of unfortunate relatives and friends into the brush on the edge of camp and left them to rot.

The bears were just coming out of den, hungry as usual, and were inevitably attracted by the constant smell of carrion. As King Bear's Paw recounted, the grizzlies began by feeding on dead bodies, and then growing bolder, they came right into camp to take Indians not yet dead and even to attack some few survivors. These understandably panicked and stampeded, leaving the place to the bears. To this day no Stonie has ever made a moccasin track in Yarrow Creek canyon again.

"The bears are very bad there," King Bear's Paw warned. "They have tasted the meat of men. Stay out of that country."

Bert recognized and appreciated the old man's concern. He gave him some small presents of tea, tobacco, and sugar, thanked him solemnly, and assured him that he would be very careful and that his bear medicine was very strong. Shaking his head, the chief left.

One day not long afterward Bert was back in the canyon cutting trail through some heavy growth of wind-twisted pine and spruce. He was chopping a way through a tangle below a series of shelving rock ledges when he noticed his horse, ground-hitched a few yards behind him, suddenly throw up its head and stare fixedly at something on the slope above. Bert could see nothing from his position, so he went back and mounted his horse for a better view. To his astonishment he saw two big grizzlies sneaking stealthily down through the low scrub growing on the ledges toward the spot he had just left.

They did not see him till he yelled. Then they milled around with their hair up, alternately rearing and snuffling, while he sat his saddle with his rifle cocked and ready. It was an early vintage .30–30, and at that moment it seemed a very inadequate arm. Bert knew that shooting one grizzly in such a place would very likely bring both animals down on him, so he held his fire. Finally the grizzlies departed. Bert was never quite sure if they were drawn by curiosity or if they had some mischief in mind. From then on, while working alone in the canyon, his rifle was always within easy reach, and on occasion he found use for it.

Some fifty years after the grizzlies' raid on the Indian camp in Yarrow Creek another incident occurred, in the spring of 1912, that at first glance seemed to corroborate a grizzly propensity for eating human flesh.

A trapper by the name of Slim Lynch was working the lower valley of Kishaneena Creek, about thirty miles west of Yarrow valley. He was the foster son of a widower by the name of Beebe, who, with three grown sons and Slim, was trapping the tributaries of the North Fork of the Flathead River in the vicinity of the International Boundary.

Slim had a line cabin built near extensive beaver colonies about ten miles up Kishaneena Creek on the Canadian side of the border; and he was busy harvesting pelts when trouble arrived. The trapper had been skinning the beaver at his cabin and carelessly discarding the carcasses in the nearby timber. No smell will draw a grizzly like the odor of fat, half-ripe beaver. A big silvertip moved in on this bonanza of feed, and as time passed the bear grew bold. Slim carried only a belt gun and quite likely was worried about the bear breaking into his cabin during his frequent absences and ruining his stockpile of pelts. So he tied the furs on a packboard and snowshoed out to his main cabin on the Flathead. He told his foster father about the bear and said something about setting a gun for it.

At that time the set gun was a common and effective way

for trappers to take a grizzly. Such a gun was light and compact and could be carried in a backpack much easier than an adequate steel trap. Although some set guns were specifically designed and manufactured for the job, most trappers manufactured their own simply by shortening the barrel and stock of a cheap single-shot twelve-gauge shotgun. The gun was fixed in the apex of a V-shaped pen built of logs, with a couple of small trees growing close together enclosed in the small end of the pen. A nail was put through a hole bored for that purpose in the butt of the gun and driven into the rear tree. The barrel was then lashed solidly to the tree in front so that it pointed towards the open end of the enclosure. A string was run from the trigger back over a convenient knot or another nail behind the gun and then forward over a crossbar fixed just in front of the muzzle, where a bait was hung on the end of it. The gun was cocked to make it ready for a tug on the bait, which would send a lethal lead slug or charge of heavy buckshot into the head of the victim that had been decoyed into position. Many a grizzly thus ignominiously shot himself.

Either Slim forgot to take a regular set gun, or he decided to use his Luger automatic pistol, a recently acquired weapon that was the last word in side arms at the time. He lashed his pistol at the back of a log pen built for the purpose, hung a juicy piece of beaver meat on the trigger string, and retired for the night to his cabin.

Sometime in the night the trapper was jerked awake by the sharp crack of the pistol. Slipping his feet into his moccasins, he went out into the moonlight to investigate. The clearing in front of the cabin was lit up like day, but there was no sign of the grizzly. Upon examining his set, Slim found that the tug on the string had somehow tipped the short gun in its lashing before it fired, so the bullet went harmlessly high.

Anticipating the return of the grizzly, he was in a hurry to reset the gun and made a fatal mistake. Somehow he forgot the pistol was an autoloader, and while he was adjusting another bait, his hand slipped and instantly orange flame stabbed at him from the muzzle of the gun. The 9 mm. cupronickel-jacketed bullet plowed into his stomach and out his back under a shoulder blade. Mortally wounded, the trapper managed to stagger back to his cabin, where he collapsed on his bunk.

What happened then was for many years fogged by the exaggeration and dramatization of a story told and retold around countless campfires. Presumably the grizzly came back and, striking the fresh blood trail leading into the cabin, followed it. Pressing through the open door, the bear grabbed the trapper off the bunk. The desperate man clutched at bedding and bunk, which was smashed, torn, and strewn across the cabin floor. The bear dragged his victim outside and killed and ate him. Later a search party found his scattered remains and buried them at the foot of a big western larch near the cabin.

When I first heard this story, I believed it; but later a better knowledge of grizzly character made me wonder. In the summer of 1952, forty years after the tragedy, I was guiding a party of geologists on the upper reaches of the Flathead in British Columbia, where I met and came to know a very remarkable man by the name of Charlie Wise. Charlie was then seventy years old, but he carried his six-foot frame as straight as an arrow and still followed his wilderness trapline. A very trustworthy and keen-minded man, he told me the facts of the Slim Lynch story.

About the time of Slim's unfortunate accident a warm, heavy downpour began that lasted several days. Augmented by fast-melting snow, the Kishaneena and other creeks feeding the Flathead River were soon roaring over their banks and the river itself was a berserk flood of completely impassable waters. When Slim failed to show up as expected, the Beebes naturally supposed he had been cut off by the floods and were not unduly concerned at first. But when the waters began to go down and still Slim failed to make an appearance, they set out to look for him, accompanied by Charlie Wise.

The mounted search party had considerable difficulty fording their horses across still-swollen streams, but finally they managed to reach Slim's cabin. Immediately they knew something was desperately wrong. No smoke came from the chimney, the door hung awry, and there was a sickly smell of death in the air. The interior of the cabin was a shambles. Mixed with a mess of debris in front of the cabin they found the pitiful remains of Slim—thigh bones, skull, pelvis, and a few other fragments. The pistol was still set in its pen, loaded and cocked, ready to blast anything that pulled the string. A dark-stained wool undershirt with a bullet hole front and back was found. Bit by bit they found evidence telling the grim story.

There were two cartridges missing from the pistol magazine, and on the ground were two empty cartridge cases, which indicated that the gun had been fired twice. Because Slim had reported a grizzly on his visit to the base cabin, they knew a grizzly bear was involved, although all sign was washed away by the flood. They did find some fresh black-bear tracks. The original story was correct except that Charlie Wise was convinced that Slim had been long dead, when a black bear, not a grizzly, had raided the cabin, torn the trapper's body to pieces and eaten it.

Because the trail to the nearest settlement was impassable and no official could be immediately contacted, they buried what was left of Slim under a huge tamarac and marked the grave with a blaze. The blaze is still visible on the old tree beside the ruins of the cabin. Later Slim's remains were exhumed and reinterred in the cemetery at Columbia Falls, Montana.

The wilderness trapper's attitude toward the grizzly has usually been one of conflict. Perhaps the most notable encounter between a trapper and a grizzly occurred in 1823. It involved Hugh Glass, a tough, irascible, fiercely independent free trapper—one of those early mountain men, a very specialized breed concerned with the exploration and early fur trade of the West. Fabulously tough and self-reliant products of their environment, such men could out-Indian the Indians: they retained their scalps in hostile country by knowing their enemies, by their ability to see and instantly read the slightest sign, to react in an emergency with the speed and sureness of a striking snake, and to fight like fury when the occasion called for it. Hugh Glass was a dour Scot with a built-in stubbornness and a power of endurance that met its supreme test up on the forks of the Grand River in northern South Dakota long before that place became a state.

He was with an organized party of trappers exploring for new beaver trapping grounds, when apparently he went off by himself against orders. Somehow he lost his horse. Proceeding on foot, he encountered a big she-grizzly with cubs, whereupon they tangled.

What happened then is somewhat hazy, but when the searching trappers found old Hugh, he was terribly mauled. They got him to camp and waited for him to die, but he refused to. So two of the trappers, one John Fitzgerald and a youth, identified by some chroniclers as Jim Bridger, were assigned to stay with him till the end. Hugh lingered on as stubborn as ever, putting them in great danger, for the country was full of hostile Indians. So they left him on the edge of his grave and hurried to catch up with the rest of the party.

Old Hugh regained consciousness to find himself alone. When through the fog of fever and pain he came to realize that he had been abandoned by his friends, his bitter rage and desire for revenge fanned a spark of life into a flame. Incredibly, he began very slowly to mend.

Eating anything he could find, completely unarmed, he started out on the most epic crawl in history—back toward distant Fort Kiowa on the Missouri River. He ate gophers, bugs, berries, roots, rattlesnakes, and the left-overs from wolf kills. He endured unbelievable torment. Each time despair engulfed him, making him wish to die, his spirit was picked up by his anger, and he set out crawling again. With the days blurring into an endless torture, he crawled more than one hundred long, suffering miles to the banks of the Cheyenne River. There he contrived a crude boat from a hollow cottonwood log, and in this he floated down the Cheyenne to its confluence with the Missouri and thence to Fort Kiowa, another hundred fifty miles. There he recovered, and as stubborn as ever, he set out once more on the trail of revenge. Having heard some details of his abandonment by Fitzgerald and Bridger through the moccasin telegraph, his anger had a focal point. He finally hunted them down and confronted them, like a spirit risen from the dead, but only after he had made still another harrowing journey alone through hundreds of miles of hostile wilderness with terrific hardship and danger. Then and only then was he persuaded that they had done the best they could, and he relented.

Hugh Glass's recovery is only one of many survivals from mauling by grizzlies. Strangely enough, this big animal rarely kills a man outright, and many men have survived such encounters. It is as though the grizzly is so nauseated by the smell of man that he goes about the business in a mincing fashion. While I have seen many full-grown cattle that have been killed by grizzlies with dispatch, for some reason the grizzly rarely chooses to kill a man. Only when the encounter involves a close-range surprise that invites a smashing blow from a paw is the outcome sudden and final.

As told by Bert Riggall, such an incident occurred while he was with the government survey party in 1903 up on the High-wood River. Intensive prospecting for coal was being done at the time in the Highwood valley. One of the claims was owned by two men whose names have been lost in the passage of time. They had built their camp on a high bench overlooking the valley and had cut a switchback trail from their cabin down to the main trail.

One evening in the fall, after work, one of the partners proposed to visit some friends who were working another prospect a mile or so down river. It was getting dark, and a threatening snow squall hung over the surrounding peaks, so he took a coal-oil lantern and set out on foot. The wind came up, and it began to snow, so when he did not return, his partner went to bed thinking his friend had changed his mind and would be away for the night. But when morning came and still the missing man did not appear, the other partner set out down the trail toward the neighboring cabin to investigate. When he got there, his inquiry was met with blank stares of surprise. The missing man had never shown up.

An immediate call of alarm was sent out to rally a fairly

large search party, including the surveyors. The light snow had melted in the meantime, and after some searching, the missing man's tracks were found where he had taken a short cut down across the first switchback in the trail below the cabin. This provided a clue to follow, and in a short time the searchers were horrified to find what was left of him.

It seems that he had been coming downhill at a run through the timber and, jumping a deadfall log, almost landed on a she-grizzly with a small cub. Acting on reflex, he apparently hit her over the head with the lantern, for it was found broken and flattened. A split second later she caught him with the full swing of her paw with such force that about all that was left holding his upper torso to his hips was the backbone. Almost completely eviscerated, the man died instantly. The bear swung on her heels and fled at a tearing gallop, as her tracks showed. It is quite likely that she was as surprised and frightened as the unfortunate miner, for she had not lingered to worry the body.

Hardly a year goes by even yet in grizzly bear country without one or two maulings occurring. What triggers these unfortunate happenings is not always clear, and generally speaking, the newspaper accounts give very little help. They are generally loaded with misunderstanding, and very little sympathy is shown the grizzly, following the unreasonable assumption that man is the only animal with license to take life.

A proportion of such incidents involves hunters who for one reason or another choose to shoot a grizzly somewhere on the outside edge and then fail to finish the job. Somehow I feel sympathy only for the bear in such a case. Having hunted the grizzly for many years as a professional guide and in predator control work, I know what it is to face a wounded grizzly. I am also aware to what lengths a grizzly will sometimes go to avoid a man, even when sorely wounded. Certainly a grizzly cannot be blamed for fighting back, and if a hunter is so witless or out of luck as to get mauled, it is but a whim of fate, the luck of the game, which should be accepted by all without recrimination.

The fast-increasing intrusion of people into the grizzly country of our national parks over the past few years has vastly increased the incidence of contact between bears and hikers. In proportion to numbers of people using the parks, the incidence of risk is very low—a small fraction of the potential hazard encountered while driving to the parks in an automobile. However where a car accident resulting in multiple deaths and horrible mangling of possible survivors will only receive terse, factual treatment in the newspapers and will cause only a slight ripple of public reaction, an incident involving a grizzly warrants screaming headlines and unduly sensational coverage. As a result, the cry "parks are for people" has been heard, and some who should certainly know better have even advocated the elimination of the grizzly bear. There can be no joy in or appreciation of the wilderness in such an attitude.

Fortunately, there are many people who enjoy adventure for the sake of adventure and would not trade a brush with a grizzly for anything. Although such an event would not be particularly welcome or enjoyable at the time, looking back on it provides a good deal of enjoyment and interest.

Mary Faegre was such a person who loved adventure for its own sake. She and her husband, Bart, and two teen-aged sons along with another boy who was a friend of the family were out on a wilderness pack-train trip as Bert Riggall's guests years ago. With Bert in the lead and a long string of horses lined out behind him the whole party was enjoying a fine afternoon in the high country of some of the best mountain wilderness of British Columbia. Heading up trail toward a timberline campsite on the rim of the Wall Lake Basin, Bert noticed fresh grizzly sign of a sow with two small cubs. The herbage of a little bench meadow was flattened out where the cubs had been playing a small grizzly version of football with a well-chewed round root. Bert was not much concerned, for grizzly sign was common, and the big bears usually moved away from the vicinity of the camps at the noise of the horse bells.

The party camped at this spot for several days, fishing and taking rides among the peaks. The trip was at its end, and on the final morning the crew struck camp and began packing up. While the packs were being put on the horses, Mary Faegre took a towel and went to a small pond a couple of hundred yards south of camp in big timber and took a bath. After her dip in the icy water she stretched out in the sun on top of a flat boulder and dozed off to sleep. She was thirsty when she awakened, so she walked up a small stream a few yards and knelt down for a drink. A noise in the bushes directly across from her made her look up, and she was horrified to find herself face to face with a big grizzly only a few feet away.

Mary's wilderness experience was limited to one or two pack-train trips, and most certainly nothing had prepared her for this. But she was a cool and plucky little lady, and stifling an impulse to scream and run, she remembered Bert's admonition: "Never run from a bear." She slowly straightened up and got to her feet, still facing the grizzly. The bear's hair was up, but it came no closer. Mary could hear her own heart beating. She tried calling, but the brisk breeze through the timber muffled her voice, and the sound made the bear growl menacingly. Afraid to call again, she edged slowly toward camp; but the grizzly circled to cut off this line of retreat, forcing her down the creek past the pond, with the bear keeping between her and camp. Mary remembered Bert saying that grizzlies do not often climb trees, so she began looking for one—with little success: the timber was big, and nearly all the tree trunks were liberally spiked with down-sloping dry branches near the ground.

As Mary moved, the grizzly kept pace with her. So long as she did not press toward camp, it seemed satisfied to proceed without showing fight. An easy tree to climb seemed as illusive and difficult to find as a path to heaven. Her route took her in a wide arc around camp, step by cautious step—a strange, unbelievable nightmare in which she and the great bear journeyed together. She did not notice the white clouds sailing against the bright blue sky or hear the soft sounds of the breeze stirring the conifers. They passed through glades spangled with brilliant alpine flowers, but these were only a part of a bad dream in color. Meanwhile the grizzly continued to pad soundlessly along beside her as though moving on velvet, never more than a few feet away, its sweet, doglike smell assailing her nostrils.

Yard by yard they went for over a half mile. The minutes were like hours, and it seemed the search for a climbable tree would never end. Then Mary's heart jumped with hope, for ahead through the trees she saw a big, bleached-out windfall lodged against a big spruce, its trunk forming a steep-pitched ramp to safety. Hardly daring to breath, she edged toward it. By this time the bear had assumed the intelligence of a demon with its mind set on preventing her escape. Mary was almost afraid to look directly at the tree, for fear the bear would cut her off from it. She finally reached out to touch the tree with her hand, paused to look at the grizzly to judge its range, and then shot up the tree like a squirrel to a safe perch.

In the meantime all the horses had been packed, and the outfit was ready to move. Repeated calls brought no response, and everyone spread out to look for Mary. When Bert found the abandoned towel and fresh grizzly tracks by the pond, he knew real alarm. The crew was set to combing the timber on horseback in every direction, calling as they went. Finally one of the boys gave a stentorian bellow from a position high up on the slope back of the camp and received a faint reply from way off to the north. Together he and Bert galloped their horses toward the sound. The crashing of horses' hoofs coming at a run caused the grizzly to abandon its vigil beneath Mary's tree, and they found her laughing and crying with relief at the sight of them. They put her on a horse and took her back to camp, where she told her incredible story.

Recounting it to me years later on another pack-train trip, Mary said with a trill of lighthearted laughter: "The experience frightened me very much at the time, but looking back on it is interesting. Besides, what a wonderful story to tell my grandchildren!"

It would seem upon the evidence concerning many incidents of humans being mauled by grizzlies that if man appreciated the true character of the grizzly as much as the grizzly does the character of man, most such unfortunate occurrences would never happen.

5. *In the Society of* GRIZZLIES

To really know him, one must
recognize his great curiosity.
—ENOS A. MILLS

In the broad and infinitely complicated world of nature there is a certain dependence of one form of life on another, much like a giant tapestry woven from myriad threads into a complex pattern; each thread by itself means nothing and is very delicate, but in the warp and woof of the design each is immeasurably strong and meaningful. From the stark tundra of the Arctic to the steaming equatorial jungles each living thing is directly or indirectly bound up with other living things, while these connections may be either commensal or predaceous, their existence is beyond any question.

It might seem incongruous to cite an association between the tuna and the grizzly bear, for each lives in totally different elements. One is cold-blooded, the other warm-blooded; and both are about as far separated in general habit as two species can be. Yet the tuna occasionally feeds on the salmon in the ocean, and the grizzly feeds on them in the rivers: the connecting thread is joined. When man decides to build a dam across the river, cutting off the salmon from access to their spawning beds, the silver hordes are wiped out in that section by their inability to create a new generation, and the thread is broken. Not only does man lose a valuable source of food and income, for which he must sooner or later find a substitute, but the bears and tuna affected also turn their attention elsewhere. This may disturb the ecology of their particular environments, and consequently more and more threads are cut.

The seed of the white pine has a tough, hermetically sealed shell designed by nature to keep it in a state of suspended fertility for many years. So it may lay buried under a thickening blanket of leaf mold until a fire or the hoof of a passing animal cracks the shell, thus allowing moisture to enter and start germination. Or a grizzly may swallow the seed whole while raiding a squirrel cache or digging for roots, and it will pass through his digestive system and be ejected with the shell sufficiently weakened by stomach acids to allow germination. The parent tree may be cut by man for match timber, but its replacement is thus assured by the bear. Another thread can be traced.

A boy wandering the wilds with his father sees the great bear stalking in majesty and power across a sun-bathed glade beneath the gnarled limbs and feathery foliage of mountain larches. This sight, one of the most impressive and unforgettable in a lifetime, may open a door to the adventure of living and show the boy an excitement and a mystery so enticing and challenging that he may bend himself toward becoming a great natural scientist. What he then discovers may be of the greatest importance to men and grizzlies. Thus the mere presence of the great bear can reveal another thread that will lead to many more, thus generating thoughts which otherwise might never have begun.

At first glance we may be tempted to believe that human life is paramount and that it is the only life in the scheme of nature worth a second thought. If we too literally and selfishly follow this view, with small consideration for other forms of life, burying them one by one with our shovel of "progress," we will ultimately destroy the vital quality of our own lives. Even if we choose to moderate too late, we will lose those two things most cherished by all men: peace and freedom.

It may not mean immediate fortune to answer the call of

the wild with a resoundingly affirmative voice, but it is one grand
way to find peace. Edward Carpenter has said: "There is a
presence and an influence in Nature and the Open, which ex-
pands the mind and causes brigand cares and worries to drop
off—whereas in confined places foolish and futile thoughts of all
kinds swarm like microbes and cloud and conceal the soul." So
if man recognize the grizzly as an associate, as an important
thread in the necessary pattern of nature and man's future,
rather than as an enemy, he cannot help but preserve the kind of
country necessary for a modicum of peace and freedom.

The animals I have encountered in my wilderness wanderings have been reluctant to reveal all the things about them I
would like to know. The animal that impresses me most, the one
I find myself liking more and more, is the grizzly. No sight
encountered in the wilds is quite so stirring as those massive,
clawed tracks pressed into mud or snow. No sight is quite so
impressive as that of the great bear stalking across some mountain slope with the fur of his silvery robe rippling over his
mighty muscles. His is a dignity and power matched by no other
in the North American wilderness. To share a mountain with
him for a while is a privilege and an adventure like no other.

I have followed his tracks into an alder hell to see what he
had been doing and come to the abrupt end of them, when the
maker stood up thirty feet away with a sudden snort to face me.
I have pursued him as a hunter for days and months on end,
watched him through powerful glasses hour after hour, and shot
him head on at close range with both rifle and camera. Never is
the thrill of such contact lessened by long association, and always I am left wondering about his way of life. There is a
fascination about the ways of the grizzly that forever prods and
calls for more investigation.

His association with other animals is a mixture of enterprising action, almost magnanimous acceptance, and just plain
willingness to ignore. There is great strength and pride combined with a strong mixture of inquisitive curiosity in the
make-up of grizzly character. This curiosity is what makes trouble when men penetrate into country where they are not known

to the bear. The grizzly can be brave and sometimes downright brash. He can be secretive and very retiring. He can be extremely cunning and also powerfully aggressive. Whatever he does, his actions match his surroundings and the circumstance of the moment. No wonder that meeting him on his mountain is a momentous event, imprinted on one's mind for life.

I have come on the grizzly in sudden and mutual surprise at close range among tangled, fire-killed down logs while riding my horse up a mountain draw, and he reared and snorted angrily at my unannounced intrusion. Then he ran; but when he had gone only a little way, he turned to come raging back. My horse and I, being in no fit place for anything but standing our ground, remained absolutely still. Again he went, this time halfway up the slope before turning to come charging back again. The third time he went over the rim of the flanking ridge. When I rode up to see where he had gone, I saw him fleeing in the distance as though pursued by devils, and I knew this to be a proud animal not wishing to lose face by instant flight.

To compare him with his lesser cousin, the black bear, is like standing a case of dynamite beside a sack of goose feathers. In grizzly country one sees aspens scarred by the claws of black bears who have escaped the embarrassment of sudden contact or perhaps are practicing in anticipation of it. The black bear is a thief, but when the grizzly chooses to pilfer, he is an arrogant brigand. The black is a sneak. While the grizzly knows how, when occasion calls for it, he makes it look like going with prudent care.

When one sees a black bear in the midst of grizzly country, it is like watching a sheep thief stealing past a vigilantes' camp. As has been recounted elsewhere, the grizzly is not averse to dining on black bear occasionally. Sometimes he chases the lesser cousin just for the fun of seeing him run. At other times the grizzly loftily refuses to recognize the existence of the lesser one, but this does not lessen the black bear's timorousness at his proximity in the same neighborhood.

One day in June, when it was warm and the air smelled of sun on new leaves and many growing things, I saw a black bear coming down a fence line through heavy aspens and cottonwoods on our ranch. The bear was mooching along toward me, completely oblivious of my presence, so I stepped behind a tree to watch him pass no more than twenty feet away upwind. Slouching along in that typical rolling walk, the obsidian black of his coat glinted in deep blue highlights in the brilliant sunlight. He shortly cut through the fence into a cottonwood grove about a hundred yards past me, and in the next moment all hell broke loose, heralded by the sharp, alarm bark of a cow elk. Then the bear reappeared coming pell-mell back along his trail with his hind feet fanning his ears at every jump. Spread out and running like race horses in pursuit came a half dozen mother elk with the hair standing on end along their necks and backs and their ears hanging in anger as though slung on swivels. A big one in the lead struck hard with her front feet at the bear's rump and missed his ridiculous excuse of a tail by a hair. The bear, in his precipitate rush to get somewhere else fast, ran into the bottom wire of the fence and broke it like a string. The whole procession went by me so fast that I had little time to do more than turn my head. The last I saw of the bear, he was gaining a bit, but the cow elk were still hot on his heels.

A grizzly wandering into an elk nursery would cause no less of an uproar, but there would be no hounds-and-hare chase. The grizzly would most likely go about his business, which might include taking a calf if one was located near enough to catch; but whatever the outcome, there would be no question for a moment as to the dominating presence on the scene. When a grizzly comes within notice of cow elk, they either edge away or stand on some lookout point barking and stamping. Bull elk pay little attention unless the bear comes too close.

The huge Alaskan and Yukon moose weigh about five or six hundred pounds more than the Shiras type found on southern ranges. Those moose I saw in the subarctic country seem to have a kind of truce with grizzlies, for I never saw either species show much sign of recognition upon passing on the tundra. A moose can employ its razor-sharp hooves and weight with telling effect when attacked. Grizzlies, being no fonder of getting caught un-

Pack horses look right in grizzly country, but snowshoes are required in winter (author and snowshoes above). A neighbor of the northern grizzly is the longtailed jaeger, web-footed predator and nest raider.

The moment of truth for the bear hunter; a shot at a grizzly in sheep country in the Canadian Rockies.

der such an animated pile driver than any other fairly intelligent animal, would have to encounter a full-grown moose under rare and advantageous conditions to be tempted into an attack.

Adolph Murie tells of seeing a grizzly being stood off by a cow moose with a newborn calf in Wyoming. The grizzly was apparently stalking the calf, and the cow became aware of its presence and came to stand over her offspring with her hair up, showing every intention of fighting. The bear did not press the issue, which might indicate some previous painful experience or just natural caution. No doubt the big bears do prey on moose calves on occasion, but it is doubtful if such predation shows any appreciable effect on the number of moose. Grizzlies have been known to take mature moose, but this is rare. For the most part the two animals live in peace throughout their ranges.

Mountain sheep will sometimes greet the sight of a grizzly with interest and curiosity as a diversion offering a break in everyday life on their mountains. My sons Dick and Charlie, while helping me make a bighorn film a number of years ago, were out scouting one afternoon when they heard a curious bawling sound up on a big avalanche track across the valley from where they sat their horses. They were astonished when through their glasses they saw two large grizzlies walking around on the open slope like two strange dogs meeting on a street corner. They were bawling and grumbling at each other while several bighorn rams looked down interestedly from an outcropping ledge twenty-five yards up the slope like ringside spectators waiting for the opening round of a championship fight. The mating season was long past, and the grizzlies were probably arguing about whose territory was being invaded. They continued their circling and grumbling for a few minutes and then, having apparently reached some sort of reasonable agreement, moved off in separate ways. All the while the curious rams looked on with no fear of these burly visitors.

Another time I was sitting with glasses glued to my eyes in rapt concentration on the activities of a band of dall-sheep ewes and lambs up in the western Yukon mountains not far from Kluane Lake. The sheep had chosen their lambing ground high on the rugged face of broken cliffs dropping from the rocky spine of the ridge—a place almost impossible to approach. Some of the ewes had just dropped their lambs. Others were lying in various attitudes of placid repose in anticipation of it. I was wondering how a man could get near the place without breaking his neck or spooking the sheep when a beautiful blonde grizzly appeared on the skyline directly above them.

Perhaps the smell of afterbirth drew the big animal, for without the slightest hesitation the grizzly climbed down the precipitous face as easily as though walking the carpet of a slightly inclined ramp. The ewes showed little alarm. The ones closest to the bear's line of descent stood up to eye the big animal as it passed. The grizzly ignored them completely, although it came within a hundred feet of two or three of them and must certainly have been aware of the snow-white sheep.

While grizzlies are good climbers, they are no match for mountain goats, for those whiskery denizens of the crags can walk ledges that are little more than figments of the imagination. They are specifically designed by nature for walking narrow places: they are slab-sided and have little width in either shoulders or hips; their hooves are rimmed with tough horn and padded with rubbery soles like suction cups, ideal for holding on to rock. When grizzlies and goats come together, it is usually as casual passers-by.

One quiet evening among the peaks of southeast British Columbia I was standing in some shintangle fir and pine on a rim overlooking a steep-sided basin. Below my level, halfway down the loose scree of a talus slope dropping from the face of a peak and adjoining ridge, two big billy goats were feeding. Both animals were venerable old cragmasters, their beards wagging as they cropped at the alpine herbage growing among the loose slide-rock. Finally they both vigorously pawed out deep beds in this loose stuff and lay down to chew their cuds.

They were hardly settled when their heads swung as one to look down the slope. They had spotted something, but the jutting shelves under me hid most of the slope on the near side of the basin, and nothing there was visible to me. Minutes went by, and the goats' attention remained no less riveted. The angle of their solemn faces had shifted my way a bit. Whatever was coming was apparently headed for the rim of the ridge on my right, following a line between me and the goats. It was a temptation to slip down over the ledges for a look; but I had the wind in my shirt pocket on top, and lower down it might easily be blowing down the back of my neck. Ten years before I might have taken the chance to be rewarded by nothing but fleeting glimpses of the south ends of things fleeing north. Now I waited, having learned the virtue of patience.

More slow minutes went by, each one dragging more than the last. The noses of the goats had swung still further, like compass needles following a magnet. Still nothing showed. Both billies elevated their tails, a sure telegraph of a desire to move. Whatever was coming was about to reach their level, a state of affairs goats do not like on general principle.

As the billies started to climb away, a big, dark-colored grizzly with fur like a silver fox ambled into my view where the ledges sloped into the slide-rock. The bear stopped broadside about a hundred yards away to look after the retreating goats. His look was not that of a scheming predator with goat steak in mind but rather the casual glance of a mountain wayfarer passing the time of day with an acquaintance met on his journey. Again the bear pointed its nose upslope and began to climb in that long, mile-eating stride that is so deceptively fast. Upon reaching the buttress ridge, he climbed easily with only a slight slackening of pace. Suddenly he hove up briefly against the blue of the evening sky and then disappeared. Meanwhile the billies had taken up a position on a jutting point of rock halfway up the front of the peak and were watching me. They were at home, unworried and content.

Violence between these species is more by chance than design. Hornaday tells of a grizzly and a goat that met on a narrow thoroughfare hung between heaven and earth. The surprise was mutual, but neither animal retreated. The bear promptly charged the goat, and that doughty warrior bowed his neck and met his attacker head on. In the fast exchange the goat buried both horns to the hilt in the grizzly's brisket, but the bear killed him. The grizzly did not go far before it too faltered, lay down, and died. Subsequent examination of the bear showed that one of the goat's horns had penetrated its heart.

Where it is possible to watch grizzlies and other game animals mingling in open country, the picture is usually one of peaceful association. Several times in Alaska we have seen caribou, dall sheep, and grizzly bears all grazing on the same slope like so many cattle. Even our pack horses pay little attention to them in the Rockies of western Canada. On two occasions I have seen a grizzly feeding with my horses. While a certain discretion is practiced by the ruminants and the horses, there is a mutual minding of one's own business that gives no indication of stresses usually associated between a predator and prey.

While rare, there are times when animals of different species form a sort of liaison to take mutual advantage of each other's specialties. Coyotes habitually follow wolves to enjoy leftovers from kills and automatically lend their senses to the communal defense bank. More than once coyotes have been seen traveling with a badger, no doubt making use of that dirt mover's underground activities to pick off prey driven from their dens. Such a partnership is more one-sided than mutual, an affair engineered by the wily coyote and tolerated by the host.

While the grizzly is largely solitary, this animal has been known to team up with the wolf. Jim Stanton has observed such a partnership, an arrangement of apparent mutual understanding and acceptance in which each animal took advantage of the other's specialties and refinements of sense. He says such teams are made up of two old animals, the wolf being one that has probably been running alone. Since wolves and grizzlies do not attain ripe years by being stupid, the reason behind such a liaison is obvious, that is, the country worked by trappers and commercial fishermen: the former covet the wolf's hide, and the latter take a dim view of the grizzly's activities on the salmon streams.

The grizzly has a supersensitive nose, fairly good ears, and poor vision. The wolf has both keen nose and eyes enhanced by excellent ears. When two such animals team up for their mutual welfare, the combination is formidable to the point of being almost impossible for a man to approach. Both animals undoubtedly realize that four ears, four eyes, and two noses working together in the same general vicinity are much better than half the defense working from one spot. Likely the wolf shares the grizzly's fish in season and the grizzly shares the wolf's kills at other times.

Grizzly-wolf association in the wilds is largely a relationship between an inveterate hijacker and a somewhat unwilling donator of snacks. My friend Steve Hatch, Alaska Airlines pilot, part-time wildlife photographer, and a naturalist of considerable talent, made an interesting observation in Mount McKinley National Park during the summer of 1964.

Up on the open reaches of Sable Pass he saw a dead caribou bull recently killed by wolves. A lone grizzly, apparently a boar, came to feed on the kill, and when he was filled up, he went over to an adjoining snowdrift and lay down for a snooze. Later a sow with two cubs appeared on the scene. She drove the boar away and also fed on the wolf kill.

Next morning Steve saw the same lone bear feeding again, this time, astonishingly enough, accompanied by a wolf. After so much attention the caribou carcass was somewhat flattened and scattered, allowing both animals to feed without crowding each other. Both animals displayed toleration with only a few steps separating them.

Later that day a lone wolf appeared at the kill while the same grizzly was feeding again. This time the grizzly moved a short distance up the slope to stand and watch as though honoring the wolf's desire to feed. Soon another wolf showed up to smell noses with the first before joining in the feeding. Then one wolf left off to trot up the slope at an angle above the bear and, coming abreast, made a half-hearted charge at the big animal as though in play. The grizzly showed no sign of reciprocating, and this wolf left the scene. The bear moved back toward the kill, and as he approached, the remaining wolf seized a big legbone and made off with it, the grizzly in hot pursuit clear over a ridge out of sight. Soon the bear came back to feed on the leftover fragments.

Steve took this most unusual opportunity to record on moving picture film such a rarely observed drama of the wilds.

The wolverine has been pictured by some as being so fearless, ferocious, and indestructible that the grizzly will give the trail to him when they meet. While there is no accounting for the actions of some individual animals, this cannot be considered the usual way of things. One swat from a grizzly's paw or a crunch from its powerful jaws would kill a wolverine on the instant. On two occasions I have seen a wolverine in the near vicinity of grizzlies, and both times the wolverine spent a good deal of time looking furtively over a shoulder and was obviously very nervous.

We were filming a big sow grizzly and two well-grown cubs up in a little hanging valley in southeastern British Columbia one day when a wolverine showed up, sifting through the undergrowth near a dead horse claimed by the bears. The big weasel took extreme care to avoid any contact whatever and was continuously on the move.

Again, up in the Carthew Lakes country of Waterton Park we saw a curious incident that revealed an aspect of the social behavior between these species. We were located with our movie cameras beside lower Carthew Lake, trying to film the erratic activities of a colony of pikas living in an old moraine. Frank Camp rode up to tell us a wolverine was feeding on a dead buck deer in the next basin below; when we investigated, the wolverine was still feeding on the buck, which had apparently slipped on a piece of old, icy snowdrift about a thousand feet above and fallen to its death. The sun was behind the mountains by then, so we left without attempting any pictures.

Next morning when we returned, we found that the deer carcass had been claimed during the night by a grizzly, which had buried it under a heap of loose earth and stones. The wolverine was not in sight, but a few minutes later we spotted him coming down across the open front of a mountain about a mile away, headed for the cache. His final approach to the place where the buck lay was very cautious, but he was soon digging furiously to uncover it, punctuating his work with frequent looks back over a shoulder at a heavy patch of shintangle scrub a few yards behind. We were reasonably sure the grizzly was bedded down somewhere in this thicket, although we saw nothing of it. When the wolverine managed to uncover a portion of the haunch, it pulled loose a piece of meat and immediately carried it away across the open slide toward a narrow watercourse. Anticipating an opportunity to get some rare film footage, I quickly climbed down a narrow sheep trail in pursuit and came out above the spot where the wolverine had disappeared. Expecting it to show up on the far side of the gully, I had just lined up the camera when the wolverine came back past me toward the deer carcass. Fortunately the wind was right, and the animal did not see me, although I was right out in the open. It dug away industriously for a few minutes and succeeded in tearing loose another very dilapidated piece of dirt-covered venison, whereupon it returned to the little stream in the gully. Obviously the wolverine was extremely nervous about the grizzly and scuttled through these actions with all the caution of a chicken thief crossing an open yard in the moonlight. It hid with its booty behind a fringe of rank herbage at the edge of the stream, and when I moved a bit to see what it was doing, I was astonished to see it washing the meat in the water by holding the piece in its teeth and scrubbing it back and forth. When it had eaten the meat, the wolverine suddenly got my scent and bolted. The grizzly did not show up.

Unfortunately we had run out of both film and food, and it was necessary to move on, so were unable to observe this unusual and interesting association any further.

Perhaps the most startling instance of the acceptance of one species by another that I have encountered in grizzly country occurred here on our ranch in the spring of 1964, when we were more or less adopted by five grizzlies. One of these was a somewhat reluctant and suspicious old male whose amorous interests in a female put him in the role of a participant with certain reservations, but the others were remarkably trusting and unconcerned.

At the beginning severe weather conditions undoubtedly

had a bearing on their strange behavior. A rather open, warm winter had culminated in heavy falls of snow, and the mountains west of the ranch were buried deep in the loose stuff. Conditions were not enhanced by a very late spring break-up, and when the grizzlies emerged from den in early May, they found their usual ranges uninhabitable. So they moved to lower ground.

One overcast evening in early June, Kay and I were in our cottage, while twelve-year-old daughter Anne was busy with some project at the lodge a hundred yards away up the hill. Son Gordon was busy in the shop back of the cottage, and the lights were on in all the buildings. Gordon heard a noise in the yard, and looking out through the open door of the shop, he was startled to see four grizzlies standing on the road not twenty yards away. A medium-sized female and two large cubs were standing in front of a huge old boar, and all the bears were obviously intrigued with their surroundings. There was much snorting, sniffing, and excited popping of jaws as the bears alternately reared up to inspect the place. Finally the female and cubs walked right past the cottage door, following the driveway about twenty feet away. The boar was alarmed and doubled back into the aspens and saskatoon brush out of sight. Meanwhile the sow and cubs continued on through the yard and disappeared into the brush down the hill. When we went up to the lodge in the misty dusk a few minutes later, we could still hear them whoofing and sniffing in the thick growth below the buildings.

Then all was quiet for an hour or more. Anne went out to get something she had left at the cottage, while we were reading around the big fireplace. None of us gave it any thought until she burst through the door and breathlessly exclaimed about meeting a grizzly on the path between the houses. The porch light was on, and we went to investigate; the sow grizzly was standing inside its ring of light in a little hollow below the veranda, huffing and snapping her jaws. Somehow she had become separated from the cubs, which we heard in the brush behind the lodge having some kind of animated argument. The light streaming through the front windows was broken into shafts by the mist, making an eerie setting for the sound of big animals moving around the perimeter of the yard. The sounds continued for some time, and then the family apparently got together again, for things quieted down for the rest of the night. Naturally we supposed that the grizzlies had blundered unintentionally into the yard and that they would leave for good. But next morning when I stepped out under a bright sky for a look through the binoculars, the female and cubs were sprawled in the sun in a little meadow surrounded by aspens about five hundred yards down the slope, just across the fence line separating our place from that of a neighbor. They had found the carcass of a heifer that had died about six weeks earlier, and they had fed on it. Later that day we saw two more grizzlies, the same big male of the previous evening and a smaller bear, another male about four years old. All were staying in the general vicinity of the carcass, but the two males were shy. The sow, however, seemed to have decided that everything was made to order for their well-being, for she and the cubs continued to be very much at home.

We were somewhat concerned, regardless of their peaceful intentions; for this is ranching country, and while it is populated by very reasonable, friendly people, we knew these grizzlies would likely precipitate some powder-burning if they proceeded to walk into ranch yards and stand about discussing the layout in bear language. If possible, we wanted to prevent them from getting into trouble before the snow melted enough to allow them back into their normal range up in the mountains. That evening Charlie and John took a horse we did not want to keep back up onto a butte west of the buildings, well inside our property, and shot it. The grizzlies must have been keeping tabs on the whole procedure, for they immediately accepted this handout. By daylight next morning we found that they had fed heavily on it.

Thus began a three-week period of the most interesting experience with grizzlies we have ever had here on the ranch. At the beginning of this session the sow was evidently mating with the larger male. We could only guess, the cover being so heavy over most of the country that keeping tabs on the romance of grizzlies would be like repeatedly finding the proverbial needle in the haystack. She often left the two cubs alone at the horse carcass, where we saw them regularly and photographed them several times at close range. Later, when the mating was over, one cub went back to her, but the other somehow got separated, staying by himself up on Cottonwood Creek a couple of miles to the west. And we grew accustomed to seeing grizzly tracks near our home, but not once did the bears show any inclination to get into mischief.

Strangely enough they did not at first show any desire to make an appearance anywhere else, although there were two occupied ranches within a mile. But then the sow found a dead cow on an adjoining property along the Cottonwood, and she and the cub and the smaller male took turns feeding on it. These activities were confined primarily to the night hours, but as time went on they became bolder. When choosing to feed in the daylight, the grizzlies could be seen from the highway beyond, and we knew it would be only a matter of time before someone took a shot at them (spring bear season was open at that time), so I decided to give them a scare.

One afternoon when Kay spotted the female going toward this carcass, I took a rifle and followed. Coming down the steep, wooded bank of the creek, I approached within fifty yards of her and the cub without their giving me more than a brief glance. The cub was a bit edgy about my presence but did not run. I fired a shot into the ground under the sow's head. The cub jumped nervously at the impact of the bullet, but the sow just swiveled on her feet and stared at me long and hard, as though to say, "What the hell did you do a thing like that for?" For answer I put another shot into the ground beside her. The cub started away, but when the mother surprisingly chose to ignore me and returned to her feeding, it came back. I then walked down toward the grizzlies and yelled. Both bears then moved toward the creek, and as they began to cross it, I put a third shot into the water close to them. I was using a powerful .358 Winchester, and its heavy bullet made a considerable racket on hitting the water; but even this did not hurry the old bear very much. Perhaps she knew I had no intention of hurting her. The more I have to do with grizzlies, the more I am impressed with their seeming ability to study and come to know what a man is thinking. Certainly she left reluctantly, although she showed no anger or desire to fight about it.

A little later I found the young male feeding on the carcass alone. Although again armed with the rifle, I decided to try something different on him. Keeping out of sight and circling down the creek to keep the wind in my favor, I came up very quietly from behind a fold of ground to within about fifteen yards of him. The grizzly was lying on his belly with his hind-quarters toward me, completely occupied with his feeding. Reaching into the rib cage of the dead cow with a front paw, he would claw out a juicy tidbit, hold it up, and lick it off his claws. If feeding on such fare could be termed delicate, he was feeding with certain delicacy, although the air was so thick with the smell of rotten flesh, it almost lifted my hat off.

After watching the grizzly for a minute or two, I suddenly bellowed, "Get out of here and stay out!"

Never have I seen a more surprised animal. He came back on his heels like a released spring, half rearing and swiveling toward me, and then he leaped away like a shot out of a gun. He covered about forty feet or more in three bounds, hit the creek throwing water high in the air, and fairly flew up the slope beyond. He took the hint, for he did not come back. My only regret was that no part of this bit of action was successfully recorded on film.

The she-grizzly and the cub continued visiting the carcass as though nothing had happened until it was almost completely eaten up. She became increasingly careless and walked up to a neighbor's door one night and inspected the box of a parked pickup truck. The neighbor was aroused by the ranch dog and fired a shot at her in the dark. It wounded her only superficially, but it taught her a lesson and marked the end of her visit in the locality.

The grapevine of the wilds seemed to pass the word around very quickly, for almost overnight all the grizzlies except the cub up at the head of the Cottonwood left for the sanctuary of the Park and did not return.

The lone cub came down close to our buildings as the season progressed, and often it came close to our door. This was a pretty, golden-brown young animal weighing about two hundred pounds. Although the sex of individual bears is always hard to determine, we decided it was a male and christened him Storm, after a bear character I had written about in a magazine story sometime previously.

Storm was a very mannerly, self-effacing grizzly with a built-in shyness, great curiosity, and amazing willingness to join the life on our ranch without undue disturbance. He was very much intrigued by our house cat and bored with Anne's noisy terrier, Blackie. His curiosity almost drove the cat into a nervous breakdown, but his restraint in taking no action against much belligerent barking and rushing on the part of the dog built that small canine's ego up to almost unbearable proportions.

One morning very early Kay and I were wakened by sounds like nothing on earth. Upon investigation we found the cat in the throes of feline hysterics on the top step of the back door. Storm was standing in the open end of the breezeway with his head cocked to one side, fascinated by the cat's vocal display but showing no inclination to investigate any further. When Kay firmly but politely told him to leave, he loped away into the brush. Meanwhile the cat shot into the house to stand in the middle of the living-room floor, the picture of outrage, her back in a bow and her tail like a bent stovepipe.

This was only one of a number of visits by Storm that were effusively greeted by Blackie, whose rushing around and shrill barking was almost ignored. Although the dog's size did not much surpass the cat's, this caused him to show not the slightest fear of the bear. What amazed us was the grizzly's tolerance of the little terrier.

When Kay began putting up preserves late in the summer, she spent a good deal of time picking the lush, tasty saskatoon berries. On these expeditions she was invariably accompanied by the dog and quite often joined the grizzly in the same berry-patch. The dog spent its time rushing back and forth with great fanfare and importance between her and the grizzly, while the young bear and Kay proceeded to pick berries, each knowing exactly where the other was located. While a bit noisy, the arrangement eliminated any chance of an embarrassing head-on encounter in the thick jungle of summer foliage, and things worked out satisfactorily for all concerned.

We had not adopted a grizzly. A grizzly had adopted us. Storm was indeed very gentle but still a wild bear. Never, as far as we know, did our acquaintance show himself in a neighbor's yard. Even when he came into ours, he came with a certain shyness, and not once did his curiosity cause him to leave so much as a claw mark on any of our possessions. Since his visits were loudly announced by Blackie, there were no surprises at close range, a circumstance he likely appreciated as much as we did. Not once did he growl or show any irritation at frequent invasions into his berrypatches. We were an honored and accepted part of his society. It was a rare and revealing look at one of the many sides of grizzly character.

By way of contrast a large black bear showed up in late spring to leave his big paw marks in the vicinity of our home. At first we paid small attention to this visitor and only saw him once or twice as he sneaked furtively through the cover. But as time went on this animal became more and more familiar, until one evening Anne saw him break into our outside cellar located near the cottage. When she came running with this news, Gordon and I immediately went to investigate.

There is only one way to deal with a bear that breaks into buildings; so we approached with cocked rifles ready in our hands. The bear was gone, but we heard him going up the hill through the heavy undergrowth toward the lodge. Gordon ran around to head him off while I trailed him. Gordon almost ran into him head-on along a path going to the ash pit. A quick shot cut a growl off right in the middle and permanently settled our problem with him. He too had adopted us, but as is the way of black bears, his familiarity had degenerated into contempt.

At first snow last fall Storm left us to head up into the mountains, and we have never seen him since. As I write this, he is likely curled up in a warm den dreaming of warm summer days and luscious berries. Maybe he will come back when the glacier lilies bloom again.

Storm proved that at least one grizzly could tolerate humans. Not only were we made aware of the relationship possible between man and grizzly, but another thread was revealed in the fascinating pattern of nature's tapestry of the wilds.

Why did these grizzlies come to stay so close to us in the first place? It may have been pure coincidence. But as I have often suspected, animals have keen extrasensory perception, which is only latent in man through lack of use. Many times while wandering the wilds, it has seemed that animals can tell if a man is of a killing or a friendly frame of mind. It is something I have strongly sensed, but of course it is almost impossible to prove. Certainly as a part of the research of this book along with our efforts to make a grizzly life history on moving picture film, we had spent the three previous years living in grizzly country, hunting them with cameras, working with the big animals, and observing them in a friendly frame of mind. Scarcely an hour has passed, day after day, winter and summer, when my thoughts have not been occupied with grizzlies. If the electrical aura of such concentration can be picked up by a sympathetic mind, then perhaps the grizzly's visit was not altogether an accident. It is a fascinating problem to which I certainly wish I could give a positive answer, an opening to an avenue of some mighty deep reflection.

In studying the association between grizzly bears and men, one thing stands out as clear and sharp as snow on a mountain slope. Grizzlies are willing and able to adjust to the complexities of that association quicker and more generously than men. In the days of the frontier, before the grizzly had learned the potency of man's character and weapons, this animal's actions were much bolder, sometimes belligerent, and often damaging to property.

In a graphic letter written to Colonel Townsend Whelen forty years ago, F. H. (Bert) Riggall has this to say:

You will note that I said that our bears are big, savage, and fearless, and I want to tell you that there is an awful lot of difference in the disposition of the grizzlies in different sections, not far apart perhaps in miles. For instance, in this particular section the grizzlies are *all* cattle killers, and come right into the corrals and kill milk cows and calves right close to the buildings, sometimes in broad daylight, but mostly at night. They run cattle for miles, like a hound and several times have been seen to chase an animal across country and kill close to the home ranch. They act a good deal like lions in Africa, and at times my neighbors have set up all night with rifles and listened to bears killing or chasing cattle 'round the houses and barns.

Now here is a strange thing. Fifty to seventy-five miles north of here the grizzlies are *quite* different, and *never* or almost never kill cattle, although a thousand head of cattle are ranged in the mountains right up to, and sometimes stray over, the Continental Divide, with grizzly tracks and diggings all over, yet for years I have never known a grizzly to touch a cow! Here the bears come out of the mountains to the ranches to kill every fall regularly, and there the cows invade the grizzlies' own territory in summer and fall with impunity.

When Stewart Edward White wrote of "Dangerous Game" in the *Saturday Evening Post,* he never mentioned "Grizzlies and Small-pox," but when you interpose the word "Indian" between, it tells a whole lot that is generally not known about bears. Forty to sixty years ago the Indians here (Stonies) camped in small groups all through the mountains in the sheep, deer, goat and bear country, and while so camped, in would ride a relative from a small-pox infested camp, and in ten days half the camp would be dead or dying, and the survivors would leave all the teepees standing and ride off to spread the plague to other camps. Pretty soon the grizzlies here found that they could invade the teepees without fear and feed on the dead, and after a while on the dying, and from that it was only a step, soon taken, to hunting the unaffected Indians in after years, and they did so hunt them in certain sections, and taught their cubs to do so also; and some of these cubs are alive today, the Stonies declare, and I believe them! When I came here this was wonderful hunting country (inside the mountains), simply because the Stonies were too afraid of these grizzlies to venture into the game country, and up the best canyons no old Indian trails led through the timber at the mouths to the basins at the heads. I had to cut these trails myself; and although each spring and fall bands of Stonies passed, none would venture over my trails, and some of them at different times told me why, and warned me that the bears there were bad actors and would smell and stalk an Indian, and myself also if I did not watch out! I had two *very* close calls from bears there the first year or two, and killed both bears within a few feet of me, and I believe that these bears were old timers who knew what human flesh tasted like, and were not averse to trying it again. I have since shot and killed grizzlies in many places as far north as the Big Smokey, and down in Montana on both sides of the Divide, and I know that without question the bears here and just across in British Columbia and Montana are more savage and aggressive than in other sections. I am sure that this is not generally appreciated or known, so I have gone into some detail, as I think you will find it interesting and probably new.

Another strange thing in this connection: Some years ago a few bunches of sheep were brought into the foothill country, but down there the coyotes were so bad in the brush that the sheep men beat a hasty retreat (and incidentally avoided serious trouble with the old-time cow-men). However, a few years ago—1915 and 1917—a bunch of 300 to 500 head were run on privately owned and fenced land 18 miles north of here by Ted Whipple of MacLeod, for the summer season, and during that time not one sheep was known to be killed by the coyotes. The reason was that the coyotes there did not know what the sheep were, or that they were good to eat. If they had ever started killing they would have killed half the herd in a month, but the sheep were not there in winter and there were no deaths in the flock in summer, so the coyotes never got a taste of mutton. Likewise I predict that if ever a cow beast is killed by a grizzly in the section fifty to seventy five miles north of here, the cattle men will have to kill all the bears off, or draw their cattle out of the mountain range, or loose a hundred head a year.

At the time these words were written, I was a boy living in the shadow of the Rockies within a morning's ride of the country described by Bert Riggall as the home of the bad bears. Later I came to know Bert personally—a very close friendship that lasted till his death some twenty-five years later. For ten of those years we worked side by side in the open wilderness country, and probably no man knew him better than I. No finer man ever wore boots. He was a truly great mountain man with an extremely keen mind and an encyclopedic memory. His store of knowledge was vast and varied. His powers of observation were tremendous. When he made the remarks quoted about grizzlies, he had very good reason for doing it. But even the sincerest and most informed men cannot always see past the obvious, and there are some paradoxical facts involved that cannot be overlooked.

At that time this area was homestead country with a population greatly exceeding today's total of resident ranchers. Most of the ranchers were just getting their start by hanging on to their small businesses by the skin of their teeth. Average herds numbered between twenty-five and forty head of breeding cattle, so if a man lost a cow by any means, it meant a good portion of his immediate future income was eliminated. If a cow died in a bog, ate poisonweed, or got killed by lightning, the loss was nearly always credited to the depredation of grizzlies for the simple reason that the bears usually found the dead animal first. There were undoubtedly more grizzlies then, and cattle were certainly killed by them; but it occurred to no one that all grizzlies were not cattle killers. There was also some light-hearted gentry of enterprising nature who were somewhat light-fingered with other people's stock. When cattle were missed, the grizzlies got the blame—a most desirable turn of events for the rustlers but overly rough on the bears.

The homesteaders were carving a living by sweat and hardship out of the wilderness, suffering in country that knows no favorites, and sometimes they stared ruin and even death squarely between the eyes. Under the circumstances it is human to want something tangible to fight—something even to hate; and so the grizzly was hated and hunted unmercifully.

To have some understanding of the grizzly, it is most necessary to have also some understanding of that species' most potent predator. Although from the very earliest times of frontier penetration men have been fascinated by bears, they have also been to a large extent bear haters. The days of the old frontier are gone. The grizzlies are still here in reduced numbers, and although some still kill cattle on occasion, they have mostly learned over the years to avoid trouble. They do not hunt men any more—perhaps modern Indians taste and smell just as bad as white men. But even yet among ranchers, prospectors, trappers, and fishermen there are many with a deep-seated and unjustified hatred of grizzlies.

Certainly if one looks for trouble, one is apt to find it. If one lives and travels with a chip on his shoulder in country occupied by grizzlies, the grizzly can sense it and may take an opportunity to knock it off. Over three years of intensive study of these animals my sons and I hunted them day after day and week after week, sometimes making five or six contacts a day with nothing more lethal in our hands than cameras. However it would be utter folly to wander grizzly country on the coast of British Columbia and Alaska without adequate arms. In those regions professional fishermen have the nasty habit of shooting grizzlies on the beach from boats with anything that comes to hand. Fishermen being notoriously poor shots, many bears escape wounded into the adjoining jungle. Some of these survive with their own developing hatred of men, and when such an animal is encountered at close quarters, the outcome may depend on some fast, straight shooting. Apart from this possibility, any grizzly approached within close range and surprised by an intruding human is a highly dangerous potential. In the almost impenetrable undergrowth and down logs of the rain forests this is another good reason to go armed, but still no excuse for shooting every grizzly encountered. Very few will press home a charge even when extremely angry.

The temper of grizzlies does vary in different portions of the country. But when one looks deep enough, it will be found that the most unpredictable and dangerous bears usually live where humans have recently come to administer their particular brand of "missionary" work. I wonder what Bert Riggall would have said, could he have lived to see his grandsons fraternizing with grizzlies, shooting them while armed only with cameras, and what is more important, sincerely liking the big animals.

II

GRIZZLY
Hunting

6. *From the Conquistadors to Here*

If bravery comes from the heart,
his heart is very big, for he is very brave.
—CHARLES M. RUSSELL

Very likely the early Spanish conquistadors, who penetrated the interior of southwest North America in the sixteenth century, were the first white men on this continent to encounter grizzlies. While they were hardy, courageous, and determined men, their interests ran to gold and Christian conversion in that order, and their talents as historians did not include a marked bent toward recording natural history; for their accounts of wildlife are largely sketchy, and it is sometimes difficult to recognize a species by the description. As the Spanish empire expanded, trade and exploration carried their galleons as far west as the Orient, from which they returned laden with rich cargoes. When Drake and Cavendish broke into the Pacific with the Jolly Roger flying impudently off the tips of their masts, they plundered these galleons and terrified the Spanish sailors. When this undesirable state of affairs was brought to the attention of the Council of the Indies in Madrid, suggestions were dispatched to

Mexico City that a port be found on the California coast to give protection to Spanish shipping. In 1602 the viceroy, Conde de Monterey, delegated Sebastián Vizcaíno, merchant mariner, to find such a harbor.

On December 16 of that year Vizcaíno sailed into the Bay of Pines, so named by Cabrillo fifty years earlier, and thinking he had discovered it, renamed it Monterey.

Father Antonio de la Ascensión, official recorder for the expedition, wrote a detailed description of the place. He noted that the Indians were friendly and that the country teamed with game such as ducks, geese, doves, quail, condors, elk, deer, and rabbits. He saw and described grizzlies coming out on the beach at night to feed on a dead whale stranded there, and he noted that their tracks measured "a good third of a yard long and a hand wide." The good Father thus displayed an honest flare for story telling, "a good third of a yard" being far more impressive than a mere foot.

This was the first accurate account of sighting the grizzly: the California grizzly, later to become extinct and also to be designated, three and a half centuries later, as the official animal of the State of California.

When the expedition sailed back toward Mexico, Captain Vizcaíno was no doubt making plans for the establishment of a permanent port in the near future; he had no inkling that fate and the vagaries of politics would decree that he would be long in his grave before the Spanish saw the Bay of Monterey again.

In the meantime, away to the north, another white explorer encountered and recorded the plains grizzly. He was Henry Kelsey, explorer and trader for the Hudson's Bay Company who traveled by canoe from the company base at the mouth of the Nelson River to Lake Winnipeg and thence to the edge of the prairies in what is now Manitoba.

On August 19, 1691, Kelsey saw his first buffaloes and grizzly bears and wrote in his journal: "Today we travelled to the outer edge of the woods; this plain affords nothing but a short sticky grass and Buffalo, and a great sort of bear which is bigger than any White bear and is neither white nor black, but silver haired like our English rabbit."

Kelsey's reference to a rabbit for comparison was purely in respect to coloration; for when he and an Indian encountered two grizzlies, the surprise was mutual. The Indian promptly took long, fast strides toward a tree with both bears hot on his heels, while Kelsey climbed into the top of a high clump of willows. Kelsey fired and killed one bear, whereupon the other, apparently noting the direction of his shot by the puff of smoke and the noise, rushed toward his hiding place. Finding nothing, this bear returned to the tree where the Indian was perched. Kelsey fired again and killed it. This was excellent shooting from such an unstable position with a flintlock musket fitted with a stock he had whittled with axe and knife from native wood when the original was burned off one night in a campfire.

Kelsey's action against the bears was so much admired by the Indians that they named him Miss-top-ashish, "Little Giant" in the Assiniboin language.

This was probably the first time a grizzly bear was killed by a white man in North America. Kelsey was very cryptic and matter of fact about the incident in his journal, as he was about everything else. He was truly a "little giant" in his tremendous explorations with Indians as sole companions most of the time. But today the student of history reading his journal of 1691–2 is left with a feeling that he could have been a bit more generous with his words.

The next page in the colorful history of encounters between white men and grizzlies opens again in California.

It was more than one hundred and sixty years after Vizcaíno's renaming of Monterey that José de Gálvez took a two-pronged expedition by land and sea to try again to discover the place. They rendezvoused on the southern coast in miserable condition. The sailors were riddled with scurvy, and the land expedition was much reduced by starvation. As they proceeded north, the priests accompanying the land expedition were much concerned by the nudity and savagery of the Indians; but the soldiers were of a more practical mind and were watching for food. On September 2, 1769, north of Point Conception, they were crossing a swamp at the head of a tidewater lagoon when they saw tracks of grizzly bears, whereupon they promptly went hunting. Each man was armed with a broadsword, lance, and musket. They found and managed to kill one of the bears.

Miguel Constanso, cartographer and engineer for the expedition, recorded: "It was an enormous animal: it measured fourteen palms from the soles of its feet to the top of its head; its feet were more than a foot long; and it must have weighed over 375 pounds. We ate of the flesh and found it savory and good."

This was likely the first California grizzly killed by white men there. Another lean, tough grizzly was killed in the same place to provide some additional supplies for the hungry expedition.

It is obvious that the modest description of the first grizzly indicates a medium-sized animal. The second one must have been sick or riddled with parasites; for at that time of year it should have been rolling with fat. These first grizzlies were easily killed, leaving the Spaniards ill prepared for the difficulties and uproar encountered a few days later.

Not far from where the town of San Luis Obispo now stands they came out on a broad, somewhat marshy valley and were amazed to see numbers of bears scattered across it busily digging for roots. Again Constanso wrote in some detail:

In this canyon we saw troops of bears; they had the land plowed up and full of holes which they make in searching for roots they live on, which the land produces. The natives also use these roots for food, and there are some of good relish and taste. Some of the soldiers, attracted by the chase because they had been successful on two other occasions, mounted their horses, and this time succeeded in shooting one. They, however, experienced the fierceness and anger of these animals—when they feel themselves wounded, headlong they charge the hunter, who can escape only by the swiftness of his horse, for the first burst of speed is more rapid than one might expect from the bulk and awkwardness of such brutes. Their endurance and strength is not easily overcome, and only the sure aim of the hunter, or the good fortune of hitting them in the head or heart, can lay them low at the first shot. The one they succeeded in killing received nine bullet wounds before it fell, and this did not happen till they hit him in the head. Other soldiers mounted on mules had the boldness to fight one of these animals. They fired at him seven or eight times and, doubtless, he died from the wounds, but he maimed two of the mules, and, by good fortune, the men who were mounted upon them extricated themselves.

They named this place La Canada de los Osos—a name which stuck, for it is still known as the Valley of the Bears.

When the Spaniards found the port of Monterey again, it turned out to be little more than a roadstead; but they set up two missions, the Mission of San Carlos Borromeo and the Mission of San Antonio de Padua, in 1770 and 1772. They depended largely on supply ships coming from Mexico. When these did not appear and the crops failed, they were reduced to eating the breeding stock brought along for agricultural purposes. The situation became very critical. Tightening their belts under short rations, the Spaniards remembered juicy bear steaks enjoyed at the Valley of the Bears. The governor and thirteen soldiers marched back to the place. Father Palou wrote in his diary that "the troops remained there for three months, eating bear meat and sending loads of it jerked to the others." During that time, he further states, "twenty-five loads, or about 9,000 pounds of bear meat," were sent back to the two northern missions, San Carlos and San Antonio. From May until August everyone at the missions ate practically nothing else but bear meat—the jerked flesh of grizzly bears. They probably abstained for the rest of their lives from bear meat as a result of this forced diet, but these early settlements were in this way saved from extinction.

The mild, salubrious climate of California, the fertility of the soil upon receiving rain, and the hardy determination of the Spaniards combined to make the settlements successful. More livestock was brought from Mexico, and the missions thrived, largely on the labor of converted Indians.

Later in 1784 large land grants were given to various officers, and the livestock increased prodigiously. These aristocratic landowners, each with an empire of grass at his disposal, rapidly developed the territory into a golden land of pastoral affluence that was almost completely self-sufficient. Each ranch was a community unto itself with its own ironworker, silver-smith, saddle maker, rawhide plaiter, wine maker, and *vaqueros* (herdsmen).

Nowhere else in the history of white man's colonization of the wilderness North America did grizzlies consequently so thrive and increase as they did in California after the arrival of the Spaniards. For nowhere else did the settlers, by their way of life, so completely train the grizzlies to join them in easy living off their livestock.

Cattle and horses ran virtually wild by the thousands. Sheep were herded in large numbers by native herdsmen. The main source of income was hides and tallow from cattle and the wool from sheep. The cattle were gathered and killed on the open range at outlying camps called *calaveras*, "place of skulls"—well named, for these places were surrounded by hundreds of yards of bleached skulls and bones. Here the cattle were slaughtered by the hundreds every day during killing season and skinned and stripped of tallow. Only the choicest cuts of meat were saved to be jerked for human consumption. All the rest was left for the vultures, coyotes, and grizzlies. At night the big bears came down off the surrounding mountains to stuff themselves with rich beef.

Cattle being much slower and easier to catch than the native deer and elk, the grizzlies did not take long to learn to kill their own meat. Horses went completely wild and increased in numbers with such speed that they became a threat. The governor forced the slaughter of these on occasion to save the range for cattle, and sometimes many hundreds of horses were corralled and lanced or driven off cliffs. This added to the bears' feasting, and some even learned to catch and kill horses.

While no records or estimates of grizzly population were possible prior to California's settlement, collected evidence would seem to indicate a thriving increase thereafter, which climbed steadily until the Americans arrived about the middle of the nineteenth century. It is estimated that there were then about five grizzlies to every twenty square miles, or ten thousand grizzlies in all, in the region; most of these were concentrated in and around the fertile valleys near the coast. Previous to Spanish arrival these animals had little respect for the primitive native Indians, and after the arrival of the white men they did not elevate their respect one bit for them.

The Spanish were not hunters in the common interpretation of the word. Very few had guns, and those weapons they did have were poor, inaccurate muzzle-loaders, largely smooth-bored. While anything resembling manual labor, especially work not conducted on horseback, was abhorred by the landowning gentry, they believed in enjoying life; and nothing pleased them more than dangerous, active sport. So they killed grizzlies with lariats, or *reatas*, as they were known there.

In the hands of the Spaniard the *reata* was more than just a tool of the cattle industry; it was a deadly weapon used with unmatched skill. The *reata* was made of four strands of plaited rawhide. These strands were cut from carefully selected hides taken from cattle of a certain size, sex, and age. Brown and red hides were preferred over black or spotted ones. It was believed that the hide of spotted cattle was weak where the different colors met. The strands were very carefully cut, trimmed, shaved of hair, and then stretched. They were then braided in continuous length to make a *reata* sixty feet long without a splice or a knot in its entire length. A running noose was plaited on one end. The very best of these were said to have been made from the hides of starved cattle, which turned black and required much diligent rubbing with tallow to keep them pliable.

With the *reata* the wild-riding *caballeros* fought and killed the grizzly. The Spaniards' inherent love of excitement and physical danger made the grizzly a challenge and a worthy antagonist. Roping the big bears became a sport enjoyed at every opportunity. The Spaniards roped them day or night all year round. Sometimes even the priests tucked up their ecclesiastic robes and joined in the fun: "Father Reál was often known to go with young men on moonlight rides, lassoing grizzly bears."

The Spanish horses of Moorish and Arab blood were ideal mounts for this kind of work, being fleet of foot and extremely intelligent. They were beautiful, very carefully trained animals with tremendous endurance in the range work required of them. It was in roping grizzlies that the training and quality of these mounts was put to its severest test.

An American, William R. Garner, who observed the Californians hunting the grizzly on horseback with the *reata*, wrote in 1846 from Monterey that "every motion of the horses, which seems as though they were doubly proud when they feel the strain of the lasso from the saddle, and appear to take as much delight in the sport as the riders themselves, is grand beyond my powers of description." He proceeded to tell that

this method of hunting the bear is one of the noblest diversions with which I am acquainted. . . . It requires an extraordinary degree of courage for a man to ride up beside a savage monster like a grizzly bear in this country, which is nearly as active as a monkey, and whose strength is enormous. Should a lasso happen to break . . . the bear invariably attacks the horse, and it requires very often the most skillful horsemanship to prevent the horse or its rider from being injured. It requires also great skill to know when to tighten the lasso, and to what degree, to prevent it from being suddenly snapped by too sudden a strain. The rider must have his eye constantly on that of the bear, and watch his every motion. Sometimes, either through fear, carelessness or inadvertence, a man may let go his lasso. In this case, another, if the bear takes off (which he is likely to do), will go as hard as his horse can run, and, without stopping his speed, will stoop from his saddle and pick up the end of the lasso off the ground, and taking two or three turns around the loggerhead of his saddle and checking his horse's rein, again detain the bear.

It might be further pointed out here that the rawhide *reata* would not stand a sudden, solid jerk, so the animal caught in the loop had to be "played," much as an angler would play a fish, by letting the rope run in its "dallies" on the pommel and then taking up slack when necessary. Only a part of the skill in this kind of dangerous game was involved in throwing the loop. The "skin-string buckeroos," as they were called in the later era of the old-time cowboy, were artists in their use of the *reata*.

Another American by the name of Davis, who married a Spanish California girl and was personally acquainted with the hide and tallow trade, relates that his father-in-law with the help of ten soldiers and a relay of horses "lassoed and killed forty bears in one night" at the killing ground near the site of the town of Mountain View. "It was the killing season, and the bears smelling the meat, had come down from the mountain to partake of it. My father-in-law said this was the most exciting event of his life, and they were so interested in dispatching the bears they forgot all danger. The animals were lassoed by the throat and also by a hind leg, a horseman at each end, and the two pulling in opposite directions till the poor beast succumbed. The fun was kept up till daylight and when they got through they were completely exhausted."

While the Californians usually roped grizzlies in groups of four or more riders, some men become so skillful and daring in the use of the *reata* that they hunted the great bears singlehanded. When this was done, the rider threw his loop on the bear's neck and then, aided by his horse, maneuvered his "catch" to entangle it around a tree. While the horse held the grizzly's head close up to the tree trunk, the rider dismounted and killed the animal with the "broad bladed *machete* or Mexican hunting knife."

A Manuel Lario employed another method one time. He got his rope on the bear and galloped away with the grizzly in hot pursuit. Seeing a tree ahead, probably an oak, with a big limb jutting out, this quick-thinking rider threw the end of his rope forward over it and, without checking, caught it as it came down beyond. Taking his dallies on the saddle pommel, he kept going at full speed until brought up with a jerk as the bear found himself suddenly hung from the branch.

Another lone bear roper, Ramón Ortoga, recounted having roped and killed seventy grizzlies in five years on the Rancho Sespe and some two hundred during his lifetime. Once he killed fifteen in a day and forty in a single month. This would require a fair-sized *remuda*, for such work was hard on horse flesh; but most certainly no one could question the skill and courage of such men.

The Californians developed other ways of killing grizzlies marauding their herds. Sometimes they dug a pit and covered it with a grate of logs, on which was placed a bait. A man hid himself in the pit with a musket or lance and, when the bear came to feed, attacked him from beneath. Another method reversed the procedure: a horse was killed beneath a tree and then a platform was built close overhead, where again a lance or gun was employed to dispatch the bear. Such attempts were not always successful, and sometimes the tables were turned, resulting in the hunter getting badly mauled or even killed.

Of all the Californians who pursued bears, the most colorful and courageous was likely Don José Ramón Carrillo, a young and very daring aristocrat who hunted grizzlies for the sheer sport of it. One day while riding hell-for-leather after a grizzly, the bear suddenly fell into a pit about six feet deep. The horse was close to the bear with no chance to swerve or check, and he too fell into the hole, where man, horse, and bear found themselves in some considerable embarrassment and confusion. The grizzly was trying to climb out, but he kept falling back. The quick-witted Carrillo, having no wish to be involved in the explosion that would develop should the bear decide to fight, grabbed the bear on the rump as it scrambled to get out and heaved upward with all his strength. Thus boosting it out of the pit, he and the horse sorted themselves out without undue interference.

Carrillo was most famous for his singlehanded duels with grizzlies in which he used a light rapier. These duels were witnessed by many men, and the accounts of them come from at least two worthy historians, W. H. Davis and Horace Bell. Of these the latter tells the more graphic story.

These grizzlies stand on their hind legs and spar, fence, parry and strike like a skilled fencing master or prize fighter. . . . Ramón Carrillo . . . overtook a huge grizzly in the Enchino Valley, challenged and fought him single handed with a light sword. . . .

This Ramón was a desperado, a man who fought for the love of it and was never defeated until finally riddled with American buckshot. General Cavarrúbias with a party which included Ramón Carrillo was journeying from Santa Barbara to Los Angeles when they sighted the bear, out on the San Fernando Plain. They surrounded the Old Man of the Mountains, who promptly stood up like a man and offered defiance.

"Stand back, please, señores," requested Carrillo, dismounting and drawing his sword. "Allow me to fight a personal duel with this grand old gladiator."

Ramón advanced like a dancing master, flourishing a rapier-like blade which he always carried. Bruin stood on the defensive, staring with angry astonishment. Deftly and with a smile—the young Californian, with all the skill and grace of a trained bullfighter, danced around the grizzly giant and got in his stinging, maddening thrusts here and there. The grizzly rushed time and again with terrific roars, but the man only waited long enough to sting the huge menacing paws with rapier point and then side stepped to safety.

The excitement of the picturesque mounted audience grew almost beyond control, and the "vivas!" first for the caballero and then for the bear, drove the animal duelist almost frantic. With utmost coolness and always laughing, Ramón Carrillo fenced with the grizzly for one hour. When all concerned seemed to be tiring of the sport, he stepped in with a quick thrust to the heart and laid the splendid brute low.

While the Californians were building and enjoying their unique pastoral, feudalistic empire, almost completely isolated and independent from the rest of the world, the remaining vast west and northwest wilderness of North America was still largely unexplored and inhabited only by Indians.

The most that was known about it was that it was there, and it was a long way from the eastern settlements of the United States and Canada to the Pacific Ocean.

In 1793 and 1794 Alexander MacKenzie made the first overland journey across the continent north of Mexico. While his route took him north of the ranges of the plains grizzly most of the way, he passed through mountain grizzly range on the headwaters of the Peace River and also in his route southwest to the mouth of the Bella Coola River. However if he saw grizzlies, he had precious little to say about them.

While on his second journey in 1795, he mentions seeing bear tracks on the banks of the Peace which measured nine inches across. He says: "The Indians entertain great apprehension of this kind of bear, which they call the Grizzly Bear, and they never venture to attack it except in a party of at least three or four."

Samuel Hearne recorded seeing a single large grizzly skin in the possession of the Eskimos on the lower reaches of the Coppermine not far from the Arctic coast in 1771. Doubtless this was one of the tundra grizzlies still found in the MacKenzie Basin.

While the grizzly does not come in for much attention by British explorers, probably because they largely journeyed by canoe through heavily wooded areas of the northwest where the big bears were hard to see, the early American expeditions across the great plains are a different story.

In 1804, shortly after the Louisiana Purchase, President Jefferson of the United States appointed Captains Meriwether Lewis and John Clark to find a route to the Pacific Ocean across the plains and mountains. The account of this great journey, which took two years to complete, is well laced with observations and detailed descriptions of animals encountered, and it is particularly interesting to the student of grizzly lore. The journals kept by Lewis and Clark are well written and accurate; so I will quote from them, from the point that Clark and Lewis encountered the grizzly bear on the Missouri River, starting in what is now Montana and including locations farther west.

On April 29, 1805, their journal says:

Captain Lewis, who was on shore with one hunter, met, about eight o'clock, two white bears. Of the strength and ferocity of the animal the Indians had given us dreadful accounts. They never attack him except in parties of six or eight persons, and even then are often defeated with a loss of one or more of their party. Having no weapons but bows and arrows, and the bad guns with which traders supply them, they are obliged to approach very near the bear. As no wound, except through the head or heart, is mortal, they frequently fall sacrifice if they miss their aim. He rather attacks than avoids a man, and such is the terror which he has inspired, that the Indians who go in quest of him paint themselves and perform all the superstitious rites customary when they make war on a neighboring nation.

Hitherto, those bears we had seen did not appear desirous of encountering us; but although to a skillful rifleman the danger is very much diminished, yet the white bear is a terrible animal. On approaching these two, both Captain Lewis and the hunter fired and each wounded a bear. One of these made his escape. The other turned

The river bars in grizzly range are often crisscrossed with his big tracks.

Caribou (below) *silhouetted on the skyline in the early morning. This animal and the moose* (above) *are commonly encountered in the grizzly's home range.*

on Captain Lewis and pursued him seventy or eighty yards, but being badly wounded the bear could not prevent him from reloading his piece, which he again aimed at him, and a third shot from the hunter brought him to the ground. He was a male, not quite full grown, and weighed about 300 pounds. The legs are somewhat longer than those of the black bear and the talons and tusks much longer. Its color is yellowish brown; the eyes are small, black and piercing; the front of the forelegs near the feet is usually black, and the fur is finer, thicker, and deeper than that of the black bear; in addition to which it is a more furious animal and very remarkable for the wounds which it will bear without dying.

Again, on May 6 their adventures with grizzlies resume:

Captain Lewis and one of the hunters met this evening the largest brown bear we have seen. As they fired he did not attempt to attack, but fled with a most tremendous roar; and such was his extraordinary tenacity of life that, although five balls passed through his lungs and he had five other wounds, he swam more than half way across the river to a sand bar and survived twenty minutes. He weighed between 500 and 600 pounds at least, and measured eight feet seven and a half inches from the nose to the extremity of the hind feet, five feet ten inches and a half around the breast, three feet eleven inches around the neck, one foot eleven inches around the middle of the foreleg, and his talons, five on each foot, were four and three eighths inches in length. This differs from the black bear in having its talons longer and more blunt; its tail shorter, its hair of reddish or bay brown, longer, finer and more abundant; his liver, heart and lungs much larger even in proportion to his size, the heart being equal to that of a large ox; his maw ten times larger. Besides fish and flesh he feeds on roots and every kind of wild fruit.

May 11, 1805.

About five in the afternoon one of our men (Bratton), who had been afflicted with boils and suffered to walk on shore, came running to the boats with loud cries and every symptom of terror and distress. For some time after we had taken him on board he was much out of breath as to be unable to describe the cause of his anxiety; but he at length told us that about a mile and a half below he had shot a brown bear, which had immediately turned and was in close pursuit of him; but the bear, being badly wounded, could not overtake him. Captain Lewis, with seven men, immediately went in search of him; having found his track, followed him by the blood for half a mile, found him concealed in some thick brushwood and shot him with two balls through the skull. Though somewhat smaller than that killed a few days ago, he was a monstrous animal and a most terrible enemy. Our man shot him through the centre of the lungs, yet he pursued him furiously for half a mile, then returned more than twice that distance, and with his talons prepared himself a bed in the earth two feet deep and five feet long; he was perfectly alive when they found him, which was at least two hours after he had received the wound. The wonderful power of life which these animals possess renders them dreadful; their very tracks in the mud or sand, which we have sometimes found eleven inches long and seven and one fourth inches wide, exclusive of the talons, is alarming; and we had rather encounter two Indians than meet a single brown bear. There is no chance of killing them with a single shot unless the ball goes through the brain, and this is very difficult on account of two large muscles which cover the side of the forehead and the sharp projection on the centre of the frontal bone, which is also thick.

May 14, 1805.

Toward evening the men in the hindmost canoes discovered a large brown bear lying in the open grounds about three hundred yards from the river. Six of them, all good hunters, immediately went to attack him, and concealing themselves by a small eminence, came unperceived within forty paces of him. Four of the hunters now fired and each lodged a ball in his body, two directly through the lungs. The furious animal sprang up and ran open-mouthed upon them. As he came near, the two hunters who had reserved their fire gave him two wounds, one of which, breaking his shoulder retarded his motion for a moment; but before they could reload he was so near they were obliged to run for the river, and before they had reached it he had almost overtaken them. Two jumped into the canoe, the other four separated, and concealing themselves in the willows, fired as fast as they could reload. They struck him several times, but instead of weakening the monster, each shot seemed only to direct him towards the hunter; till at last he pursued two of them so closely that they threw aisde their guns and pouches and jumped down a perpendicular bank twenty feet into the river. The bear sprang after them, and was within feet of the hindmost when one of the hunters on shore shot him in the head and finally killed him. They dragged him to the shore and found that eight balls had passed through him in different directions. The bear was old and the meat tough, so they took the skin only.

The reaction of this bear is typical of the kind—they fight when attacked. Captain Clark's description of the battle would seem to indicate that excited hunters did not shoot any better then than they do now.

June 14, 1805, at the Falls of the Missouri [where Great Falls, Montana, now stands].

Captain Lewis met a herd of at least one thousand buffalo, and being desirous of providing our supper, shot one of them. The animal began to bleed, and Captain Lewis, who had forgotten to reload his rifle, was intently watching to see him fall, when he beheld a large brown bear, which was stealing towards him and was already within twenty steps. In the first moment of surprise he lifted his rifle, but remembering instantly that it was not charged and that he had no time to reload, he felt there was no safety but in flight. It was in the open, level plain—not a bush or a tree within three hundred yards, the bank of the river sloping and not more than three feet high, so there was no possible mode of concealment. Captain Lewis therefor thought of retreating at a quick walk, as fast as the bear advanced, towards the nearest tree; but as soon as he turned, the bear ran open-mouthed and at full speed upon him. Captain Lewis ran about eighty yards, but finding the animal gained on him fast, it flashed in his mind that, by getting into the water to such a depth that the bear would be obliged to attack him swimming, there would be some chance of his life; he therefor turned short, plunged into the river about waist deep, and facing about, presented the point of his espontoon. The bear arrived at the water's edge within twenty feet of him; but as soon as he put himself in this posture of defense, the bear seemed frightened, and wheeling about, retreated with as much precipitation as he had pursued. Very glad to be released from this danger, Captain Lewis returned to the shore, and observed him run with great speed, sometimes looking back as if he expected to be pursued, till he reached the woods. He could not conceive the cause of the sudden alarm of the bear, but congratulated himself on his escape when he saw his own tracks torn to pieces by the furious animal, and learned from the whole adventure never to suffer his rifle to be a moment unloaded.

June 20, 1805.

As one of the men, who was sent a short distance from camp to bring home some meat, was attacked by a white bear, closely pursued within forty paces of camp, and narrowly escaped being caught, Captain Clark immediately went with three men in quest of the bear, which he was afraid might surprise another of the hunters who was out collecting the game. The bear was, however, too quick, for before Captain Clark could reach the man, the bear attacked him and compelled him to take refuge in the water. He now ran off as they approached, and it being late, they deferred pursuing him till next morning.

June 27, 1805.

As the men were hunting on the river, they saw a low ground covered with thick brushwood, where, from the tracks along the shore, they thought a bear had probably taken refuge. They therefore landed without making a noise and climbed a tree about twenty feet above the ground. Having fixed themselves securely they raised a loud shout and a bear instantly rushed towards them. These animals never climb, and therefor, when he came to the tree and stopped to look at them, Dweyer shot him in the head. He proved to be the largest we had seen. His nose appeared to be like that of the common ox, his forefeet measured nine inches across, the hind feet were seven inches wide and eleven and three quarters long, exclusive of the talons. One of these animals came within thirty yards of camp last night and carried off some buffalo meat which we had placed on a pole.

June 28, 1805.

The white bears have now become extremely troublesome, they constantly infest our camp during the night, and though they have not attacked us, as our dog, which patrols at night, gives us notice of their approach, yet we are obliged to sleep with our arms by our sides for fear of accident, and we cannot send one man alone for any distance, particularly if he has to pass through brushwood.

These were plains grizzlies described in the journal so far, bears which ranged the prairies with the buffalo in great numbers at that time. Doubtless, having met only primitively armed Indians, they were not much afraid of white men and reacted either in anger or curiosity upon seeing them. These bears were bison-eaters. The migration routes of buffaloes ran at right angles to the big rivers, and while crossing them, the millions of big grazers suffered much mortality. Many were drowned, bogged in quicksand, and injured and killed while climbing up steep banks from the bottoms to the plains above. Consequently there were easy pickings for the bears. Undoubtedly many grizzlies learned to kill mature animals. It was small wonder that these bears were arrogant, fearless animals not particularly inclined toward self-effacement at human intrusion.

The Lewis and Clark expedition also met the mountain

grizzly, as is recounted by the journal on May 13, 1806, near the Kooskooskee River.

The hunters killed . . . a male and a female bear, the first of which was large, fat, and of bay color, the second, meagre, grizzly, and of smaller size. They were of the species common to the upper part of the Missouri and might well be termed the variegated bear, for they are found occasionally of a black, grizzly, brown, or red color. There is every reason to believe them to be precisely the same species. Those of different colors are killed together, as in the case of these two, as we found the white and bay associated together on the Missouri; and some nearly white were seen in the neighborhood by the hunters. Indeed, it is not common to find any two bears of the same color, and if the difference in color were to constitute a species, the number would increase to almost twenty. Soon afterward the hunters killed a female with two cubs. The mother was black with a considerable intermixture of white hairs and a white spot on the breast. One of the cubs was jet black and the other of a light reddish-brown or bay color. The poil of these variegated bears is much finer, longer and more abundant than that of the common black bear, but the most striking differences between them are that the former are larger, and have longer tusks, and longer as well as blunter talons, that they prey more on other animals, that they lie neither so long nor so closely in winter quarters, and that they never climb trees, however closely pursued by hunters. These variegated bears, though specifically the same as those we met on the Missouri, are by no means so ferocious, probably because the scarcity of game and habit of living on roots may have weaned them from the practice of attacking and devouring animals. Still, however, they are not so passive as the common black bear, which is also found here, for they have already fought with our hunters, though with less fury than those on the other side of the mountains.

These amazingly perceptive observations place Lewis and Clark in the leading ranks of the "lumpers," and it is interesting to note that after about two centuries, during which we have wallowed up to our ears in a bog of species nomenclature and confusion, we have about completed the circle to common sense.

The return journey to the east put the expedition back through the Missouri River bear country, where a man by the name of McNeal had a stirring experience with a grizzly not far from the Falls.

July 15, 1806.

At night McNeal, who had been sent out in the morning to examine
the cache at the lower end of the portage, returned, but he had been
prevented from reaching that place by a singular adventure. Just as he
arrived near Willow Run, he approached a thicket of brush, in which
was a white bear, which he did not discover till he was within ten feet
of him. His horse started and wheeled around, throwing McNeal
almost immediately under the bear, which started up instantly. Finding the bear raising up on its hind feet to attack him, he struck him on
the head with the butt end of his musket; the blow was so violent that
it broke the breach of the musket and knocked the bear to the ground.
Before he could recover, McNeal, seeing a willow tree close by,
sprang up and there remained, while the bear closely guarded the foot
of the tree till late afternoon. He then went off; McNeal being
released came down, and having found his horse, which had strayed
off to the distance of two miles, returned to camp.

Reading these accounts makes one grateful to Lewis and
Clark for valuable information, which could have been written
much less accurately and full. Certainly the grizzly made a great
impression on them, and it was a wonder that someone in the
party did not get severely injured or killed in their adventures
with the big bears. It is also fairly obvious that the grizzly was
not nearly so ferocious as the Indians had led them to believe.
Furthermore, some of the attacks by the big animals were likely
begun in mere curiosity, which ended in a fight when the hunters fired at them or ran from them. The incident at the Falls on
June 14, 1805, when Lewis ran into the river, might have ended
the same way had he stood his ground in the first place instead of
running.

This great journey opened a door to an era of exploration
and fur trade in the West in which the mountain men played a
major role at the beginning in their search for the valuable
beaver skins. These were a tough breed, the refinements of
survival of the fittest, who wandered in groups, pairs, and sometimes even singly all through the West from Taos to the northern Blackfoot country. They penetrated the Rockies, finding
passes across the ranges, as they searched out rich beaver valleys. At least once a year they gathered at a great rendezvous to

trade their pelts for powder, lead, trinkets, and bright-colored cloth for their squaws; and together they joined in one huge celebration well lubricated with strong trade whisky. At night, while the flames of the campfires leaped and danced, the jug was passed freely as these raconteurs of the wilds traded the stories of their adventures. Stories of encounters with grizzlies likely took second place only to run-ins with Indians. Unfortunately these men were for the most part not particularly literate, and their stories died with them.

But there were exceptions, and one of these was a bearded, buckskin-clad trapper by the name of Jedediah Smith, who, with a band of trappers, penetrated California in November 1826 by way of the Mojave Desert. While engaged in taking beaver there, he tells of shooting grizzlies for their meat. They had some roaring mix-ups with the bears, and on April 7, 1827, he recounts one of these in his journal. The incident occurred about three miles up Mill Creek from its confluence with the Sacramento River.

In the evening we shot several Bears and they ran into the thickets. . . . Several of us followed one that was Badly wounded. . . . We went on foot because the thicket was too close to admit a Man on horse back.

As we advanced I saw one and shot him in the head when he immediately fell. . . . Apparently dead. I went to bring him out without reloading my gun and when I arrived within 4 yards of the place where the Bear lay the man who was following me close behind spoke and said "He is alive!" I told him in answer that he was certainly dead and was observing the one I had shot so intently that I did not see one that lay close by his side which was the one the man behind me had reference to. At that moment the Bear sprang towards us with open mouth and making no pleasant noise.

Fortunately the thicket was close to the bank of the creek and the second spring I plunged head foremost into the water. The Bear ran over the man next to me and made a furious rush on the third man Joseph Lapoint. But Lapoint . . . had a Bayonet fixed on his gun and as the Bear came in he gave him a severe wound in the neck which induced him to change his course and run into another thicket close at hand. We followed him there and found another in company with him. One of them we killed and the other went off Badly wounded.

Then I went on horse Back with two men to look for another that was wounded. I rode up close to the thicket in which I supposed him to be and rode around it several times halloeing but without making any discovery. I rode up for a last look when the Bear sprang for the horse. He was so close that the horse could not be got under way before he caught him by the tail. The Horse being strong and much frightened . . . [exerted] himself so powerfully that he gave the Bear no opportunity to close with him and actually drew him 40 or 50 yards before he relinquished his hold.

The Bear did not continue the pursuit but went off and [I] returned to camp to feast on the spoils and talk of incidents of our eventful hunt.

This portion of Jedediah Smith's journal was one of many similar adventures recorded by him. Although his party had some casualties in their battles with grizzlies, no one was killed—an occurrence that was to become more commonplace later, when the Americans came to settle in California in numbers. At this time the grizzly population of California was probably at its all-time peak, and the growing pressure of human population put bears and men in an almost continuous state of war.

The Americans, traditional hunters, were armed with rifles, but it must be remembered that these weapons were still far from the power and mechanical development of modern guns. They were single-shot muzzle-loaders prior to 1848, when Sharps introduced his famous line of breech-loaders, which spelled the ultimate doom of the plains grizzly and the buffalo. Loading a long-barreled weapon of this kind from the muzzle took time—so much time that what started as a grizzly hunt often dissolved into a spirited foot race for the nearest tree. These rifles fired a lead ball of varying caliber propelled by a charge of black powder. The most effective range was inside one hundred yards, and apart from a brain or spine shot, killing depended largely on hemorrhage. A grizzly's heartbeat is relatively slow, and consequently the animal takes a long time to bleed out even when struck in the heart. Sometimes the hunter was desperately mauled or killed minutes after shooting his quarry through the heart.

In the period between 1828 and 1848 many men emerged as being superior bear hunters in California. These were specialists who took great care to get close and make that first shot count, and who practiced a strategy that took many things into account, including the location of a suitable climbing tree, should the strategy fail.

One outstanding hunter, George Nidever, wrote: "I think I must have killed, on this coast, at different times, upwards of 200 grizzlies." Another, Colin Preston, claimed to have killed two hundred grizzlies in a single year. George C. Yount was a famed bear hunter of such renown that his gravestone is adorned with a bas-relief of a grizzly bear.

Apart from the use of guns in the usual manner, these early bear hunters devised some thoroughly original methods of taking the bear. One particularly unique device was a spring pole with its butt fastened to the base of a big tree so it projected out parallel to the ground. A heavy weight—likely a rock—was lashed to its tip. A keg containing a bait was sunk in the ground directly under the weight. Presumably, when the bear tried to get the bait, it heaved the weight to one side and the springy pole then swung it back with some force to strike the animal on the head.

Another spring-pole version of a trap was rigged with the butt of the pole caught between two stumps with an eighteen-inch knife fastened to the other end. The pole was sprung back by means of a "Spanish windlass" and caught in a "figure-four trigger" with a bait fastened in such a way that a tug on a cord tripped the device. The pole then snapped around with great force, and the knife was supposed to stab the bear. The two inventors of this contraption admitted that the knife missed the bear; but the pole gave it a mighty smash, and it left their camp site, never to return.

An inventor of a whaling gun, Oliver Allen, was a rancher near the mouth of the Tuolumne River in 1852 and used his own device for killing grizzlies. His method was described by a reporter at the time: "Mr. A. loads his gun in the same manner as for shooting whales, with a harpoon and line attached. The gun was then secured to a tree, and the end of the line attached to the harpoon is tied to a broken limb or some movable object, and a bait is attached to a string pending from the gun in such a manner that the instant it is touched the gun discharges its contents into whatever is before it. The gun is so arranged that it cannot be approached except in a direct line with the muzzle, and sure destruction awaits whatever dare touch the bait, either a piece of fresh meat or a salmon. Mr. Allen has recently killed several bears in this manner. . . ." Set guns of different kinds were also used employing a conventional charge.

Colin Preston, a hunter of some note in the San Luis Obispo region, described a most unique method of hunting grizzly bears:

We make large and dangerous bears drunk, when they have cubs in February, and are too savage. The bear goes to and from his den or cover—usually a hollow among rocks—by certain paths, called "beats." A bear will use the same beat for years, going by night on one beat, and in the day taking another, more circuitous. You will often find a tree fallen across a beat, or you fell one, and wait till the savage has examined the new barricade, and finding that it is not a trap and willing to climb over it. Then you make a hole in it with an axe large enough to contain a gallon of rum and molasses. Bears are greedy for sweets. In countries where there is wild honey they will overturn all obstacles to get at it. Of sugar and molasses, and sweet fruits, strawberries, mulberries and the like, they are passionately fond. The bear reaches the log; he pauses over the hole full of sweet liquor; examines it, tastes of it, drinks all in a draught, and is drunk. And what a drunkenness is that! The brute rolls and staggers, rises and even bounds from the earth, exhausts his enormous gambols, and falls at last stupefied and helpless, an easy prey for the hunter.

This description indicates that the grizzlies were already acquiring some considerable cunning from contact with the American settlers. Preston's sense of sportsmanship may also have been somewhat assaulted, for he states: "We have killed many bears this way, but it is treacherous and I do not like it."

Probably the most potent and infamous means used by Americans for decimating the California grizzlies was strychnine during the period 1870 to 1890. Little is said about this method in available records, but it is very likely that the bears were wiped out with it in certain areas. Probably because poisoners have never been viewed with much popularity anywhere, they did not advertise their activities.

During the height of the gold rush in 1849, when wealth ran like water from the miners' pockets and food of high energy value and a change from available beef was in high demand in the camps, grizzlies came to the attention of market hunters. At the camp of El Dorado the meat of a grizzly weighing eleven hundred pounds sold for $1300, netting the hunter $1.25 per pound. Grizzly meat was sold at the markets in Sacremento and San Francisco in 1850 at prices ranging from $.50 to $1.00 a pound. Records exist of prices up to $2.00 a pound being paid for grizzly meat; apparently it was considered an unusual delicacy at that time. Perhaps the well-fed California grizzly had a superlative flavor in comparison to meat from those grizzlies farther north, or maybe the miners were simply hungry. The one time I tried to eat grizzly meat, it had a texture like that of old boots and a flavor so strong that it was almost impossible to stay in the near vicinity while it was cooking.

Accounts of methods, means, and reasons for grizzly hunting in California at that time are legion. The big bear was hunted for food, sport, and to eliminate a danger. Without a doubt the most colorful and outstanding figure to emerge from the history of grizzly hunting throughout its entire reach across the years from the seventeenth century until today was "Grizzly" Adams. He hunted the bears with his rifle, but he went further toward a true understanding of this great animal than any other man of his time, and he still towers as a historical figure in North American frontier history because of his ability to capture the grizzly alive, tame it, and even make it a beast of burden.

John Capen Adams was born on October 22, 1812, at Medway, Massachusetts. As a youth he was trained to be a shoemaker, but the adventurous heart of the man and his born instinct and interest in animals lured him away from such a prosaic trade. He arrived in California in 1849 by the overland route from St. Louis, Missouri. He had some experience training and handling wild animals from a job he had held in the east with a traveling circus; he was a keen shot and a good hunter, as well as being skillful with tools. An enterprising Yankee of a tireless, courageous, and very resourceful nature, he set about carving his niche in history.

After a four-year period of odd-jobbing around Stockton, he began catching live wild animals for display. It was a good excuse to wander widely, exploring, hunting, and trapping live animals across the mountains to the east and north into Washington Territory. While in the Territory in 1853, he captured "Lady Washington," a mountain grizzly cub about a year old. She was big and old enough to be very savage and had, as he put it, "a dangerous mouth." She met his advances to tame her either by sulking or flying into a roaring rage, until he came to realize something drastic would have to be done if he was ever going to gentle her. Kind treatment had not worked, so he forthwith decided to try some grizzly type discipline. Cutting a stout club, he beat her unmercifully from end to end until she quit fighting him. She apparently appreciated his determination and understood the kind of language he was now talking, for she never fought him again and became a devoted and docile pet that followed him everywhere.

On a summer expedition into the Yosemite country the next year, Adams captured "Ben Franklin" as a small cub and took him along on a trapping trip to the Rocky Mountains across the Sierra Nevada. Upon returning to his wintering camp in early winter at Yosemite, he built a great live trap and captured an enormous grizzly, which he named "Samson." After taking his collection of animals, including Samson, down to the settlements, he left them with an assistant and returned to the mountains.

While he, Ben Franklin, and his dog, Rambler, were hunting one day in the Sierras, a big she-grizzly surprised him in some thick brush. Before he could raise his rifle, she knocked it out of his hands and almost scalped him with another blow of her paw. Adams was knocked down, and the grizzly jumped on him to rip and chew at his back. He was wearing a buckskin shirt and jacket, which turned her blunt and broken teeth to some extent, but he was taking a severe mauling when he sang out for his pets to help. The dog streaked in to grab the bear by the heels, while Ben piled on her head tooth and claw. Adams rolled out from under the fighting bears and dog, grabbed his rifle, and climbed into a small tree. There he pushed back the flap of scalp that was hanging down over his forehead and wiped the blood from his eyes. The she-grizzly had Ben down and was chewing his head and neck in a killing rage. The hunter let out a "bear screech," which he sometimes used to arrest a charging grizzly; and as the bear rose to look for him, he shot her through the heart. She went over backwards in a heap, whereupon Ben, finding himself free, headed for camp at a high gallop, bawling and crying every jump. By this time the downed grizzly was showing some signs of getting back on her feet, and Adams jumped in close to finish her off with his belt knife.

Then he returned to camp, where he first attended to Ben's wounds with the help of two Indian companions and then proceeded to patch himself up as best he could. He used a woodsman's concoction of "snake root and blood root" for poulticing his wounds, washing them and changing the dressings every few days; but it was a long time before he recovered sufficiently to leave his cabin.

Both Adams and Ben Franklin carried the scars of this fight for the rest of their lives, and had it not been for the faithful bear and dog, Adams likely would not have survived. It was not the only hand to paw encounter with a grizzly that he took part in, but it was by far the worst. He had little fear of the consequences of his work, taking animals alive and hunting them for hides; but being something of a fatalist, as are many such adventurers, he had great self-confidence in his ability to take care of himself in any kind of situation.

Both Ben Franklin and Lady Washington remained faithful and helpful wilderness companions. Sometimes when hunting in country too steep for horses or mules, he used them for pack animals to move his gear from one camp to another.

During the fall of 1856 he took his animals to San Francisco and exhibited them publicly at the Mountaineer Museum, a rented basement. The writer Theodore H. Hittell, who wrote a book about "Grizzly" Adams's life, graphically describes the exhibit:

Descending the stairway, I found a remarkable spectacle. The basement was a large one with a low ceiling, and dark and dingy in appearance. In the middle, chained to the floor, were two large grizzly bears . . . Ben Franklin and Lady Washington. They were pacing restlessly in circles some ten feet in diameter, their chains being about five feet long, and occasionally rearing up, rattling their irons, and reversing their direction. Not far off on one side, likewise fastened with chains, were seven other bears, several of them young grizzlies, three or four black bears, and one cinnamon. Near the front of the apartment was an open stall, in which were haltered two large elks. Further back was a row of cages containing cougars and other California animals. There were also a few eagles and other birds. At the rear, in a very large iron cage, was the monster grizzly, Samson. He was an immense creature weighing some three quarters of a ton; and from his look and actions, as well as the care taken to rail him off from spectators, it was evident he was not to be approached too closely.

Adams was a natural-born showman, very much admired and liked by all who knew him. The newspapers of that time were well sprinkled with accounts of him and his animals. He always dressed the part of the mountain man and lived with his animals even while in town. He was a "character" who towered among the characters commonplace at that time in the West in his well-earned fame as a hunter and wild-animal tamer.

Hittell was a great admirer of Adams. He further tells of interviewing him at this time and noted that both Ben Franklin and Lady Washington had the hair worn from their backs. Upon query about this, Adams unchained the bears and threw loaded grain sacks over their backs to demonstrate their ability to carry loads.

Adams finally took his show to New York in 1860, where he enjoyed some brief success. He died in Neponset, Massachusetts, on October 28 of that year.

At this time the buffalo hunters were rapidly slaughtering the great bison herds of the western plains for their hides in what was the greatest concentrated killing of wildlife in world history. At the same time the plains grizzly came in for considerable attention from these hunters, who were armed with the breech-loading Sharps rifle. This weapon was highly accurate, long range, and delivered a heavy bullet at a velocity sufficient to rake a large animal through heavy muscle and bone. The Indians found out just how effective it could be at the Battle of Adobe Walls when a buffalo hunter took a solid rest and shot the chief out of his saddle at a thousand yards. This one shot lifted the siege, for the Indians were so discouraged that they rode away.

The last great stronghold of the plains grizzly was in Canada, but even here they were doomed. On an overload expedition of exploration and trade for the Hudson's Bay Company in 1871 and 1872 Isaac Cowie reported in his journal some facts about grizzly numbers in the region just east of the Cypress Hills in what is now southwestern Saskatchewan.

His records show 750 grizzly skins and 1500 elk skins taken in trade within a few months, and he estimated that as about half the kill. He measured one grizzly skin that was thirteen feet long from nose to tail, but he neglected to say whether it was stretched and dried out of proportion or was fresh off the bear.

Both he and Kelsey make the interesting statement, however, that the plains grizzly they encountered was as large or larger than the polar bear, which they had undoubtedly seen along the coast of Hudson's Bay.

Cowie also left an interesting account of seeing six young Peigan braves, armed only with spears, attack a two-year-old grizzly on foot. Stripped down to breechclouts and moccasins, they surrounded the bear in a hollow at the foot of a hill, and one of them prodded bruin in the rump with a spear. The grizzly swapped ends like a flash and rushed after the fleeing Indian; but before his tormentor could be overtaken, another brave jabbed the bear in the rear again. Once more the enraged grizzly whirled to chase this attacker, and so the game proceeded until the Indians tired of their sport and dispatched the grizzly.

The West rapidly grew tamer. The beleaguered grizzlies

were pushed into the wilds of hills and mountains. The buffalo were gone, replaced by the tame cattle of the ranchers. On these the grizzlies preyed on occasion, thus sealing their doom in many remaining portions of their ranges. While the ranchers hunted grizzlies without mercy, few paused to study the big animals and learn something of their ways.

Montague Stevens was a rare exception. He was a very successful cattle rancher of the 1890's in New Mexico who left a classic of personal experience in his writing of ranching adventure for posterity. Of English extraction and having considerable formal education, he also had that rare gift of understanding—he was a man of analytical mind who studied nature and crawled into the skins of those animals he used and hunted to try to reason as they reasoned; and consequently he enjoyed a great measure of success in his dealings with them.

He was the only man in the history of bear hunting who successfully trained and consistently used hounds in pursuing and killing grizzlies that raided his cattle. This use of dogs has been tried by many, but few ever enjoyed much success because of the grizzly's superlative ability to fight a fast-moving retreat until the hunter loses touch with his pack and the pack is reduced by casualties to the point of complete rout.

Stevens's hounds were cross-breeds specially bred by him for the job, with a strong strain of bloodhound in them. He not only taught his dogs obedience in highly developed form, but also trained what he called "liaison dogs," a pair of pure bloodhounds, which trailed the fast-moving hunting pack, thus keeping him in touch with them regardless of what route they took in pursuit of their quarry over the heavily wooded mountains and very rough terrain of New Mexico. His use of his pack of hunting dogs on both grizzly and black bear between 1893 and 1896 was without doubt the most remarkable development of the hunting dog in the history of North American sport.

In hunting the grizzly Montague Stevens became particularly interested in this animal's obvious intelligence, and he recounts an incident of two cattle-killing grizzlies being pursued by trappers. The trappers tried to take the grizzlies first in steel traps, but the cunning bears made fools of them and did not even bother to leave the vicinity. During the course of events, the bears came into the trappers' camp one night and took a deer which they had killed and hung in a tree. This gave the men an idea, and they built a small cabin of heavy logs about 8 x 10 feet in measurement, with a trap door at one end. Inside they hung another deer, so fixed that when pulled, it would trip the trap door. During the night one of the grizzlies entered this oversize box trap and sprung the door shut. But when the trappers came, they found no grizzly. The wily bear had dug his way out under the wall, but what was most remarkable about the escape was that dirt which had been removed outside the enclosure was thrown away from it, showing that the hole had been dug from both sides. This was definite proof that while one grizzly dug busily from the inside, the other heard the activity from the outside and proceeded to help by digging on the opposite side of the wall. This amazing example of cooperation demonstrated a very high order of intelligence and ability to think.

Not only did Stevens have a tremendous insight into the potential intelligence of animals; he also knew men and took a particular delight on occasion to slaughter certain "sacred cows" in his quiet yet piercing way. In speaking of being contrary to some popular beliefs, he says: "I have tried to solve the riddle of why so many popular beliefs are erroneous. The best answer I have been able to evolve so far is that someone starts a rumor which is false. The next person who hears this rumor remarks: 'You cannot believe all you hear,' but never-the-less repeats it and by constant repetition it merges into: 'Everybody says so.' When everybody says so, it becomes an acknowledged fact and popular belief is thus born. After this, if anyone ventures to assail its truth, he is likely to be looked at and considered queer."

Most certainly this penetrating observation is interesting to the avid student of the natural history of the grizzly bear. It is prophetic, for few animals in the world have been so cursed and harried by popular beliefs.

By 1890 the last plains grizzly had been killed or driven into the shelter of the mountains. The great California grizzly was on the swift, steep, and final toboggan slide to extinction.

While there were still grizzlies scattered through the southwest and western United States, they were being hunted as vermin and were saved from being totally wiped out only by the formation of the great western national parks. By 1915, the year that I was born, the era of the plains hunter was long gone, and the prairies were tamed by the shackles of wire fences—a prickly, preternatural symbol of the affluence and selfishness of civilization cutting the land into private claims.

During the latter years of the nineteenth century and the early part of the twentieth there was a great poison campaign set up against wolves, coyotes, and ground squirrels in the northwestern United States and the prairie region of Canada; it not only decimated the intended victims, but it also killed uncounted other wildlife. The badger suffered heavily and was wiped out in some portions of its range. The kit fox was almost exterminated completely. While it takes a heavy dose of strychnine to kill a bear, some were undoubtedly killed. Many more were likely made very sick and were so trained to leave dead carcasses alone.

W. H. Wright, a very observant hunter and naturalist who knew the grizzly well, discussed the feeding habits of the big bears thoroughly and particularly mentioned some vagaries in their feeding ways in different areas. While most of his observations detail the results of environment and the grizzly's habit of taking food where it is most readily found, Wright mentions one instance of food choice that may well have been forced on the bear by human interference. He says:

Here [in the mountains of Wyoming] the grizzly does not dig to any great extent for roots, nor is he the confirmed grass and fish eater that he is in the Bitter Roots; but, aside from the berries that all grizzlies love, and the ants and grubs they never refuse, he is, Spring and Fall, very decidedly carnivorous. In this Wyoming region there are thousands of head of elk and other game. During the winter many perish, and their bodies lie until spring under the snow. During the Fall many are shot, and their carcasses left lying where they fall. These the grizzly feeds on. In the Bitter Root country, strange as it may appear, not one in fifty would touch a carcass thus found.

It did not occur to Wright that the Montana grizzlies lived in a country where one of the most devastating poison campaigns in history had been carried out, and no doubt many bears had tasted strychnine in sufficient quantity to make them deathly sick but insufficent to kill them outright. A grizzly bear, being no kind of habitual fool, would not need a second lesson. Furthermore they would teach their cubs to avoid the temptation of feeding on any carcass found on their range. The Bitter Roots were not protected by a national park and were largely intruded upon by domestic stock, thus coming under the scrutiny of the poisoners. While elk, regardless of park status, were being poached wholesale in Yellowstone for their teeth—in high demand for Elk's Club jewelry—and thus were providing grizzlies there with a bonanza of feed, the Bitter Root bears trusted little but vegetation for their diet.

The sons of the pioneers were lavish in their eulogies of their fathers, but at the same time they went to almost unlimited lengths to wipe out the last vestiges of remaining, living romance and value of the wilderness from which their empire had sprung. Aldo Leopold, North America's classic writer on the subject of conservation, writes nostalgically and sadly of this in his description of the last great grizzly in Arizona.

Life in Arizona was bounded under foot by gramma grass, overhead by sky, and on the horizon by Escudilla.

To the north of the mountain you rode on honey-colored plains. Look up anywhere, any time, and you saw Escudilla.

To the east you rode over a confusion of wooded mesas. Each hollow seemed its own small world, soaked in the sun, fragrant with juniper, and cozy with the chatter of pinon jays. But top out on a ridge and you at once became a speck in an immensity. On its edge hung Escudilla.

To the south lay the tangled canyon of the Blue River, full of whitetails, wild turkeys, and wilder cattle. When you missed a saucy buck waving his goodbye over the skyline, and looked down your sights to wonder why, you looked at the far blue mountain; Escudilla.

To the west billowed the outlines of the Apache National Forest. We cruised timber there, converting the tall pines, forty by forty, into notebook figures representing hypothetical lumber piles. Panting up a canyon, the crusier felt a curious incongruity between the remoteness of his notebook symbols and the immediacy of sweaty fingers, locust thorns, deer fly bites, and scolding squirrels. But on the next ridge a cold wind, roaring across a green sea of pines, blew his doubts away. On the far shore hung Escudilla.

The mountain bounded not only our work and our play, but even our attempts to get a good dinner. On winter evenings we often tried to ambush a mallard on the river flats. The wary flocks circled the rosy west, the steel-blue north, and then disappeared into the inky black of Escudilla. If they reappeared on set wings, we had a fat drake for the Dutch oven. If they failed to appear, it was bacon and beans again.

There was, in fact, only one place from which you did not see Escudilla on the skyline: that was the top of Escudilla itself. Up there you could not see the mountain, but you could feel it. The reason was the big bear.

Old Bigfoot was a robber baron, and Escudilla was his castle. Each spring, when warm winds had softened the shadows on the snow, the old grizzly crawled out of his hibernation den in the rock slides and, descending the mountain, bashed in the head of a cow. Eating his fill, he climbed back to his crags, and there summered peaceably on marmots, conies, berries and roots.

I once saw one of his kills. The cow's skull and neck were pulp, as if she had collided head-on with a fast freight.

No one ever saw the old bear, but in the muddy springs about the base of the cliffs you saw his incredible tracks. Seeing them made the most hard-bitten cowboys aware of the bear. Wherever they rode they saw the mountain, and when they saw the mountain they thought of the bear. Campfire conversation ran to beef, "bailes," and bear. Bigfoot claimed for his own only a cow a year, and a few square miles of useless rocks, but his personality pervaded the country.

Those were the days when progress first came to the cow country. Progress had various emissaries.

One was the first transcontinental automobilist. The cowboys understood this breaker of roads; he talked the same breezy bravado as the breaker of broncos.

They did not understand, but they listened to and looked at, the pretty lady in black velvet who came to enlighten them, in a Boston accent, about woman suffrage.

They marvelled, too, at the telephone engineer who strung wires on junipers and brought instantaneous messages from town. An old man asked whether the wire could bring him a side of bacon.

One spring, progress sent still another emissary, a government trapper, a sort of St. George in overalls, seeking dragons to slay at government expense. Were there, he asked, any destructive animals in need of slaying? Yes, there was the big bear.

The trapper packed his mule and headed for Escudilla.

In a month he was back, his mule staggering under a heavy hide. There was only one barn in town big enough to dry it on. He had tried traps, poison, and all his usual wiles to no avail. Then he had erected a set-gun in a defile through which only the bear could pass, and waited. The last grizzly walked into the wire and shot himself.

It was June. The pelt was foul, patchy, and worthless. It seemed to us rather an insult to deny the last grizzly the chance to leave a good pelt as a memorial to his race. All he left was a skull in the National Museum, and a quarrel among scientists over the Latin name of the skull.

It was only after we pondered these things that we began to wonder who wrote the rules for progress.

Since the beginning, time had gnawed at the basaltic bulk of Escudilla, wasting, waiting, and building. Time built three things on the old mountain, a venerable aspect, a community of minor animals and plants, and a grizzly.

The government trapper who took the grizzly knew he had made Escudilla safe for cows. He did not know he had toppled a spire off an edifice abuilding since the morning stars sang together.

The bureau chief who sent the trapper was a biologist versed in the architecture of evolution, but he did not know that spires might be as important as cows. He did not foresee that within two decades the cow country would become tourist country, and have a much greater need for bears than beefsteaks.

The Congressmen who voted the money to clear the ranges of bears were the sons of pioneers. They acclaimed the superior virtues of the frontiersman, but they strove with might and main to make an end to the frontier.

We forest officers, who acquiesced in the extinguishment of the bear, knew a local rancher who had plowed up a dagger engraved with the name of one of Coronado's captains. We spoke harshly of the Spaniards who, in their zeal for gold and converts, had needlessly extinguished the native Indians. It did not occur to us that we, too, were the captains of invasion too sure of its own righteousness.

Escudilla still hangs on the horizon, but when you see it you no longer think of bear. It's only a mountain now.

But thanks to time, rough country, hard climate and the very bigness of the land, the encroachment of progress is not accomplished in a day, a month, or even years. For I was to be born, grow up, and live on the edge of the wilderness and in its folds, where horses and man's two feet were—and in certain holy places still are—the only means to get where one wants to go.

7. *Some Early Recollections of My Own*

He only loses interest and dignity in the eyes of those whom fear alone impresses.
—WILLIAM H. WRIGHT

In the spring of 1921, when I was five years old, my father showed me the first grizzly track I ever saw; it was pressed into the mud on the edge of a willow-ringed slough on our ranch at the foot of the Rockies in southwest Alberta. It was the track of a big bear—long-clawed and deep from his weight—and the sight of it made my heart jump with a mixture of fear and the stirring thrill of coming adventure. Little did I realize that my tracks would be inextricably woven with those of grizzlies for the rest of my life, from the prairies to the blue waters of the Pacific, from the rugged northern rim of Montana to the tundra-carpeted country among the stark fangs of snow- and ice-capped peaks in interior Alaska and Yukon Territory. I was, that day on the edge of the slough, something like a hound pup put on the tracks of game for the first time—a bit afraid and a bit confused, but strangely stirred by an awareness that destiny was calling, and excited by the faint hint of what it had in store.

136

The business of growing up is unfortunately very painful and cruel for many children. Very few are blessed, like my brother John and me, with the opportunity of attaining the status of men in the midst of a natural paradise trapped between civilization and the wilderness. Too few ever become aware of man's association with and relationship to other forms of animal life. And still fewer are blessed with parents who have a sense of adventure and an appreciation of beauty and a love of living for the sake of living, all of which allows them to join their children on an equal footing in their pursuits of vocation and play. How many mothers walk with their offspring under the trees in the cool of the evening and stand with them in silent awe of a flaming sunset? How many fathers can teach their boys to ride and shoot, to swing and throw a lariat, and to look at danger with respect but little fear? How many parents take the trouble to point out and explain the wonder of a butterfly emerging from a cocoon? How many give their children a female pet and allow them to see the wonder of birth?

To be sure, our schooling was primitive by modern standards, administered by young ladies with a teacher's certificate, often hard pressed to cope with the young savages they taught. Our education, my brother's and mine, might even be considered sketchy, but a good portion of what was missed in it was taught by our parents and the country we lived in.

Our ranch was by a small lake cradled among folded hills, part of a vista of aspen and cottonwood parks in the lee of Drywood Mountain, which stood over us with massive shoulders humped up close to its rounded dome as though frozen in an endless shrug of patient endurance. Down deep, twisted canyons on either side ran the forks of Drywood Creek to join on our ranch meadows. Its waters were clear as crystal and cold as a flowing, liquid ice. Its highly colored, stony bottom moved and undulated with shadows of fish—brilliant and pastel-colored cut-throat trout, Rocky Mountain whitefish, and big Dolly Vardens. The woods were full of grouse and mule deer. The limpid mirrors of sloughs and lakes scattered among the hills reflected the mountains on still mornings and were the nesting grounds of countless waterfowl. The furbearers—coyotes, beavers, musk-rats, minks, and weasels—wrote their stories in their tracks everywhere for sharp eyes to read. The slopes of the mountains, two miles from our door by crow wing, were the stamping grounds of bighorn sheep, mountain goats, black bears, deer, and grizzlies. Behind and beyond the outside range were mile upon mile of tumbled peaks and twisted canyons, making an almost trackless and uninhabited wilderness reaching from Glacier Park north to the arctic, and from our door to the fruit-growing country of British Columbia, two hundred and fifty miles to the west.

We met old mountain men, colorful in dress and speech, who still clung to their primitive, free life and spurned the comforts of civilization. There was "Kootenai" Brown, an Englishman fugitive from a shooting scrape in far-off India, where he shot a fellow officer in a duel over a woman. He came to the Waterton Lakes country about 1860 and was one of the first white men allowed to stay in Blackfoot country by those warlike tribesmen. He was a trader and hunter at first, and later he became the first superintendent of Waterton Lakes National Park, in which office he died. There was Joe Cosley, a college-educated half-breed Indian who trapped and hunted widely through the mountains. He was a quiet-spoken man, a deadly shot with both rifle and pistol, and apart from being a great hunter, he was something of a naturalist and journalist. His name still appears clearly on a giant aspen not far from our door, where it was scratched with his lonesome-heart insignia in 1922. There was Henri "Frenchy" de Reviere, son of a French aristocrat and nephew of a cardinal of the Roman Catholic Church, who was likely the most efficient hunter and trapper of grizzlies I ever knew. He had deserted as a young man from the French Navy in New Orleans and made his way north and west to finally settle with a warm-hearted Scotch-Cree woman in this country. Neither last nor least there was George Gladstone, Frenchy's brother-in-law, who was the son of a Hudson's Bay man and a direct descendant of the famous British politician of the same name.

George was a natural-born wilderness comedian and raconteur with a rich fund of stories he would tell with great glee at the slightest excuse. A happy bachelor with absolutely no fear of anything walking on two legs or four, he had a sense of the ridiculous that towered. He loved youngsters, and they invariably loved him. Nothing pleased him more than to sit with young folk sprawled at his feet and tell them a story. Sometimes the story would have done justice to Baron Munchausen, and sometimes they were true. We were forever left wondering where truth left off and fabrication began—a minor detail, for the tale was inevitably uproarious. George was an irresistible version of a Rocky Mountain Uncle Remus. One story he often told, illustrates his fun-loving nature and is even stranger for being true.

One fall George was employed as guide by a couple of hunters from Duluth, Minnesota. They were away back in the mountains one bright day hunting along some skyline ridges high above timberline when George spotted a grizzly. The big bear was digging for a marmot, and only his hind end was projecting from the small mine he had excavated. He was a long way off, and the only possible approach was to cut a circle and come in against the wind over a ridge crest above him. So George led the way over a mountain shoulder with the hunters toiling at his heels for more than an hour across one steep canyon and gully after another. Finally they climbed up the back of the ridge where the grizzly had last been seen.

Was the bear still there? Breathless from exertion and mounting excitement, the hunters trailed George up to a lookout point of rock and peered over. About a hundred fifty yards downslope the grizzly was still engrossed with business at the bottom of the hole, his furry rump projecting ever toward the sky. Nobody with a shred of sense shoots a grizzly in the south end when he is heading north; so they waited in ambush for their trophy to back out into full view. The hunters were slowly dying of acute suspense. George, meanwhile, calmly studied the animal through his binoculars. Suddenly George stood up and softly announced, "You boys get set. I'm going down and give him a good kick!"

Before either of the dudes could open his mouth or move, George put his hands in his pockets and blithely sauntered down toward the grizzly—not even bothering to take his rifle. To their popeyed horror he strolled up behind those big hindquarters and planted a rousing kick on them. Nothing happened. The bear was stone dead.

Wiley George had spotted bluebottle flies swarming on the grizzly's fur and immediately had known the truth. The opportunity for a joke was too good to miss. After he had managed to calm himself and the jelly had somewhat receded from the hunters' knees, they proceeded to examine the grizzly.

The bear had dug deep trying to dislodge the marmot from under a subterranean boulder, but the little animal's fortress proved impregnable. Although the grizzly could get close enough almost to touch it, he could not quite reach his prospective lunch. Under such circumstances a grizzly is quite likely to lose his temper, as has been said previously, and this one must have worked up an apoplectic rage. Herculean efforts to haul the boulder out of its bed, coupled with a burst of temper, had apparently caused some kind of internal hemorrhage; for the bear's head lay in a puddle of blood and his paws were still holding the boulder. No evidence of any external injury could be found.

Regardless of story content, the natural acting that went along with the telling of such stories leaves me painfully aware of my shortcomings in describing the natural talent of such wilderness elocutionists—a vanishing breed, for radio and television has largely killed the art. Certainly their stories opened vistas of adventure to their listeners—especially to small boys and to this one in particular. Small wonder that my fascination with the wilds grew by leaps and bounds until I could think of little else.

This preoccupation must have been noticeable, for I have not forgotten a bit of advice George Gladstone gave me one day in one of his rare moments of absolute seriousness. "You will be good in the mountains," he told me. "Go learn what they have to tell you. It is the way your moccasins are pointed, and you will be happy."

This I was eager to do, and as it does to all young people, the process of growing up seemed very slow to me. Dad and mother both loved to hunt and fish, but never at the expense of neglecting their work—a virtue neither of their sons inherited. A crack shot in his own right, dad schooled us early in the correct use of firearms. Going hunting with him was an occasion to be looked forward to for weeks, even when we were still too small to hold a gun.

Guns were never far from anyone's reach in those days. Sport shooting was purely a by-product of hunting for meat and protecting livestock from preying grizzlies. Sometimes it seemed as though the bears resented our intrusion into the portals of their mountain strongholds and went to some length to show it.

Certainly, at that time they were bold, and many were the flurries of excitement when they raided the cattle. Once a big grizzly climbed into a homesteader's corral in the dead of night and massacred his milk cow within easy hearing distance of the owner. The homesteader, Alex Campbell, a misplaced British sailor with a good deal of courage and recklessness, ventured forth with a shotgun and a coal-oil lantern to avenge the untimely death of his cow. Everyone agreed his luck was not all bad, for he failed to close with the bear. Next day George Cairns, an adjoining neighbor, trailed and killed this grizzly.

For all their brashness the big bears rarely raided buildings. On the one occasion when this occurred, the incident took place under somewhat extenuating circumstances in the village of Waterton Lakes National Park, a few miles to the south.

Late one fall a particularly bold grizzly made an appearance in the village, where he proceeded to raid garbage cans at night. The Park residents were accustomed to shooing black bears out of their way, but they had no desire to fall over a grizzly some night in the dark. Forthwith a delegation went to the superintendent demanding the bear's removal.

The superintendent was of British army stock, a spit-and-polish type who ruled exactly by the book of regulations and did not believe that laws were written for the direction of wise men and the eminence of fools in their administration. The rulebook said clearly and emphatically that no animal within a national park shall be hunted, killed, or otherwise molested. So he looked down his prominent patrician nose in some disapproval and quoted the book verbatim, ending his peroration with: "By Jove! It just can't be done, don't you know. Completely contrary to regulations. Impossible to consider such a notion!"

The delegation departed muttering under their breaths, while the grizzly went his unsuspecting way. Some days passed, and then came a night with stormy, gusting winds blowing snow squalls down off the peaks. It was as dark as the inside of a cow.

As was their custom, the superintendent and his wife left home early that evening to play bridge with friends. Some enterprising character, unrecorded by history, chose that opportunity to smear a bucket of honey all over the back door of the official residence.

It is safe to say that the superintendent had no suspicion of this development; for he did not return until nearly midnight and was horrified to find his home occupied by a large, well-fed grizzly. The animal had shattered the rear door in his enthusiasm for honey and so gained entrance to the larder of winter supplies. There he proceeded to enjoy a variety of fare, the likes of which he never dreamed existed. In the course of his feasting he ripped open a hundred-pound sack of flour and a twenty-pound pail of syrup, then he happily tramped the mixture all over the place. The house was a complete shambles.

The worthy official lost no time in sending word to the nearest warden, who lived on the far side of the village. "Come quickly! There's a blawsted grizzly in my house!"

The warden, one McFarland, an inscrutable western type whom nothing could excite except perhaps the dismal expression of an empty bottle, arrived in due course. He came weaving through the storm, carrying a dim coal-oil lantern in one hand and a very dilapidated Winchester in the other. The rifle, the only official weapon in the Park, was an ancient .30–30 carbine, battered and rusty. Its magazine would not function, the trigger was broken, and the only way it could be fired was to load it single-shot fashion and then slip the hammer off the ball of the thumb.

By this time the grizzly had prudently decamped into the forest, leaving his big fresh tracks in the snow. Several people who had arrived to commiserate with the superintendent as well as to enjoy both the excitement and his discomfiture tried to dissuade the indomitable McFarland from following the bear. But he was of a rather unreasonable frame of mind and went weaving off through the pines to be swallowed in the gloom. Ten minutes went by, twenty minutes—half an hour—and then the single boom of the rifle away off on the mountain. Those waiting, watching, and holding their breaths as they listened for some further sign of Mac's well-being were not particularly cheered by the lonesome howling of the wind.

Then there appeared a swaying dot of light glimmering through the timber, and McFarland emerged, just as inscrutable and unhurrying as when he left.

He went up to the superintendent, steadied himself, and managed to focus his eyes long enough to report: "Your grizzly is dead."

"Dead!" exclaimed that unbelieving official.

"Christ yes!" reiterated the gruff-voiced Mac. "Deader'n hell!" Whereupon he turned on his heel and wove off toward his cabin.

Subsequent investigation next morning proved this to be true. The grizzly was lying inert at the far end of his tracks with a neat bullethole at the butt of his ear. How close McFarland had to get to administer the quietus with such a weapon in the dim light of a lantern is anybody's guess, and he never said. At any rate Mac assumed immortal status among bear hunters, for the story is still told around mountain campfires.

From the time we were big enough to sit a horse, my brother and I adventured and explored the creeks and canyons cutting back into the mountains from our backyard. Sometimes we went with Dad, but most of the time we went alone. Our parents believed experience to be the best teacher, and when our chores around the ranch were done, we were given free rein. Our first excursions into the wilds were short, but as we grew to know the trails and the country, we went farther and farther until there was hardly a square yard of ground within ten miles that we did not know.

Many times we found the big, long-clawed tracks of grizzlies, sometimes so fresh that we tiptoed away, looking back over our shoulders just to make sure. The half-expected appearance of a bear never occurred. We finally came to think our fears were groundless and ceased to worry much about the prospect. I was nine years old before I had the supreme adventure of first acquaintance with a grizzly at close range.

I was fishing alone at a favorite spot, a secluded beaver dam on a small fork of Drywood Creek, just under the face of the mountain. A couple of miles from home, the place was one of real wilderness splendor. The dam had partially flooded a willow grove at the foot of the trees, and this was a maze of beaver channels, which were also the thoroughfares of the cutthroat trout swarming in the pond.

These were the most unsophisticated trout imaginable. As George Gladstone would put it, the fishing was so good, you almost had to hide behind a tree to bait your hook. For a while I fished the open side of the pond, but this was so easy it soon palled, so I went around among the willows to stalk the bigger ones lurking in the cover. With all the guile and patience of a great blue heron I moved like a shadow among the willows, preoccupied with the game of keeping my line from fouling on the numberless hazards while presenting my impaled grasshopper to trout cruising and resting in the clear waters of their hiding places.

This was the purest kind of sport for a boy—sport fraught with anticipation, the thrill of sighting individual fish without disturbing them, planning a step-by-step stalk and presenting the lure. It was close-range hunting of shy individual fish in surroundings of pristine wilderness, and it required the greatest care.

The tops of the willows spread overhead in a screen that allowed the sun through in dappled patterns. The waters beneath were contrasts of brilliantly lit spots, where every detail of the bottom was revealed, and mysterious dark lairs. A small boy was one with all of it. The only sounds were the sporadic slurping and splashing of rising trout, the gentler song of the breeze among dancing cottonwood leaves, and the music of birds. It was a bewitching place where I was utterly at home and content, especially when my fish sack hung comfortably heavy on my shoulder as proof of my prowess.

Completely absorbed in the business of presenting my lure to a beautiful trout lying in six inches of water just beyond a snag, I noticed little else. Every flowing line, each brilliant black spot and detail of delicate pastel coloration was visible as the fish lay motionless in a small patch of sunlight on the jet-black bottom—an electric suspension of promised action, only its gills moving gently. The grasshopper was lowered over the trout's nose when the tiny snap of a breaking twig sounded behind me. Moving only my head, I swung my eyes to look.

Twenty odd feet away, behind a scrubby black birch clump, an indistinct mass of fur began to rise up and up, till I found myself confronted by an enormous grizzly bear standing at full height with big front paws hanging over a vast expanse of hairy belly. It was a sort of wilderness confrontation of David and Goliath—with David sadly miscast, for he did not feel very brave. He stood frozen, every detail etching into his mind. He did not know it, but Goliath was equally transfixed with astonishment and curiosity. The giant's eyes glowed with a deep flame. He looked as huge as the end of the earth, his shoulders mantled with shining silver that contrasted with his dark brown coat, those great front paws hung with long, brilliant ivory claws. Apart from his probing nose he was motionless.

Some movement, sound, or smell of me must have triggered him, for he suddenly dropped to all four feet with a great whooshing snort and bounded away through the cottonwoods and up the slope beyond. I did not linger to ponder the manner of his going. With pounding heart and flying feet, unmindful of deep channels and brush, I flew for my horse and home.

For some time the trout of that secret place were left undisturbed by one small boy. But after thinking about the incident, the fact that the bear had chosen to retreat first took some of the threat out of the encounter. Finally the irresistible lure of the place drew him back to enjoy its magic, somehow enhanced now by the knowledge of a great presence. Where he had gone before as a mere angler for trout, his going now had the added feeling of real adventure, tuning eyes and ears to a fine pitch for signs and sounds. The wilds were teaching their lessons.

Early one morning later that same summer I was riding up the trail to the pond when my horse suddenly snorted and shied, throwing me off on the edge of a small meadow. I landed on my belly across an ant heap, knocking my wind so far out that it was some time before I could do anything but grimace and roll feebly on the ground. By the time I got back on my feet, the horse was gone, and I stood wondering if it would be easier to walk the rest of the way or to go back to the ranch gate for my mount. Then something strange caught my eye behind a willow a few yards away, and I went over to investigate.

Rooted in a mixture of awe and horror I stood gazing wide-eyed at the torn and bloody carcass of a cow, so freshly killed that the bluebottle flies had not yet found her. The smell of blood and torn intestines was strong on the damp morning air. There was no sign of the thing that had caused this carnage, but I knew what it was as I crept closer for a better look.

One of the cow's eyes hung clear of its socket, dangling grotesquely on the optic nerve and giving the carcass a look of frantic horror. The whole front of the skull was crushed to a pulp, and the nose was almost torn away. High on the shoulders were great claw marks channeled deep into hide and flesh and merging in a great gouge on top of the withers that revealed naked bone. One whole flank was ripped out, spilling a mass of

Grizzlies are interesting partly for the gorgeous country they inhabit. R. H. Russell took the bottom shot near Mount McKinley. The upper picture of a sow and two yearling cubs was taken in a blueberry patch.

Buffaloes and grizzlies once used the same range on the prairies. Two very heavily antlered bull moose feed on lily pads in the McKinley area (above).

guts and torn, grass-filled paunch in a tangled messy heap. A big chunk was eaten out of one haunch. When I put my foot on the tip of an upturned horn, the whole head folded a little under my weight with the sickening feeling of jellied bone. Suddenly I wanted very badly to be somewhere else, and in two strides my feet were flying toward home.

When I blurted out my story to Dad, he exclaimed, "Grizzly kill! Bad business for you to be getting too close to that. It must be one of Butcher's bunch. We had best tell him."

It did not take long to ride up to Butcher's ranch, which adjoined ours up the valley. He immediately dispatched a rider to summon Frenchy from his place over on Pincher Creek, the next valley to the north. Frenchy was the recognized bear hunter of the country, and he added to his income with bounty paid for killing grizzlies raiding cattle on Butcher's sizable property.

As Dad stepped back up on his horse to go back to his work, Butcher suggested, "I wish you would leave the boy. I would like him to guide us to the cow."

To my huge joy Dad nodded in agreement. I was bursting with self-importance, and by the time Frenchy rode over the skyline, my impatience was almost choking me. Frenchy reined his big sorrel down into the yard off the shoulder of the hill, with a buckskin pack horse jogging behind him loaded with a huge trap, shovel, axe, and other gear. Stopping his horse and dismounting in one smooth motion, he flashed his teeth in a smile and said in that curious soft accent, probably borrowed from the Creoles who hid him from indignantly searching Navy men years before, "I heah you got a demised cow, Butch."

"She's dead all right," Butcher replied. "The boy here found her this morning over in the south pasture. From what he tells me, she was killed last night. Let's go have a look."

As we rode out a few minutes later, I was trying to sit tall in the saddle—not very easy bareback on a fat old horse. Frenchy and Butcher rode along talking and paying no attention to me. When I thought he wouldn't notice, I would sneak a look at Frenchy. From the top of his high-crowned, broad-brimmed Stetson to the soles of his beaded moccasins he filled me with awe and fascination. There was a wild strangeness about him, and a hard shine in his blue eyes spoke of thinly veiled vanity and temper. He sat his saddle with indolent grace, like a part of his horse, and always as he rode, his eyes prowled restlessly, seeing everything. All items of his equipment and apparel were somewhat different from that used by anybody else. I wondered about them and wished for some like them.

Hanging from his saddle horn by a leather thong was a curious quirt about two feet long, gradually tapering from the grip to its frayed-out tip. It was gray in color and looked something like bone, but it was obviously something else. My eyes went back to it again and again. Finally Frenchy reined his horse over beside mine.

"You like my quirt, eh?" he said. "I bet you can't tell me what it's made from." Then he passed it over to me.

It had the hard dry feel of rawhide, but it was almost an inch thick at the grip and I knew it could not be hide. I admitted I didn't know. An amused glint came into Frenchy's eyes as he said, "That's what a genuine sun-dried penis looks like, kid."

Still mystified, I asked, "What's a penis?"

"Ho!" chuckled Frenchy to the world at large. With a grin and a flourish of his hand he announced, "This kid, his education is neglect!"

Butcher snorted through his big nose, and I burned with embarrassment.

"How do little boys call it, eh?" Frenchy drawled. "Maybe a pecker, eh? That's it—a genuine sun-dried bull pecker!"

Completely speechless and red to the top of my ears, I handed the quirt back as though it were red-hot. Frenchy took it with another chuckle and hung it back on his saddle horn.

My embarrassment was quickly forgotten when we reached the dead cow. Here Frenchy took command and ordered me to stay on my horse and out of the way, while he and Butcher unpacked the buckskin. Taking his axe, he went into a grove of aspens and cut down several trees, which were quickly cut into shorter lengths. These were dragged to the carcass. Long stakes were then driven into the ground. The short logs were wired and spiked to these, enclosing the carcass in a rectangular pen open at one end. More logs and brush were fastened on top to cover it with a rude but heavy roof. The trap was ready to set.

Such traps were huge double-springed affairs with offset jaws armed with staggered teeth, all forged from solid steel and weighing close to fifty pounds. The springs could only be depressed one at a time by the use of a heavy screw clamp. Such a trap would hold anything that stepped squarely into it.

Frenchy cut and trimmed a heavier section of log. The big steel ring on the end of the trap chain was fitted over the smaller end of this, then wired and spiked securely to it. When the trap was set, Frenchy placed it in the open end of the pen, a bit off side from center. Then he sharpened some small, thin stakes of dry willow at both ends and planted them cunningly around it to induce the bear to put its foot directly on the trap. When everything was arranged to his liking, Frenchy stepped back to survey his work with a critical eye.

"I think we will pinch his toes tonight," he said.

I wanted to ask if I could come in the morning to watch, but my courage failed me. I rode home to supper wondering what would happen when the grizzly came back. Excited and stirred up by the day's adventures, I made plans to stay awake all night, sneak out at dawn, and ride to the kill. Somehow my plans went awry, and before I knew it, Dad was shaking my shoulder.

"Come quick!" he said.

Outside on the back step mother and John joined us. The sun was just tipping over the eastern horizon, and the morning air was still, cool, and very clear. Then from away off toward Drywood Mountain in the direction of the trap came the most terrifying sound I have ever heard. For pure, unadulterated savagery and outraged hurt no sound on earth can match the mad bawling of a trapped grizzly. High and wild, full of hate and a primal desire to kill and rend to bloody ribbons, it also has a strange pathos. Once heard, it is never forgotten. On a morning like this the sound of it carried easily for more than a mile. My desire to go closer had evaporated.

"It's awful!" my mother murmured with a shudder.

Then the roaring rose to an almost insane crescendo and was abruptly and cleanly cut off by the single slatting roar of a heavy rifle.

Dad broke the silence by stating flatly, "That one will kill no more cows." And we went indoors for breakfast.

When we had eaten and the morning chores were done, Dad, John, and I rode out to look at the bear. Frenchy was gone when we arrived, and so was the trap. Among freshly scarred aspens and torn-up willows at the kill the great bear lay stretched out obscenely on his back, teeth bared in a frozen grimace. His mighty paws were cut off, and his belly gaped open. The male appendage was cut away. The worthless summer hide, which Frenchy had not bothered to take, was gummed and matted with blood and filth. Somehow the cutting appalled me.

"What did he do that for?" I asked.

"You can bet he had a reason," Dad replied. "He'll sell the paws and the gall to the Chinese in town. They make some kind of soup from the paws and a medicine from the gall." Then he noticed where my eyes were pointing. "I don't know why he took that part."

"Maybe to make a quirt?"

Dad laughed and said, "He caught you on that one, did he. This time he had something else in mind. Not big enough for a quirt. No telling what Frenchy might do with it."

Years later I found out. He made a hand-carved letter opener from this white, hard ivory bone unique to bears, and doubtless he trapped some curious people into asking questions about it. Frenchy had a singular sense of humor.

The bears coming down out of the wild fastnesses of the mountains were no doubt intrigued by cattle when they ran into the scattered herds on the edge of the wilderness. Maybe some inherited a taste for beef from bison-eating ancestors. Perhaps some pursued stampeding cattle out of curiosity and thus learned how easy they were to kill. In spite of trapping and hunting the bears, cattle were lost to them every year. In our wanderings we found many kills. Well I remember one such incident that wound up in the most unusual foot race I ever ran.

My parents' hospitality, the beautiful location of our ranch, and the excellent fishing resulted in many summer visitors. Naturally John and I enjoyed showing these around the creeks and hills of our playground, and among the friends thus cultivated was one lad about my age by the name of Mac.

Mac was a town boy with little experience of the big open country we called home, but he was strong and active and took to it with enthusiasm. He was helping us put up hay one summer when a night rainstorm followed by a heavy fog gave us a chance to take the day off and go fishing.

By the time breakfast was over, the sun was cutting through at higher levels, and the tops of the mountains were sticking up like rocky islands from the great silvery ocean of mist that filled the low ground and valleys to the brim.

Mac and horses did not get along too well, so when he suggested that we walk, he came in for some good-natured ribbing; but I agreed. We picked up our tackle and plunged down the slopes into the fog-shrouded valley of the Drywood. I led the way down to the forks, where we turned up the south branch toward the mouth of the canyon.

About two miles upstream, still a mile or so short of the canyon, the trail crossed some rocky flats where the stream meandered through scattered willow thickets and cottonwood groves. The place was eerie in the fog, the big trees looming silently, their wet leaves drooping motionlessly. We were not talking as we padded silently up the wet trail in still wetter sneakers. Everything was adrip with clinging moisture. Suddenly we came to a yearling heifer lying torn and dead right beside the trail. For a few long moments we stood absolutely still, looking and listening.

Then Mac gasped in an awe-struck whisper, "What happened?"

"Grizzly kill," I whispered back. "Be quiet!"

Mac was quiet for a while, and then he urgently whispered, "Let's go home."

I was half of the same mind myself, but the idea of giving up our plan to fish the canyon did not sit too well, and anyway I was supposed to be the leader.

"Phooey!" I said softly. "Who's afraid of a bear."

"Me," Mac admitted with complete honesty.

"Shut up!" I instructed unceremoniously. "He's gone."

With that I led off up the trail ahead with Mac following somewhat reluctantly at my heels. We came to a sharp elbow of the creek, where the trail forded it and passed through a thick grove of birches and willows. We waded across and were about halfway through the brush when we were jerked up short by a long-drawn sniff that ended in an explosive snort followed by a great crashing of something big tearing a hole through the thick growth. I was aware that the grizzly was running away, but Mac did not linger to find out which way the animal was heading. He soared over a big dead log like a startled buck and lit running. His fishing rod got caught in a branch, and he dropped it, never looking back to see where it fell. In a moment he was out of sight. My impulse to laugh faded away when I suddenly realized what was about to happen; for he was heading straight away for the wild slopes of Drywood Mountain. His instinct for direction and his desire to go home were far from being meshed. It might take a search party a week to find him.

Dropping my rod, I sped in pursuit. For a while I thought he was gone, but when I broke out onto the open flats, the mist was beginning to thin a bit and there was Mac running like a spooked jack rabbit a good hundred yards ahead. He was a track runner, and now he was going wide open over rocks and rough ground as though it were as flat as a table. Wishing I had a horse, I stretched out my stride to catch him. When he got snarled up in some brush in a gully, I gained some ground. But then he heard me hit the brush behind him, and I lost it again. For a good quarter of a mile I failed to gain an inch. I tried yelling but gave that up when he threw a wild look over one shoulder and fairly flew, as though I were the bear.

We were crossing the valley on a long angle toward a steep slope covered with a tangle of wind- and snow-bent aspens. Just before he came to this, Mac tripped and fell hard enough to slow him up for a moment. I gained some ground and veered a bit toward a spot on the slope where the brush was not so thick. With some luck I might be able to head him off. Tasting salt in my mouth, I made one last desperate dash up this break and stopped to get some wind into my tortured lungs. I couldn't see Mac any more, but I could sure hear him plunging and breaking brush, trying to smash straight through the middle of the thick stuff.

Seized by an inspiration, I roared with the last wind left in me, "Hey, Mac! Quick! This way!" Then I fell over flat on my back.

Mac must have heard me, for the crashing turned in my direction. He finally came into sight right in front of me, staggering glassy-eyed with his mouth wide open like a fish out of water, and fell in a heap.

For a while he just lay there, frantically gasping for air, and then he managed to gasp, "We gotta go home."

"Sure," I agreed, "just take it easy for a while."

But he got up and started away up the slope again.

"Hey!" I yelled at him in exasperation. "Where do you think you're going?"

"Home."

"You darn fool!" I barked at him. "Keep going this way and you'll be in British Columbia!"

That snapped Mac out of it, and he sat down to rest again. But it was a long time before I could talk him into going back with me for the rods. That was the only time in my life that I almost ran myself to death trying to keep somebody from getting lost. I doubt if I ever fully convinced Mac that he did not outrun that grizzly bear.

The only time I ever remember the cattlemen showing some grudging magnanimity toward bears was when some sheepmen leased a part of the mountain range. Both grizzlies and blacks found mutton to their taste, and on one or two occasions the grizzlies played a sort a gruesome game with them, resulting in many casualties. Once a bear stampeded a herd into a steep draw, which was literally filled with smothered sheep when the herder found them.

The herders were largely prairie men unaccustomed to mountains and had dealt with no marauding animals larger than a coyote. When they saw the burly form of a grizzly, looming twice as large as life in the light of the moon, as the big animal stampeded their flocks off the bedgrounds at night, it was demoralizing. It was not long before sheep were scattered far and wide. For the most part the sheepmen retreated back to the more hospitable prairies.

But there was one exception. His name was Alvin Ecklund, a burly, powerful man of medium height and florid complexion who could best be described as a sudden, short-tempered, somewhat bullheaded man. If mountain grass seemed desirable when he moved his sheep onto it, it became a great deal more valuable after the bears killed some sheep. He scoffed at the retreating sheep owners, shamed his herders into staying, and declared war on bears in general. Whatever his shortcomings, Alvin was one of the most fearless men I have ever met.

One night he caught a big marauding grizzly in a trap up on the Yarrow Creek range, and when he and his herder came to the place next morning, they found the grizzly had dragged the clog down into a steep, narrow defile choked with fallen logs and alder brush. It was hidden from view, but they had no trouble locating it by the sound of its bawling among the quaking brush.

The herder made no bones about wanting no part of this place, so Alvin went in alone with his rifle and dog to dispatch the animal. The cover was thick, forcing him in close before he could see any part of the bear. Like most everything else he owned, the rifle was a hard-used piece of equipment, and when he tried to shoot, the gun refused to fire. Then the grizzly saw him and lunged straight at him with a great roar. Only one toe was hung up in the trap, and the straining ligaments parted. In the twinkling of an eye Alvin was almost under the raging animal. Most men would have tried to retreat, but with typical, headstrong, reckless courage he stood his ground and rammed the rifle barrel straight down the grizzly's throat. At the same moment the dog streaked in to fasten on the bear's heels. No other combination could possibly have saved Alvin from a terrible mauling, for as the bear, trying to spit out the rifle, turned toward the dog, it gave him a chance to retreat. He ran back to grab the spare rifle out of the paralyzed herder's hands, then he tore back into the fight again. Before the grizzly could make another rush, he shot it through the head.

His brother, Jack, a man of much sunnier disposition but equally fearless, occasionally helped with the sheep, although he preferred working with horses and cattle.

Once when John and I were riding up Yarrow canyon, we came across fresh sign of a grizzly having been in a trap in a thick stand of lodgepole pines. We were sitting our horses speculating on the skinned and chewed second-growth trees when Jack Ecklund rode up. We asked what had happened.

"Come," he said. "I'll show you."

At a spot above the trail, where a grizzly had killed a sheep on the upper edge of the thick growth of young pines, Jack had set a trap. Because the grizzly was a big one, he chained the trap to the middle of a green pine log, a foot thick at the butt end and perhaps ten feet long. It weighed two or three hundred pounds and seemed more than adequate for a drag.

Jack woke from his sleep in the middle of the night at the sheep camp a half mile up the valley when he heard the grizzly bawling and smashing timber as it fought the trap. At daylight everything was quiet, and as he rode down the valley to investigate, Jack was wondering if the grizzly had somehow managed to escape. When he arrived at the set, he found grizzly, trap, and clog gone; but there was a well-blazed trail beaten through the pines straight down the mountainside and plain enough for a blind man to follow. For several hundred yards the bear had pulled the drag through a tangle of down logs and second growth. Every few yards the clog had jammed up solid, whereupon the grizzly had chewed and torn up everything within reach until it was free again. When it finally reached the creek, the grizzly could slide the log much easier in the water and had turned downstream. Then the creek narrowed in a canyon and leaped down over a series of small waterfalls. The first of these did not slow the bear up very much; but as the animal headed down over a bigger drop-off, the log jammed solid crosswise in a water-worn slot at the lip of the falls, and there the grizzly hung helplessly with the water playing over him. The creek was low, so the bear was still very much alive when Jack found him.

As he showed us the place, Jack said with a grin, "When I saw him hanging there, I did something I've always wanted to do—pet a real live grizzly bear. So I climbed down over the rock alongside him and stroked his back."

"What did he do?" I asked.

"Why, he sort of bowed himself up like a steel spring and roared and rattled things to beat hell!" Jack grinned. "Reckon you couldn't blame him much. I've never felt anything so powerful. That old bear was all guts and fight. I purely hated to shoot him."

To be sure, it was a reckless thing to do, but somehow the idea appealed to us. Even if it was a sort of left-handed compliment to the bear, Jack was one of the very few stockmen I ever heard express any admiration for the grizzly.

Although the use of steel traps was a way to make our spending money in winter, somehow the trapping of bears never sat right with me. If someone had asked me why, I doubt if I could have given a satisfactory answer. I used steel traps to take small furbearers without a qualm about cruelty, and logically the gradient of suffering is not steepened by the size of the animal. My aversion to bear trapping was something deep and unexplainable, and I kept it to myself. Seeing a bear in a trap left me with the taste of having observed an obscenity.

This feeling was sharpened one day up on the north fork of the Drywood. I was fishing a bit downstream from the mouth of the canyon along a magnificent stretch of trout water, where the stream, the mountains, and the forest conspired to form a place that was truly a wilderness paradise. My fish sack sagged with the weight of a four-pound beauty of a Dolly Varden along with several fat cut-throats. My day was full, and the whole world seemed to be smiling.

Suddenly I heard a queer wailing sound from up in some spruce timber along the top of the bank, and upon investigation I found a cub fast in a grizzly trap. The little animal was moaning and crying feebly, almost dead from shock and thirst. The jaws of the trap had him high on one front leg, which was broken with the bone protruding. Matter and tears streaked its little furry face. When I approached, it could do little more than hiss and wail in a choking fashion that tore my heart.

If I had been able, I would have turned him loose. But I knew this would be useless anyway, so I did the first thing that came to mind. I went home, got my .22 rifle, came back, and shot him. What might have happened, had the cub's mother shown up, did not occur to me until later. But she likely had two cubs and had abandoned the one in the trap, for I never saw her.

That day I swore a mighty, private oath never to set a bear trap, and to this day that oath holds good.

By no means did my antipathy for bear traps dampen my desire to become a bear hunter. From the time I owned my own rifle, I hunted bears. If my parents had known how many hours were spent unsuccessfully rambling the hills in search of bruin with my .22, they would undoubtedly have put a curb on my ambitions. The bears did not find out either, which was probably just as well. It was not till I was sixteen years old that I got my chance to trail a grizzly with an adequate arm.

There came a sudden storm one October night, dropping eight inches of snow. Next morning, with the typical swiftness and caprice of mountain weather, the clouds rolled away, and when I rode out to bring in some loose horses from the pasture, the whole country sparkled and glistened under a brilliant sun. Not more than five hundred yards from the barn I was astounded to see the fresh trail of a big grizzly crossing an open hay meadow. It was unusual to find a grizzly track that far out of the mountains so late in the year, for by that time they were usually back among the peaks close to their denning grounds. Whirling my horse on his heels, I galloped back to the buildings. I left the horse in the barn, and I grabbed my latest and dearest possession—a sleek Ross sporter in .303 British caliber.

A horse could be a nuisance hunting, especially where wire fences cut up the low-country range, so I headed out on the grizzly track on foot. In a short time I was coursing along the track like an eager hound, trotting in the open and slipping through the willow and aspen groves at a fast walk. The grizzly was heading into the wind in a southwesterly direction. The snow was soft and quiet, making trailing conditions perfect.

For a couple of miles the bear led me straight across country, but then he came to a place where sheep had grazed the previous summer. On a willow- and birch-covered dry swamp a number of them had died from eating poison plants, and here the grizzly began uncovering and investigating the carcasses.

I had been going with all the headlong enthusiasm of a long-geared, wiry youngster to whom hunting was not just a sport but a passion. The fresh tracks were now even fresher. The grizzly was close, and the knowledge made my heart pound, my ears singing with the excitement in my blood. The cover was thickly hung with clinging snow, cutting my vision to short yards. The possibility of a close-range fight put an edge of prudence on my going.

Now the bear was wandering, bending his trail from one sheep carcass to another. Sometimes he only clawed the bones and rags of wool out of the snow, but here and there he apparently ate some fragments, which held him up a bit. Every few steps I stood very still, looking and listening, particularly when some thick cover forced a detour. The breeze was dead. There was not a sound. Once or twice I could have sworn I smelled the sour-doggy smell of bear. I was caught in the meshes of suspense and nerve-tingling anticipation that occur only in danger faced alone in the wilds—the wine, zestful and heady, known only to the hunter. The tension built up till it seemed to hum. Back and forth the tracks led me, until finally they came to a heavy growth of willow and cottonwoods on the edge of the swamp.

Step by step they led over fallen logs among big trees, past one possible ambush after another. Finger on trigger, ready for instant action, I followed. Then a strange set of man tracks broke into the bear's tracks from the side. A great surge of angry, disgusted disappointment welled up in my throat—this was my bear!—to be swallowed again with a gulp of dismay when I recognized them for my own! The tables were turned. Instead of the hunter, I was now the hunted. I swung with the rifle pointed down my backtrail, half-expecting to find the big bear stalking me from the rear, for I knew now the grizzly had tolled me around in a complete circle.

A stick suddenly broke behind me, followed by a swishing of dislodged snow from branches. Tiptoeing toward the sound. I found where the tracks broke off the circle in a great bound and led up toward the rugged flanks of Drywood Mountain.

I trailed the grizzly up across steep gullies and hogback ridges, through the deepening snow of higher levels, but not once did the length of the bear's stride show any sign of slackening up. My legs began to cramp. I was tired, hungry, and suffering from a great letdown. The grizzly had outwitted me so easily that I was ashamed; but I had learned some lessons that day—lasting lessons. We had played a game, and I had lost. When I came to think of it in this light, my disappointment lifted toward cheer. I realized that for him who relishes experience, there will be other games to be played—and maybe won.

8. *Crossed Trails in* GRIZZLY *Country*

When he stands tall like a man,
he looks very dangerous and fierce,
but he does so only to see better.
—ANDY RUSSELL

Some dogs are born to hunt and some destined to live in sedentary style, never getting very far from the comfortable fireside of home. Men are not much different. While some abhor leaving the wall-to-wall carpets and central heating of their civilized abodes, others are restless unless rambling under the big open sky with just a scrap of canvas over their heads at night and the small comfort of a campfire to cook a meal and hold off the evening chill.

The world of the wilds is like a theater where the action goes on without stop. The dramas can be watched from in front of the footlights or participated in. Some men may be satisfied to sip the juices of vicarious adventure from the experience of others, but there are those for whom nothing will do but to dip in the stewpot with both hands clear up to the elbows. Thus my first job away from home found me in wilderness grizzly country working as broncobuster, packer, and guide in the employ of Bert Riggall.

Bert's well-appointed pack train was famous among the wealthy sportsmen of North America. He was the reason for the fame; for not only was he a superlative big-game hunting guide with many trophy records to his credit, some of which still stand today, but he also specialized in photographic, sight-seeing, and fishing trips in summer. He enjoyed a clientele that was something like a big family rendezvousing with him year after year for a wilderness holiday. He was a first-class naturalist, a botanist well versed in the lore of the mountains, a man with a genius for interpreting nature, and a great teacher. As one friend put it: "He knew what the bighorn ewe said to her lamb." Work with such a man was a university, and the instructor was a hard taskmaster by the very virtue of personal ability, but at the same time he was a warmhearted and trusted friend.

Life on the pack train was a delight of gypsying through the mountains, with everything we needed for living on the trail packed on good horses. We wandered from camp to camp with the long forty-five-horse string winding up and down trails through rich valleys and alpine meadows, singing streams and tall timber hung in great pictures between mountain cliffs, the cloud shadows racing across rugged country to lose themselves over the rim of the horizon. It was a life of contrasts, where sometimes we loafed in the sun and on occasion worked and froze in sudden storms. There were times when split-second judgment and deft handling of horses and people spelled the difference between chaos and safe going.

The pack train was something like a sailing ship, where the guiding hand of the captain was the difference between rank danger and zestful adventure enjoyed to the hilt in sunshine and storm. No two days were alike, and there was little repetition; life was never boring.

The pack outfit naturally depended entirely on horses for its mode of operation, and these were a conglomeration of breeds and personalities, no two individuals exactly alike and all something of a reflection of the skill and character of those who handled them. Some were utterly dependable under the most frightening and unusual circumstances, while others were timid and inclined to precipitate an uproar at the smallest excuse. They were tough, strong, active as cats, and as sure-footed as mountain goats. Like mountain weather, they were also somewhat unpredictable. Treating them like the weather, one never fought them but used skill and patience in bending them to their best use. We rarely picketed a horse and never hobbled them; for horses understandably hate picket ropes and hobbles, and angry horses make trouble. We simply tied one horse to a tree with a halter, while the rest were turned loose at night; the tied horse was used in the morning by a wrangler to round up the bunch. Every seventh horse wore a hand-wrought Swiss bell, each pitched to a different key. These bronze bells make the sweetest music in the world to a horse wrangler's ears. We came to know them so well that it was possible to tell which horses were within earshot before they could be seen.

Because they were so much a part of traveling through and coming to know something of grizzly country, I have always considered horses synonymous with it. Many of them were born, lived, and died on the trail with us over the years. Some of these four-footed milestones of history are well remembered for various reasons.

There was the epic occasion of killing my first bear. The actual shooting was over in a moment as the bear fed all unaware in a patch of kinnikinnik berries on a timberline ridge top in the dusk of late evening. Being very young and inexperienced, I was savagely jubilant under the first pale stars as I headed for camp after gralloching the animal. If I had had a tail, it would have wagged clear off in sheer exuberance. What I did not know was that the adventure of the hunt was a long way from being over.

Next morning, while Bert Riggall and another hunting companion rode up the valley to hunt among the mountains, I saddled up a half-broken thoroughbred mare and a pack horse to bring in my trophy and meat. It took much longer to get up onto the ridge with the horses than I had anticipated, for the whole slope was crisscrossed with down logs. It was mid-morning before I was able to find and blaze a passable trail for the horses through this labyrinth to my kill. It was almost noon before the job of skinning and cutting up the meat was completed, and everything was packed in the canvas alforjas ready to be packed on the horse.

I had purposely picked what I thought to be a gentle horse for the job, a big brown mare by the name of Steamboat. Now, Steamboat proved to have a decided antipathy for bears in any form, dead or alive. She was, in fact, a decidedly ornery old blister about it, snorting and blowing like a steam whistle. The load finally got tied onto her saddle, but not before I had hobbled her front feet and blindfolded her with my jacket. She stood humped up like a goat in a hailstorm as I pulled the diamond hitch down snug over her pack, with her breath going out in long purring snorts foretelling stormy weather ahead.

When all was ready, I led my saddle horse in close on the upwind side, unfastened Steamboat's hobbles, and stepped up in my saddle. Snugging my hat down and ramming both boots deep in the stirrups, I reached over and pulled off the blind.

Old Steamboat stood for a while as though in a state of shock, absolutely still, with a mad, glassy look in her eyes; then she rolled an eyeball back toward her pack and broke wind like a string of giant firecrackers going off. She soared like a rocket and tried to kick my hat off on the first jump. She bogged her head and bucked like a three-star rodeo bronc. I spoiled her style a bit by jerking her off balance with the halter shank every time she took to the air, but this did not slow her down very much.

Then my saddle horse got a noseful of fresh blood and bear smell and joined in the festivities. Between the two of them I had my hands full. It was one of those lonely rides a man makes sometimes in wild country with only the jays and himself for an audience. The jays would likely be jeering anyway, and he is likely too busy to watch his shadow and enjoy the show. The slopes were steep and the footing rough, but the horses never noticed. So long as they contrived to go together, things went along all right; but when they headed in opposite directions, I lost my hold on the lead rope and came within a whisker of getting unloaded.

Finding herself free, Steamboat stampeded for camp. When my horse discovered she was being left alone, she quit bucking and lit out in pursuit like the wind. Steamboat never bothered with my trail, being of no mind to mess around with detours. She just pointed her nose downhill, and what she did not go over, she broke through. My horse elected herself the tail of the hurricane, and we joined in tearing a hole through the scenery. We went over logs that would have given a moose second thought. The take-offs were not too bad, but the landings were a long way down, and some of them would have scared a buck deer into a slow walk. Dry limbs broke against my legs and green ones flailed me like whips. When we finally hit the open flats at the bottom, the pack was miraculously still in place, and though somewhat battered, scratched, and scared, I was still sitting straight up in my rigging. Like the Virginian who drove the runaway team and buckboard off a cutbank into a wash and came to a stop right side up, I was feeling "about halfway between good gosh and thank the Lord."

My black bear hunt was all over, but it was then there sprouted an awareness that hunting was a great deal more than just going out to kill something. There were other skills involved and additional satisfactions to be enjoyed—sight and smell and feel of many things, all parts of the adventure. To overlook them would be like picking the tasty bits of mushroom out of the soup and ignoring the rest.

To see a bear track causes a measure of anticipation to the hunter, but to see the bear that made it calls for some art in reading sign lost to the uneducated eye. To be a good shot is one thing; but if one does not also develop some knowledge and skill in using a keen-edged knife, the reason for the shooting may be wasted. To point a rifle and pull the trigger might be shooting, but to place bullets with pinpoint accuracy from any position and under all conditions is something reaching well into real science. To be a successful hunter and guide requires some skills smelling of saddle leather and powder smoke, but also a wide understanding of animals and men and a kinship with some of the secretive ways of nature.

Such men as Yount, Stevens, and Adams were famous frontier hunters who still live in history for their part in the early development of North America. They were not just killers, but men of many skills with keen powers of observation and an ability to make the best use of their minds and tools. The edge of their skill was whetted on their satisfaction and pure enjoyment in making the most of their opportunities. Above all they had an appreciation for the things they saw.

Such men could look at an Indian teepee and see something more than just a primitive lodge. For to their eyes the teepee was a mighty pretty and useful kind of tent, and it looked good pitched along a stream against a mountain background. It was shaped so the wind helped hold it down, and it shed rain perfectly if properly pitched. It was cool and airy in summer and warm in winter, with its central fireplace holding just a small fire. Given sufficient poles to pitch it, no tent was ever designed to be more practical and useful. Yet unless it is pitched properly, this tent can be a most infernal smokehouse and absolutely useless.

Many the enjoyable hour I have spent around evening campfires with hunters discussing the pros and cons of different rifles, calibers, and combinations of ammunition. It is a happy part of the game, this choice of weapons, yet how often we have seen people forget the necessary skill that spells the difference between disappointment and satisfaction.

Bert Riggall and I were guiding three hunters one fall up on the headwaters of Cataract Creek. One of the hunters was armed with a flossy, hand-engraved European carbine stocked to the muzzle and weighing only about 6½ pounds. It was bored and chambered for the big .375 Holland and Holland cartridge. The resulting recoil of this combination was something to make strong men weep and the wise ones take to the hills. The other two hunters were also armed with imported European weapons of the more conventional 7 mm. caliber, but as it turned out, they too apparently suffered from the illusion that the skill of the gunmaker's art imparted some kind of magic to the owner which turned an ordinary Joe into a Daniel Boone.

One morning we rode up under a rim and dismounted and walked up to where we could look down into a steep-sided little basin on the front of the Continental Divide. There were five fine billy goats lying asleep in the basin. The effect on our hunters was remarkable.

Oblivious to our entreaties to sit down and take plenty of time, they promptly unlimbered the artillery, stood proudly on their hind legs, and laid down a terrific barrage. Strangely enough, the goats, though obviously very much surprised, did not seem to mind. In spite of the hunters' most valiant attempts to shoot them, bullets slamming into rocks and dust flying, they were in no hurry to move to safer and less noisy places. Bullets continued to shatter rock and ricochet where goats were not.

The shooting finally died down into a heavy silence, partly because of a lack of ammunition and also because neither Bert nor I could think of anything adequate to say. The goats were still within easy rifle range. Suddenly a rock rolled and clattered above and behind us, and when we turned to look, we saw a magnificent silvertip grizzly galloping for the top of the mountain. The bear had apparently been sound asleep among some broken rock, and it waked to discover that the storm was not ordinary thunder.

With a certain dryness, Bert quietly remarked, "If one of you gentlemen has any ammunition left, here is a bear!"

A frantic search by all turned up a single 7 mm. Mauser cartridge in one hunter's pocket, but by the time he had fed this into his rifle chamber, the grizzly was about four hundred yards away. Just as the bear topped out on the skyline with little but the seat of his pants exposed, the hunter threw up his rifle, skeetshooting fashion, and fired. The bullet struck the grizzly squarely in the root of the tail and ranged up along its spine to kill it instantly in mid-stride. No one can deny that Lady Luck suddenly turned her back on that bear and put her arms lovingly around that hunter's neck. Not even the blindest, most conceited man could honestly deny her presence. Whether or not gathering a trophy in such a fashion would remove some of the potential satisfaction is a question, but certainly there is no substitute for the ability to use one's weapons efficiently.

The years in grizzly country have served to show me that the choice of the weapon is not near as important as pinpoint accuracy in its use. A man hunting for sport most certainly owes it to the game and himself to be as efficient and clean about his killing as possible.

Hunters once killed the grizzly for food, to make the country safe, and to put money in their pockets from the sale of the hide. Some of us still do, although hunting the bear for meat to fill the larder is no longer a factor. Occasionally the grizzly is killed in a real or misdirected case of self-defense. Now we hunt mainly for sport. It is in the interpretation of this that some clouds are found; for in the name of true sport, killing is an anticlimax, and though some might accuse me of wishy-washy Bambi-ism, sometimes it is not even necessary. Just the same, there are times when a man can get himself into a difficulty in bear country in which shooting fast and straight is the only way out. At such a time his scalp is his main concern—or perhaps his pocketbook—and sport is strictly something viewed in retrospect.

In the dark of a summer night years ago, a huge bear came down out of the mountains onto the range country on the upper Cottonwood Creek just west of our ranch. It was one of those black, velvety nights with a million stars and a slight cool breeze thermaling down the valley and carrying the soft sounds of birds, insects, and sleepy cattle. The creek talked and chuckled drowsily to itself among the willows.

When the bear came to it, he turned upstream against the wind along a well-worn cattle trail, padding along with his head swinging low and his nose full of the warm, sweet smell of the cattle bedded on the meadow above. Blacker than the black shadows, the bear came silently up the trail and stopped on the edge of the clearing to read things with his nose and listen. Twenty odd head of cows were lying bunched in various attitudes of repose, their breathing sounding in a soft cadence of grunts and snores. Without the slightest whisper of sound the bear ghosted into a scattered string of willow clumps leading toward the cattle. He went to the last cover and again stopped to stand like an obsidian statue.

Then he erupted into their midst like an avalanche of chopping teeth and flying paws to land on a husky Aberdeen Angus heifer. She let out a terrified bawl and half lurched to her feet, only to fall rolling and kicking under his weight. A moment later her bawling was cut off sharp and clean by a broken neck.

At sunrise Frank Allred, the local game warden, came down the creek fishing for his Sunday dinner and suddenly was face to face with the bear. The big animal stood his ground, growling over the kill, as though he knew Frank carried nothing more lethal in his hand than a trout rod. It was a time to back away discreetly into the brush, where Frank returned to his horse and was soon riding swiftly toward home for his rifle.

But this big killer had not attained his size and age by being stupid. When Frank returned, there was no bear to be seen. The bear did not return to that kill, but pulled down another steer on an adjoining ranch a few nights later. A trap was set for him, but he knew about traps and contemptuously flipped it over with a paw to spring it harmlessly on the ground. This bear went on killing cattle all summer and into early fall, until his score tallied close to $3,000 worth of beef. No one so much as caught a glimpse of him for the rest of the season.

When I returned from the last hunt of the year with the pack train that October, the whole neighborhood was buzzing with consternation and stories of the big bear's depredations. Most of the ranchers were of the opinion that it was a grizzly, although Frank Allred was convinced that it was a monster black. Being somewhat reluctant to take for gospel anything that I hear about bears, I wondered.

Black bears do not usually kill cattle, and when they do, it is usually calves they pick. Only once had I known a black to tackle a mature cow, and this attack had aborted. The bear jumped the cow on top of a hill and rolled and fought with her clear to the bottom of an adjoining valley, where the cow escaped, chewed and mauled from end to end, but not sufficiently to prevent her recovery.

Before I had time to look for signs of this big killer, hard weather set in and the bear returned to the high mountains for the winter.

The following spring, in early May, we were suddenly wakened one night by our collie dog making a fuss in the yard by the house. It was a cold, blustery night with snow squalls blowing down off the peaks. Thinking it was only a skunk that had wandered in by the buildings, I did not go out to investigate. Next morning just after I lit the kitchen fire, I found some enormous black bear tracks in the fresh skiff of snow not more than twenty feet from the door. Apparently the big animal had been attracted by some beaver hides that were stored in a shed. But the dog had jumped him and driven him into a heavy patch of brush about fifty yards behind the shed, where there had been a considerable argument that the dog had been lucky to survive. Then the bear had made a break for more hospitable country.

I grabbed my rifle, and trailed him for about an hour, and then the sun melted the snow and I lost the track completely.

A couple of nights later a storm blew in out of the north and dropped eight inches of heavy snow. Three days of hard hunting revealed not a single sign of the bear. It was as though the big animal had vanished into thin air. On the third day I came home for lunch at noon, tired and disgusted. The weather was warm again, the snow was melting fast, and it began to look as though the bear, which I was now convinced was the killer, had escaped.

Then my wife, Kay, reminded me of a spot on the north end of the ranch where a horse had died the previous winter. The coyotes had left little but clean-picked bones and a ragged piece of hide. It was unlikely that the bear would be attracted to it; but on the off-chance that something of importance had been overlooked, I set out to investigate.

About a half mile from home I discovered that I had left my bandolier of ten extra cartridges behind. There were five loads in the rifle magazine, so I did not go back.

Along the way I hunted out a swamp on the Cottonwood, but there was not a sign of the bear. It was late afternoon before I broke out of this place, tired and wet, and headed up over a low ridge into the valley of Pine Creek to have a look at the remains of the horse. More out of a feeling of duty, garnished with very little hope, I strolled over to look at the scattered carcass with my rifle resting on the crook of my arm as nonchalantly as though hunting grouse.

To see the place it was necessary to come out on top of a low bank about forty feet from it. Upon doing this I was suddenly transfixed with sheer surprise. There, lying sound asleep, flattened out like a great rug, with head resting on forepaws, was a great black bear. He was dead to the world, sleeping soundly on top of a big nest of old dry leaves and debris scratched into a heap among the wreckage of the horse. What was even more surprising, the only tracks in the snow around him were some leading to the creek a few feet away, where he had gone for a drink periodically. He had been there since the storm began.

Then a little whirling cat's-paw must have given my scent to his nose, for the bear leaped to his feet with a great sniff. His movement brought me back to life, and I slammed a shot into his near shoulder, knocking him flat. But he was up again in an instant, running for some thick cover a couple of bounds beyond. I shot him again as he went, which made him bawl but did not slow him up very much. A third shot, taken just as he entered the thick stuff, struck a cottonwood.

The wounded bear was headed for an open gravel bar about a hundred yards beyond this patch of cover, so I ran upstream to cut across and head him off. Trotting across a beaver dam on a half-sunken slippery log, I rammed into a tangle of second growth and down logs at a run. After a few steps in this it came to me that this place was one for some caution, so I stopped for a look around, and it was well I did; for the bear had turned and was coming straight toward me about fifty feet away. I could see little but the black bulk of him looming through the brush.

Then he must have got my wind. There was a big stump about six feet high just in front of him, and when he got a noseful of my smell, he must have thought it was me; for he reared to full height and bit it savagely near the top. As he twisted his head to rip off a chunk of the bark, I got a clear shot at his neck and dropped him.

Had it been a grizzly, I would likely have taken some time before approaching; but I had killed many black bears by then, and none had shown any inclination to fight. This one looked stone dead, and I went straight up to within ten feet to look at him where he lay behind a log. Something about the look of his eye made me start to raise my rifle, when suddenly he came to life as though prodded by a sharp stick.

His broken shoulder was under him. The toes of his sound paw on top of the log suddenly flexed and spread to grip the wood, and in a flash he was coming over it with mouth wide open straight at me. Involuntarily I stepped back as I raised the rifle, and at that moment a forked stick beneath the slush and snow caught the heel of my rubber boot and down I went. Without conscious thought of it and with a distinct impression of everything occurring in slow motion, I simply poked the rifle under his jaw and fired. The bear came down with a soggy thump so close that I could have poked him in the nose with the muzzle of the rifle; but with my last cartridge gone, such a waste of time did not occur to me. I did not look back till fifty yards were behind me.

Next morning we took this bear without cutting him up and weighed him on a scale with a five-hundred-pound limit. He took it to the bottom with a solid bump. A most unusual giant of his kind, this bear must have weighed somewhere between five and six hundred pounds. Laid out loose on the ground, the hide measured six feet nine inches from nose to tail and seven feet four inches across the front paws. The pads of the front feet were seven and a half inches across. The skull was very mediocre, of a size no way relative to his general bulk. The teeth were yellow and broken with age. But in spite of age and the time of year the carcass was still extremely fat with a heavy layer under the hide and more filling the abdominal cavity, proof that bears can emerge from den with little of this store of energy used up.

Following the killing of this animal, no cattle were lost to bears in our neighborhood for several years. Then one fine spring morning my neighbor Vermont Nixon rode up to tell me that a grizzly bear had killed one of his cows and that he had seen it feeding on the kill that morning. We made plans to lay an ambush for the bear that evening.

Shortly before sunset we walked up a little valley along a small stream above his ranch buildings and took up a position in some low brush about a hundred yards downwind from the kill. Logistically the position was excellent, although it was remarkably uncomfortable otherwise. We were directly downwind from the cow, and the weather had been hot. The cow was so high that we could not only smell but also taste it. When Vermont finally suggested that it might be better if we moved along the open slope a bit, I readily agreed.

We had not moved very far when Vermont suddenly gave an exclamation under his breath and stopped. At the same time I saw a big grizzly coming down through a strip of second-growth cottonwoods across the creek off the adjoining hill. The bear was too well screened to allow for a shot, and he reached the heavy belt of willows beyond the kill without either of us getting the chance to place a bullet in him.

We waited, and for a few moments we saw or heard nothing. Then the grizzly's light-colored face showed on the near side of the willows just back of the kill, but before either of us could shoot, the wind shifted and blew down the backs of our necks. With a sharp snort of alarm the grizzly whirled back out of sight.

After a long moment or two while we stood poised waiting for the bear to come into view on the far slope again, Vermont whispered, "He's standing behind that big willow. I can see him through the top of it."

When Vermont lifted his rifle to shoot, I was confident the bear would be anchored in his tracks. Perhaps a twig deflected the bullet a bit, or maybe the failing light spoiled Vermont's aim, for when the .30–06 bucked and roared, hell promptly broke loose.

The grizzly let out a choking roar, leaped straight up in the air, and did a spectacular backflip to come slamming back into the willows straight at us. We heard him smashing willows and rattling rocks in the creek, but the bear did not charge as expected. Instead he came running out on the far side of the creek, again straight up his back trail. We both threw a shot at him, but both bullets hit trees, and the bear disappeared into the heavy growth farther up the slope.

We were in a fine mess. Letting a wounded animal of any kind get into such a jungle is bad. To lose track of a wounded grizzly in such a place can be a horror—especially in view of the fact that two of my boys were going back and forth through this part of the country to school every day. To make things even worse, it was getting dark.

Upon examining the ground where the grizzly had been standing when wounded, we found a bullet gouge in the ground and a bit short of it a short length of gut attached to a piece of fat. As we stood looking at it, Vermont was swearing softly under his breath, for he was not one who normally throws bullets wide of his chosen target. Although there was little blood sign, the tracks were easy to follow, for the long claws of the front feet had torn into the damp leaf mold on the ground. Going abreast so that both rifles could be brought into play on the instant, we trailed the bear through the timber and undergrowth. We had gone only a hundred yards or so when we came onto the grizzly standing broadside behind a clump of saskatoon brush. From where I stood it was impossible to tell which way the animal was facing, for only a bowed-up hedgerow of back hair was visible along the back. I waited, ready to cover Vermont's shot, but as it turned out, he could see little more than I. For a long moment we were at a complete stalemate. Then the grizzly coughed and lunged away. I took a flying shot at him, but my bullet only lifted a ribbon of hair off the top of his shoulder hump.

The next instant there was a protesting squeal of breaking barbed wire as the grizzly tore through a fence. We could plainly hear him breaking brush, growling, and rumbling as he turned up the fence line. The big animal was badly hurt, for he was not going fast.

We held a brief council of war, fully knowing we had to move fast. I suggested that Vermont circle up onto the open top of the hill while I followed the bear through the thick stuff. It would be taking a chance, but with the noise the grizzly was making, it would not be difficult to keep track of him.

The plan worked well for a while, but then suddenly everything was quiet as the grave. Even the thrushes quit singing, and not a whisper of breeze stirred the aspen leaves. It was as though everything was holding its breath in suspense. I stood listening for the welcome crash of Vermont's rifle, but it did not come.

For all its bulk a grizzly can move as quietly as a cat. If one so chooses, it can plan and lay an ambush with all the guile of the most wily bushfighter. Stepping ahead a few feet where it was possible to see clearly for a few yards between some bigger aspens, I waited, hoping the bear might run short of patience and give his position away.

Perhaps five minutes went by—each one an age longer than the last and collectively the most prolonged I have ever lived. Then there came the jarring snap of clashing teeth, and up the slope on a brushy bench beyond the aspens the greenery began to shake. The grizzly did not rush but came deliberately. It was so nearly dark that it was useless to try a shot through the tangle. Finally the bear's face broke into the clear, and in the gloom I simply centered the bear's head in my scope and fired.

The bear lurched and rolled clear over on his belly, kicking and clawing while I poured more bullets into him. I hit him hard three more times as he rolled ten feet. When everything came to a stop, the grizzly was dead.

This bear's hide squared out close to nine feet. The claws of its front paws were five and half inches over the outside curves. A rough autopsy conducted next morning showed the first wounding shot to be far back through the animal's guts. My first shot had struck under the left eye. The next one had duplicated the point of impact under the right eye, while the third had smashed through the butts of its ears. The fourth shot had torn out a section of spine on top of its shoulders. These last three shots had been completely superfluous, but under the circumstances the waste of ammunition did not seem out of reason.

Both this adventure and the one with the giant black bear are classic examples of the rivalry between men and bears—a competition wherein the bears prey on beef cattle and men prey on the bears to preserve their interests. Both of these bears were definitely predators; but on many occasions innocent bears were killed by cattlemen merely because they were seen in cattle country or had the bad luck to run afoul of a trap set for a real killer. On one particular occasion the ranchers were totally responsible for educating and developing one of the most devastating and cunning killer bears that was ever known in western Canada.

It has often been said that to know a man well, study his friends. It might also be well to take a long, thoughtful look at his enemies. The same thing can be said of the grizzly, for if one is to reach a fuller understanding of the great bear, then it becomes necessary to know and understand something of his only real enemy—man.

Many frontiersmen have shared my campfires with me: fishermen out on the Pacific coast, professional guides of the West and North, prospectors searching for the pot of gold at the end of the rainbow, trappers of the wilderness country, and my neighbors the ranchers. Tough, sometimes generous to a fault, quick to laugh, and courageous, such men are the kind who help carve out empires. Almost to the last man they have a queer blind spot when it comes to bears, and their favorite view of the grizzly is the one seen over the shining blue barrel of a rifle. Many times over the years I have known of grizzlies being killed and left to rot for no other reason than their presence. To suggest to these men that most grizzlies are not trouble hunters and ordinarily are not destructive is to receive a long, silent, quizzical look, perhaps momentarily generous of your opinion but still only veiling the thought that you have lost your marbles.

Yet strangely enough these are the men who get the greatest kick out of recounting their experiences in bear country. If all the bears were suddenly gone, most of these men would sorely miss them; for they enjoy the presence of the grizzly and take a certain satisfaction in their association with the big bear.

However inclined towards such single-track thinking, my outspoken, hard-working neighbors the ranchers are noted for their thrift. This is an admirable kind of thrift for the most part—a most necessary characteristic for the sake of their continuance. They have to be thrifty to exist. But sometimes, if overworked, the exercise of thrift can backfire with disastrous results. One group of ranchers making up the membership of a local stock association and representing enough collective wealth to buy out the nearest town, lock, stock, and barrel, niggardly decided to purchase a cheap black bear trap instead of a much more expensive and adequate one for grizzlies. Thus for the sake of a few dollars they lost the price of a foundry equal to producing all the bear traps the world would likely ever see, much less need.

Following this thrifty purchase, decided upon at a meeting with sage and solemn nods of heads, a small, somewhat nondescript mother grizzly with two small cubs came out of den one spring. She was likely somewhat depressed by a shortage of feed and the burgeoning responsibilities of her new family; for she proceeded to kill a cow in an unfortunately conspicuous place. Consequently the new trap was set for her, and shortly thereafter the mother grizzly unwisely put her foot in it.

As is often evident among men, size is not always a measure of strength, sagacity, and determination. Following her first flurry of disorganized bawling and fighting, she got down to serious business and pulled out of the trap. Undoubtedly her foot was sore. Perhaps she blamed this discomfort on the dead cow, for she promptly went on a cattle-killing spree as though she had invented the pastime. Through experience she was now very careful and wary, avoiding any further contact with the trap, which followed her hopefully around the hills from one kill to another. When fall arrived, she returned to her high denning ground in the mountains, leaving the ranchers to tally their losses and blame everything but the trap.

The following spring she came back with her cubs, now rollicking yearlings, and promptly opened a spring festival in bear country by killing another cow. Once more the trap was set for her. She must have been a bit fuzzy in her mind after the long winter's sleep, for she walked into it a second time.

Once more she fought it and successfully escaped, although this time she injured her paw in the process—a lingering hurt that honed her cunning day and night. Thus a killer of truly psychopathic proportion was developed by a misdirection of thrift and further cultivated toward new heights of bovine murder by the very men wishing to destroy her.

Her kills were easily recognized by a missing ear. Probably because of her injured foot she developed a unique method of killing cattle. Instead of striking them down in the usual fashion with simultaneous blows over the head and spine at the top of the shoulders, she ran up alongside her quarry, grabbed it by an ear, set her feet, and threw it end over end. Then she fell on it to worry the unfortunate beast to death. In due course her cubs joined in this mayhem, and so two more killers were well on the way.

This she-grizzly had developed into a habitual killer as wary and cunning as a three-toed wolf. To set a trap for her was an open invitation for her to kill again. In fact she would immediately abandon a fresh kill if a man so much as handled a twig within a hundred yards of it. One rancher lost sixteen head to her in one summer, removed his cattle from the Forest Reserve summer ranges, and to this day has never put another animal to graze there.

Finally a heavy bounty was placed on her head. This had the advantage of bringing her to the attention of the best trappers and hunters in the country, but it also had the disadvantage of attracting sufficient inexperienced ones to spoil the chances of the others. I briefly joined the hunt for her, but I quit after a few days in a split frame of mind, divided between admiration for this bear's wonderful cunning and intelligence and complete frustration at interference from other hunters. About all that happened to the bear was that she was kept continually on the move, so that she rarely fed on any kill twice and was thus elevated to a new crescendo of killing.

Had Frenchy Reviere been on the scene, this grizzly would likely never have survived her first brush with a trap. His youngest son, Jim, a keen-eyed, rawhide-tough trapper of real wilderness stamp, took up her trail with an adequate trap; but as he admitted, his medicine was no good on this one. He found a fresh kill one day and set a carefully concealed trap by it. When he came next morning, a grizzly was caught in it—but the wrong bear as it turned out.

Jim approached the set through a thick stand of aspens on horseback, and on coming within easy range of the grizzly in the trap, he stepped down from his saddle to shoot it. As he reached for his rifle hanging in its scabbard, a big boar, likely the mate of the sow in the trap, came boiling out of a clump of alders in a roaring charge. The horse pulled back, taking the rifle out of Jim's reach, but fortunately he had a short hold on the bridle reins with the other hand. As his mount whirled and plunged past him, he grasped the pommel and vaulted into the saddle. The horse shot back through the aspens, knocking him on trees as it went, but Jim managed to stay with him. When he pulled the wild-eyed animal to a stop on the far side of an open bench to look back, the pursuing grizzly had vanished. It had been a close shave, for the horse had long scratches from grizzly claws down its haunch.

In this way other bears paid the price for the killer's work. As her second year of terror among the herds came to a close, she once more headed back up among the high peaks, a smoul-

Charles Tillenius examines a spent spring salmon (below, left). Grizzlies gorge on the salmon run. Sometimes the photographer's camp (below) in grizzly country is a welcome haven from the inevitable mosquito (above).

Toklat Joe (above, right) *stands for a better look. Joe and his kind regularly feast on the remains of wolf kills, such as the young caribou bull below. The bull elk* (foreground, above) *sports an "imperial" head.*

dering promise of more hell to come. By this time the bargain bear trap had become a most valuable piece of equipment, its price reaching a substantial five figures, somewhere in excess of $10,000. Though adequate traps were now being used, no one but the most reckless gambler would have risked a well-worn dollar bill on their success.

There came another spring and with it came the bear—hungry for beef as usual. In the meantime the stock association had hired Roy Marshall, an old hand of about sixty winters who had spent all his life in this country since he left Texas as a boy.

He was the kind who did not wait for trouble to come hunting for him without making some preparations for its proper welcome. When the grizzly made her first kill of the season, down on the Carpentier Creek flats, he was ready. He had worked out a plan that was about as cunning as anything the grizzly had improvised in her most inspired moments. Furthermore fate took a hand, and the kill was ideally located for his plan to be carried out.

Fate and human ingenuity had conspired, for in the late weeks of winter Roy had taken a grizzly trap and sundry other gear and boiled the lot in a strong solution of wood ashes. After a thorough scrubbing to remove any dirt, rust, and clinging man-smell, he had boiled everything again for hours in a soup of willow bark, aspen, and a handful or two of bunch grass. When this was done, the trap was not only completely cleansed but also smelled of odors blending into the country in which it would be used. He hung his entire trapping outfit in a tree to weather and mellow until needed.

Now he loaded it into his wagon and drove his team toward the kill. He did not go to it but swung wide and went to an old kill made the previous summer by the wanted bear. It was located beneath a big aspen tree, and there Roy made his medicine to cure the country of its most notorious murderer of cows.

Standing in the wagon box, Roy threw out a canvas tarpaulin and then stepped down on one corner of it to arrange it as a sort of platform from which to work. He took a shovel and dug a shallow hole for the trap in the midst of the old hair and bones, piling the dirt on another bit of canvas. From this hole he dug a shallow trench around the tree to conceal the logging chain that was to hold the trap. When this was ready, he set the trap and cunningly hid it in the hole, the chain looped around the tree. Using carefully cleaned canvas gloves, he touched nothing with his bare hands, nor did he set foot on the ground. When finished, he stood up to survey his work with critical gaze. Not even the most practiced eye could tell where the trap was hidden.

Fate chuckled softly—and directed his eye to a triangular piece of old weathered hide lying a bit to one side. With a touch of pure genius he picked it up and nailed it as high as he could reach up on the tree, where the breeze made it flop like the wing of a wounded bird. When he left, he took everything away with him, including the unused dirt rolled in the canvas. That evening a heavy shower fell and washed away any possible trace of man-smell that might have lingered.

The grizzly came back to her kill that night, hungry but wary as usual. Wise to the ways of her enemy, she circled slowly, testing the wind and the whole flat with her nose for those tiny telltale smells of danger. Finding none, she went to the carcass and fed heavily on it. When she struck out for the slopes of the mountains at the first waking squeaks of dawn, her path took her past her old kill.

Perhaps old memory of it drew her close without her being entirely aware. Maybe fate was now singing a siren song, for the she-grizzly saw the piece of hide flapping against the trunk of the tree. She forgot everything of her usual caution, drawing closer and closer to it, filled with a consuming curiosity. She looked at it and smelled of it. She wanted to feel of it too. So she reared and took a staggery step forward to mouth it. But it eluded her momentarily, and as she reached, the ground sagged beneath a hind foot and there was an upheaval followed by the ominous metallic clank of the closing trap. The soft quiet of the morning was torn to shivering shreds by her high, wild bawl of rage and pain.

Nothing fights like a grizzly in a trap. It is the great power and the wild, free-roaming spirit of the mountains ignominiously shackled in steel, fighting in almost maniacal rage and mercilessly flogged by the need for freedom. It is a kind of desecration—an obscenity. There is a lurching and a stench that does not fit the dignity of this animal. No matter the need, it does not fit the principles of the true hunter.

This one fought even harder than most, her will steeled by former experience. She plunged against the chain over and over again until her breath came in great sobbing gasps and the slobber fell from between her splintered teeth in bloody ropes. Her coat was full of filth and dirt. She pulled and clawed in desperate efforts to escape until the tree stood in the center of a fresh mound of torn-up earth.

Then she saw him coming astride his horse, black against the reddening sky. She checked her wild plunging to stand as still as her favorite mountain, as though listening to that last verse of the song fate was singing far away. She did not cower or cringe but stood her ground. And when the man got down from his saddle and walked toward her with something shining in his hands, she eased back, throwing a little slack in the chain. Then she roared and plunged straight at him. There was a flat, cracking whiplash of sound and everything was still.

That fall there was much less red ink in the ledgers, and the market for cheap bear traps was at an all-time low.

9. *Along Wilderness Trails*

Hunting, as an art, can be refined
to its highest degree through the
medium of photography.
—ANDY RUSSELL

When I first saw the country along the upper reaches of the north fork of the Flathead River in southeast British Columbia, it was wild and grand. We came from the east by pack train over the Continental Divide on the historic South Kootenai Trail, a great Indian and fur trade route of the old days, used so much by so many horses that it was worn into a dozen terraces where it dropped sixteen hundred feet in the first mile off the steep western slope. It was the kind of place where anything could happen to a pack and sometimes did.

On occasion Bert Riggall would stop the pack outfit on the summit overlooking the vast panorama of peaks and the depths of the canyon below, whereupon he would announce to our guests with a flourish that we would now tie all the horses together, nose to tail, with the last one anchored to a tree; and when all was ready, we would chop down the tree to get them all going in the right direction at once as they slid. Even if he was only making some lighthearted fun, he was not so far from wrong.

In wet weather that particular portion of trail is about the closest thing to a prolonged otter slide imaginable, and it is no joke when absolutely dry. Upon reaching the bottom of the first long pitch into the canyon by the most reckless use of gravity, it goes straight up the opposite side with typical Indian disregard of contours and horse flesh, to hang itself precariously on ledges and lose itself in the brush. Then it plunges in a most irresponsible fashion for another mile into the main valley of Kishaneena Creek. There it winds down the valley, resting from its exertions, past waterfalls, rapids, and gorges, through meadows and forest. It tangles itself mischievously in stiletto-thorned clumps of wild hawthorn brush here and there, and it gives the pack horses nervous fits when it goes through chains of beaver dams in the lower reaches of the valley.

Here it goes through some of the most magnificent natural parks in the mountains, where great western larches tower a hundred fifty to two hundred feet against the sky, and we rode stirrup deep in grass and flowers. In June rare and lovely yellow orchids lift their rich-throated blooms in thick clumps beside mouldering logs to add an exotic touch to this mountain heaven. At every step our horses crushed blooms beneath their feet, and we lay on them at night in camps where the muted rush of streams and the soft murmur of the gentle Pacific breeze lulled us to sleep.

We rode past curious moose and herds of elk. We saw the flashing flags of whitetail deer as they scampered from the sound of the Swiss bells. Goats gazed solemnly down at us from the crags. Grizzly and black bear tracks flattened the soft loam of the trails with their broad pads. Sometimes mule deer came right into our camps, drawn by the smell of salty, sweat-soaked leather. Once I woke in the small hours of morning to find a buck with his massive antlers filling the open front of the tent as, salt hungry, he ate the laces out of my boots. Hardly a shot had been fired in that country for fifty years, and it held about as much game then as it did when white man first saw it.

Upon coming to the International Boundary, we left the old trail to turn directly west along the open cut of the forty-ninth parallel. This man-made line between two great countries is a monument to peace, unguarded by guns along its entire four thousand four hundred miles, and proof that men of different nations can live as friendly neighbors.

Leaving the Kishaneena, the trail went up and up to the top of a high, timbered ridge and then took us down in a long, steep swoop into Alder Creek. Again it soared up another steep slope, where sometimes a dozen times in a mile we immigrated from Canada to the U.S. and back again as we switchbacked to find an easier grade for our loaded horses.

On the timbered crest of the summit between Alder and Sage Creeks the whole length and breadth of the upper Flathead Valley lay exposed—huge, sprawling, and fading into the bluish distances to the west and north. Flanked on the west by the rugged limestone peaks of the McDonald Range and on the east by the main range of the Rockies, it was a rolling ocean of green and deep, hazy blue, five days wide and seven days long by pack train. With the silver loops of the river showing here and there down its middle, it was so beautiful that a man's breath caught in his throat just looking at it.

It was pretty, smiling country, but it could show its teeth in a different humor, too. Parts of it were easy to travel, but through the main valley and the many side valleys dropping into it there was every kind of hazard from soft, quaking muck to steep rock.

Much of it was old burn, blanketed with dead logs lying from four to twelve feet deep and thick with second-growth lodgepole pine. In the worst of the *brulé* travel by pack train was utterly impossible. Here it was only possible to go on foot by walking logs. On such exploration trips about the only time we came to the ground was to eat and sleep. Where logs upwards of a hundred feet long and three to five feet thick at the butts are lying strewn three or four layers deep, the way is no place for daydreaming. In places it was even too tough for moose to get through, and when deadfall timber gets that bad, it is purely awful.

In most stretches of the valley we could use the horses, although it often meant days of chopping and sawing to clear the way. Even then the pattern of our detours was like a maze, where one could see his destination a rifle shot away and it would take hours to reach it.

The down timber was well sprinkled with standing dead trees—tall, bleached-out ghosts of the old living forest merely balanced on their roots that long since had failed to function as anything but props. Traveling among these with a long string of loaded horses was something we carefully contrived to arrange on calm days. Sometimes I woke at night bathed in the cold sweat of a nightmare wherein I dreamed of being caught out in such country in a wind with the pack outfit.

It was relatively windless down along the main valley, where the big dead timber stood the thickest, but sometimes a passing line squall or thunderstorm would set up sufficient thermal drafts to rock the big dead trees past their angle of balance. The tall spire of the trunk would then pause for a long moment as though reluctant to take that final plunge, and there would be a rising swish of sound culminated by a great crash as the log hit, smashing everything under it, sometimes splintering itself and often throwing debris for many yards. If the tree missed a man, there was still a good chance of his being hit by flying splinters and dead limbs. Either way the results could be final.

I remember being caught out once in such a place with six heavily loaded pack horses in the dusk of late evening, when a big thunderhead blew past a mile or so up the valley. Although we missed the hail and the rain, we got caught in the wind along its turbulent perimeter, and then the big trees began coming down. One snag—a bone-hard Douglas fir about two feet thick—fell across the trail in front of us, and another fell behind us, pinning us down like we were in a corral with all the gates locked. As the wind howled like a banshee in the weather-

checked wooden tombstones all around us, there came the
earth-shaking splintering crashes as the trees fell. It was a
frightful place to be, and we were practically helpless to do
anything about it. Out there in the dark, with the wind's
tortured wailing and the logs crashing down, it sounded like a
prelude to being suddenly squashed like a bug. I cannot remember ever being more frightened in my life.

Yelling at the horse wrangler bringing up the rear of the
string to get off his horse and under something big, I dived from
my saddle and lay flat under a three-foot fire-killed fir. All I
could do for my horses was hope they would be lucky. When it
was over and everything became still about half an hour later, we
crawled out to find the horses standing patiently—all unscathed.
I distinctly recall that my scalp felt sore from the prolonged
extreme tension.

We were within a quarter mile of the open flats, but it took
hours to clear a way through and around the debris blocking our
trail. One does not blithely attack fire-killed logs, even with a
razor-sharp axe. When we finally jingled into camp at 3 a.m.,
dawn was breaking. We unpacked, turned the horses loose, and
fell into our sleeping bags utterly exhausted.

Upon arriving in the valley on that first exploratory expedition years ago, we dropped leisurely down the last long slope to
the banks of the river. There in the midst of a clearing well
grown with small trees and dotted with old stumps was an old,
abandoned log building with doors ajar and windows staring
blankly through empty sashes like sightless eyes. It was the old
customs house on the wagon road coming up from Montana to
no particular destination in Canada. It marked a past era of
human occupation near the turn of the century, when coal prospectors teemed in the valley, aflame with the anticipation of a
bonanza from its great coal deposits. But even more coal was
then discovered in Crowsnest Pass along the railroad a few miles
to the north, which burst the Flathead bubble, leaving little to
mark its passing but a mouldering cabin or two smelling of pack
rats in a couple of stillborn villages, where a few rotting oak

stakes in the encroaching rabbit jungle of new pines still marked off the lot boundaries of the proposed towns.

A couple of abandoned wooden oil derricks of a somewhat later oil-drilling prospect stood as a silent threat of what was to come. But largely speaking, the whole valley had been reclaimed by the wilderness. It was unoccupied except for two or three trappers and a small customs house of later vintage located across the river to keep tabs on summer visitors.

As though to prove the wilds were reclaiming their own, a big grizzly scat lay within ten yards of the old customs house door. Indeed, from one end to the other and from the deepest deadfall patches to the rugged shoulders of the high peaks, this was grizzly country, where we were to have many adventures with the big bears. Such adventures often came unannounced and unexpected. There was, for instance, my discovery of a bear bridge across the river.

It happened near a camp we made on a ten-week trip with a group of geologists making a survey of the area. At the head of a big pool on a bend of the river flanked by giant spruces, a huge log spanned the stream just at the tail of the rapids coming in from above.

We arrived at the place in the middle of the afternoon. When the tents were all set up and the camp ready for a prolonged stay, there was still plenty of time to catch some trout for supper; so the cook and I went fishing in the pool. I waded upstream in the shallows at the tail of it to cast upstream with my flyrod, while he took his ancient steel telescope rod and ensconced himself in the middle of the log. With his back comfortably supported by the broken-off snag of a big limb, he baited his hook with a piece of bacon and let it float down into the pool. In no time we both had good fish on.

I fought a fat cut-throat trout down into the shallows and beached it on a little gravel bar. When I looked up, I saw the cook unceremoniously horsing its twin brother up onto the log. Killing the fish and hanging it on a string, he looked self-satisfied and half-asleep as he lowered his bait back into the river. Then the jungle growth of dogwood and willows on the bank at the butt of the log shook and quaked as a big grizzly ambled out on it. The bear came about two steps out over the water before he discovered the cook blocking the way. He stopped dead with about the most comical expression of astonishment and sheer disbelief that a bear was ever known to wear on its face.

Meanwhile the cook was utterly oblivious of the fact that he had company on the log. The grizzly made the first move by executing a most spectacular belly-flopping dive into the swift water on the high side of the log. He lit with a huge splash and began to swim powerfully, but strong as he was, the current swept him down almost under the log. The cook roused himself to see what had fallen into the river behind him. His reaction upon finding a grizzly almost within touching distance was sudden and almost disastrous. He started for the bank, but his feet slipped and he came within a whisker of falling into the river with the bear. Fighting desperately for traction, he fell down three times in about as many seconds without moving away from the spot. Accomplishing miracles of recovery of balance every time he slipped, he looked like some sort of strange, giant, fledgling bird threatening to fall out of the nest. Eventually he reached the bank, partly on his feet and partly at a sort of gallop on his hands and knees. In the meantime the grizzly came out on the gravel bar across the river, threw a disgusted look at the cook, and galloped into the timber.

When the cook came crashing and banging through the undergrowth down to my end of the pool, he found me rolling helplessly on the gravel bar holding my sides. Somehow he failed to see anything funny about the whole thing just then, and he went stomping off to the tents.

There are three versions to this story: mine, the cook's, and the grizzly's. Naturally I have never heard the bear's version, but likely it is just as funny as the other two.

Later, upon examining the log, I found it thickly pocked by bear claws. It was a regular bear bridge undoubtedly used by every bear in that portion of the valley at one time or another.

Sometimes I am very sure that bears have a well-developed sense of humor. Certainly they seem to create situations about as comical as anything can get. About a week after the cook's adventure on the log I saw another comedy of the wilds.

I was out scouting some new country on foot and had had a rough morning crossing a stretch of bad burn, where the logs were lying like straws and the second-growth lodgepole pine was as thick as the hair on a dog. I came out on a little benched meadow by the river about noon, feeling a bit the worse for wear and ready for something to eat. Old rotten logs and stumps were scattered on the meadow, and among these the wild strawberries were growing so lush and thick it was impossible to walk without squashing them. In ten steps my boot soles were wet and red.

I am somewhat addicted to strawberries—any kind of strawberries. Surely no fruit can come near the strawberry for pleasurable eating. But whatever horticulturists have done for the size of the tame ones, nothing can match the flavor of the wild ones.

Without moving from one spot, I got down on my hands and knees and ate a pint or two. Then I crawled into the shade of a little spruce to eat the sandwiches the cook had put up for me, cool off with a drink at a little spring nearby, and proceeded to have another feed of strawberries for dessert. Full to the ears, I lay back against a log in the shade to contemplate the trials and tribulations of being a guide.

I was only about half awake when a slight movement on the edge of the willow-grown riverbank caught my eye. Before I could raise my binoculars for a look, a grizzly stepped up into full view. He was a big shaggy bruin with old winter hair still clinging to his back and shoulders in patches. His head was shed off slick and smooth, but around his neck he still wore a collar of old fur, all tattered and unkempt, making him look like a hobo who, for want of money or by dint of just plain laziness, was still wearing a part of his winter clothes. He acted like one, too. He was feeding on the wild strawberries, eating them leaf, stem, and all, in about as lazy a fashion as could be imagined.

He did not walk very briskly but mooched along, indolent in the sun, as though the effort of putting one foot ahead of the other were almost more of a responsibility than he cared for. At one spot he lay down on his belly to eat around the base of a big stump, hitching himself along without even getting to his feet. Then he crawled over the log that had fallen from it and lay draped like some kind of big animated rug across it while picking berries on the other side. Upon coming down off the log, he rolled over on his side for a nap. Through my glasses I could see the berry juice glistening on the bottoms of his big feet.

But the sun was too hot for him. He came up on his feet and angled across the meadow toward me, and again he lay down in the shade of some little spruces with his noise pointing my way and not more than a hundred yards from where I sat. Through my glasses every whisker of his craggy countenance was visible, his eyes half-shut, and now he looked more like a fat, lazy old hobo than ever.

Perhaps fifteen minutes passed before I heard the querulous chirping of an excited chipmunk somewhere near the bear. A search with the binoculars finally located him on top of a section of dead log lying with its butt overhanging the river bank and its broken tip about three feet ahead of the bear's nose.

The little animal was in a perfect ecstasy of excitement, curiosity, and alarm. With his jerking tail seeming to trigger his tiny barks, he appeared to be propelled against his will out along the log closer and closer to the snoozing behemoth. This nightmarish development seemed to galvanize the little animal's terror. Here and there on his mesmerized journey he started as though to streak for safety; but inevitably his fascination turned him back toward the bear. If living dangerously was intoxicating to this chipmunk, then he was on a real bender.

As he progressed closer and closer to the grizzly, his spasmodic actions speeded up until finally he was sitting on the broken end of the log looking down into the bear's face. The grizzly seemed not to know that the little animal existed. It was a feeling not mutually shared; for now the chipmunk's chirps were almost lifting him off the log, and his tail was snapping back and forth like a whiplash.

Both animals were clear and sharp in the field of my glasses, and I saw the bear's ribs swell in a great breath. When he expelled it in a gusty sigh, the chipmunk seemed to be blown from the log three feet into space. He was running frantically in the middle of his jump, and when he hit the ground, he was streaking for cover over the lip of the bank with a long, quavering string of panic-stricken chirps. The grizzly roused himself to look after his departing visitor and then dropped his head back on his paws.

A moment or two later a little twister of breeze crossed the flat to give my scent away. Instantly the grizzly leaped up with a horrified sniff, as though something had set fire to the seat of his ragged pants, and went barreling over the bank of the river, going whoosh-whoosh-whoosh every jump clear across the river. It was about as comical as anything in the wilds can be.

Apart from the pleasures of mountain travel with congenial company in constantly changing scenes and adventures, these summer expeditions were an important part of our way of living. Not only did they provide a major part of the annual profits from our business, but they also provided the opportunity to scout and study the movements and numbers of various game animals. This information was valuable in planning and conducting the fall hunting expeditions into the mountains.

Then the atmosphere was entirely different, for we reverted into the part of those things that prey on other animals—a fact we did not often think about at first, for hunting is interesting and often exciting. Certainly we enjoyed the camaraderie about the campfires on frosty evenings, when the hunter's moon rode high, and away off somewhere there would often come the high, quavering, and infinitely lonesome call of a coyote or the eerie hooting of a hunting owl. There were pleasant people to talk and hunt with. There were challenges of high peaks, storms, and rough trails, sometimes spiced with an element of danger. In summer we lived in almost complete harmony with this country.

In the fall we jarred the harmony a bit by joining the predators in their hunting. While this was not as peaceful or carefree, it provided another kind of experience, opened a door to new understandings, and provided lessons that could not be learned in any other way.

I came to learn that matching wits with the grizzly in the heavily timbered, precipitous country of the Rockies was not particularly hard on the population of bears, although it almost invariably gave the hunter much vigorous exercise. One did not hunt grizzlies exclusively in such country, unless he was so dedicated to the sport as to care nothing for the small chance of success. One traveled through grizzly country hunting other animals and took the bear when opportunity afforded. Grizzlies are will-o'-the-wisps in hunting country, secretive, shy, and very difficult to find. Even when found, the big animals can disappear into thin air with the suddenness of a puff of smoke on a windy flat.

We watched for them in the timberline berry patches. Sometimes we stalked them as they dug roots or excavated for marmots and gophers. Occasionally we came on them as they fed on the offal of a previous kill we had made. Most often we ran into them by the purest kind of chance. One never knew for sure just where a grizzly bear might be seen.

I remember riding several miles up a valley one morning with a hunter for a day in some high basins. We tied our horses at timberline and climbed hard for an hour or so before sitting down on a comfortable ledge to rest and glass the surrounding country for game. The breeze was cool up high, but on the lower slopes of the mountains it was baking hot.

To see a grizzly out in the sun in such country was about as remote a possibility as seeing a chorus girl practicing her steps on that mountainside. When I chanced to look back down the valley toward camp, I saw three grizzlies feeding on a steep goat pasture about fifteen hundred vertical feet above our tents. Airline from us, they were about three miles away, but by trail it would take two hours to reach them. Knowing they would be long gone, we did not try a stalk but proceeded on our way.

No matter how carefully a stalk is planned and executed, a grizzly sighted is by no means a dead one. Sometimes when things appeared to be all in our favor, we failed even to get a shot; for no animal can fade into the surrounding scenery so quickly and easily, and few animals are less inclined to take second readings on the faintest hint of human intrusion. Many times when things appeared to be going just right and the bear was almost within range, some slight puff of wind gave us away, and we found ourselves looking at a place recently emptied of grizzly.

The reaction of hunters to the presence of a grizzly is also something of interest. More than one professed grizzly hunter has rapidly lost his desire to shoot a grizzly upon seeing his first silvertip. Most hunters are afraid of them, even when carrying the most modern magnum rifle—a weapon of such power and accuracy as to make those of the early pioneers and frontiersmen look like peashooters in comparison. Actually the modern hunter could be much more dangerous and deadly than he is. A grizzly sighted within three hundred yards offers a cool and accurate shooter an opportunity with his scope-sighted weapon that leaves the bear not a ghost of a chance. Contrary to popular belief, the grizzly is not a particularly difficult animal to kill. Certainly they are no more bulletproof than an elk, a moose, or similar game. To my way of thinking, the prairie antelope and the mountain goat are much harder to kill. Like any animal of comparative size, the grizzly can display an astonishing vitality if hit in the wrong place by the first bullet. Perhaps fortunately for bears in general, cool and accurate shooters are not really common in the hunting fraternity.

On occasion I have heard men say that they would not shoot at a grizzly inside a hundred yards. They want them way out there, where they feel safe from a charge. But too many fail to consider what they will do, should a long-range bullet just wound the bear and he get into heavy cover. Other hunters have a horror of getting under a grizzly on a steep slope.

I remember spotting a grizzly on a high rockslide one day. The bear was busily digging for ground squirrels on a small bench. I wanted my hunting guest to take his shot from the cover of some boulders directly below the bear, but he was utterly horrified at the idea. What if he wounded the bear and it came down on us? This eventuality was exactly what I had in mind, for I have a deeply ingrown dislike of pursuing wounded grizzly bears any place, and I would far rather have that second shot at a sure range. But my hunter was adamant and insisted on taking his shot from where we stood, about three hundred yards from the bear. The bullet just nicked the grizzly across the brisket, just back of the front legs, whereupon it let out a great roar and came barreling down the slope right past the boulders I had marked for our position to take the opening shot. As things progressed, my guest contrived to run his rifle dry shooting boulders while the bear was behind them. The last we saw of the big animal, it was heading at top speed into a mess of old burn. We trailed it, but the bleeding stopped after a quarter mile, and we were forced to give up. Understandably enough we did not see that bear again.

Another hunter came out on our pack train so full of a desire to kill a grizzly that he could talk of little else. He had never seen a grizzly outside a zoo, and when we came upon a three-year-old on the second day of the hunt, he was so hugely impressed by its size that he forgot to shoot. Right there he lost all interest in bear hunting. When I contrived to get him out of sight of our tents, he was extremely nervous. In spite of this reluctance, he was uncommonly lucky and collected some excellent trophies of other species of game.

Toward the end of the trip we were out in some top bear country amid a huge burned-over area at timberline. The whole region was carpeted with huckleberries, and the bears—both grizzly and black—were everywhere. Along about noon, after a hot, fruitless search through a crisscross pattern of bear sign, we rode down into a strip of green timber along a little creek. About the first thing we saw upon reaching it were the marks where a big grizzly had jumped down a clay bank into the water, leaving the three-foot skid tracks of his hind feet in the wet mud with big toe and pad prints at the bottom. My hunter took one goggle-eyed look at these tracks and refused to get off his horse to eat lunch. When we proceeded to hunt out a partially burned basin in the afternoon, he was at first preoccupied and very quiet. If he had known the way back to camp, I think he would have gone there and left me behind. Then he suddenly burst forth singing grand opera at the top of his lungs. My disgust gave way to amusement and also some pleasure, for he had a very good voice and had been a professional in younger years. Even though the ringing melodies of *Carmen* may be somewhat out of place on a grizzly hunt, he was paying for it, and who was I to say he could not sing? Needless to say, we saw nothing beyond tracks of bears, which was the general idea my hunter had in mind.

It was not until next day, when we were heading out for civilization with the pack outfit, that I suddenly realized he had thought those long skid marks were bona fide grizzly tracks, and I scared my horse by bursting into a great roar of laughter. No doubt this hunter returned home with a story about seeing grizzly tracks a full yard long!

Under the best of circumstances hunting and trailing grizzly bears in the Rocky Mountains is no soft excursion. Many times over the years I have been hugely amused by letters from high-pressure, ambitious junior executives who requested a ten-day hunt with a grizzly bear guaranteed. One would have thought grizzlies come packaged for sale at the corner grocery!

In the first place, a ten-day pack trip through wilderness country is admittedly somewhat better than no pack trip, but not very much. It is like rushing to catch a train for the city to do some shopping and then tearing off home again, only to find that the most important and badly needed item has been forgotten. In the second place, the weather, grizzlies, and other unpredictable norms of a mountain pack-train hunt usually conspire to arrange things so that ten days is far from enough time.

Such a hunting trip is more than just a hunt: it is one of the most effective means of relaxing recreation possible to enjoy. It is a wonderful way to let the springs of tension unwind—a means to cleanse the mind and cheer the soul, wherein the killing of bears is a thing most secondary in importance to escaping the raucous jingling of telephones and the rising crescendo of rumbling wheels.

I know of one man who made many trips before he managed to bag a grizzly. When he finally did collect his bear trophy, it was with some expression of regret, for part of his excuse for coming was thus removed. It was his firm conviction that no real sportsman with any sincere regard for the future has the moral right to kill more than one grizzly in a lifetime. It is a thought I am bound to support. For if all sportsmen adhered to such a self-imposed limit, no finger of accusation could be pointed at them for endangering a great species.

Although the aura of danger usually connected with a grizzly hunt is much exaggerated, it does understandably enough afford some spice. For somehow if a man encounters dangers and avoids it, or even thinks he has met it when the fact be otherwise, his experience assumes a certain unforgettable quality in his mind, especially in hindsight, and he enjoys telling about it over and over again.

There is no doubt in my mind, from the vantage point of looking back on many years of wilderness travel in grizzly country, that if the bear were half as dangerous as held by popular belief, hundreds of people would have been mauled and killed who actually came away not even knowing that they had been close to grizzlies. Time and again I have found sign of the big bears very aptly demonstrating their ability in looking over visitors without revealing their presence. To fully understand the grizzly bear one must consider this animal's great curiosity. Things out of the ordinary fascinate the grizzly. Even when the unusual involves a human, of which he may be very much afraid, the bear will often take the time to examine the visitor closely without the man knowing it.

Years ago I saw evidence of this when one of my British Columbia guides and I were hunting with a couple of sportsmen from the United States. We were coming into camp on foot just before dark one rainy evening. I was about a hundred yards ahead with one hunter, and we were slogging along a winding trail through a stretch of lodgepole pine forest looking forward to a hot supper in the camp about two hundred yards ahead of us.

The hunter and I slid down a steep little bench where, although we had not the slightest suspicion of it at the time, we passed a big grizzly lying hidden behind a bush. After letting us pass by, the grizzly noiselessly came out onto the trail behind us and leaped up onto the bench heading away. There it almost bumped noses with my guide and his hunter in a head-on collision. The big animal reared to full height and looked at them in astonishment, while they stood transfixed by surprise, dwarfed by the towering bear. The bear recovered first and leaped away out of sight in the timber. The hunter did not even unsling his rifle from his shoulder. Upon being quizzed jokingly about this later, he said that shooting the grizzly never occurred to him. It was likely just as well. Involuntarily both men did exactly the right thing, for they were almost within handshaking distance of the bear, and any kind of movement might have provoked him into taking a swing at them.

Later examination revealed that this bear had spent some considerable time examining the camp from all angles. Probably he was intrigued by the activities of the cook and the horse wrangler who had been sawing and splitting wood.

Again on a wilderness hunting trip I was out riding alone trying to find some of our horses that had managed to hide themselves very thoroughly among the mountains. At dark I found myself riding in very rough country far from camp. Having found horse tracks but no horses, it was expedient that I make camp for the night—a siwash affair wherein I covered an empty belly with a tired back and a small Navajo saddle blanket and slept under the wide-spreading branches of a big spruce.

Sometime during the night it snowed a little skiff to just whiten the ground. When daylight came, I was somewhat surprised to find big grizzly tracks all around my improvised bed. He had come up the canyon with the wind and had been close on discovering me. There is no telling what had intrigued the bear. The big tracks were in complete circles around me not more than six feet away. The big animal had come and gone without my being aware of his presence.

Such incidents are too rarely recognized for the harmless things they are. But all grizzlies not being alike, there are enough offbeat characters among them to put the whole species in something of a bad light, whether they deserve it or not. To be sure, for a long time we have been prone to look for the worst in these animals. Sometimes man's natural tendency to be a killer pushes him into doing things he would not do in his more generous moments.

During the years I spent as a professional guide and outfitter, killing a grizzly mother with cubs was not illegal, although it was a practice I abhorred. Not only was it extremely bad business in view of the fact that the orphaned cubs usually died and were thus wasted; but it was most inhumane, for the cubs died slowly of starvation. For these reasons we had a hard and fast rule in our hunting camps never to kill a mother bear with cubs—a rule that was rigidly observed with just one exception. The incident involved a very cranky she-grizzly up on the headwaters of Grizzly Creek, a tributary of the Kishaneena.

My guide, Wenz Dvorak, a veteran of many years on the hunting and trapping trails of the British Columbia mountains, was out hunting with one of our guests, and they had the opportunity to kill a very fine mountain goat at the foot of a precipitous face. They skinned the trophy out and were proceeding toward camp through some huge boulders at timberline, when they came upon a she-grizzly with two second-year cubs at fairly close range.

She did not choose to retreat but led her cubs past in front of the hunters, showing every indication of being very angry at their intrusion into her mountain stronghold. With head slung low and her back hair standing on end, she stalked along, giving them sideways looks as though of half a mind to charge.

Most guides would have asked the hunter to shoot her on the spot, but Wenz showed remarkable forbearance. He attempted to scare her away by shooting close to her head, but instead of being alarmed, she only growled at him. However she did take the hint and left, although with obvious reluctance.

A couple of days later, following a snowstorm, Wenz and I were back in the area with two other hunters in search of another huge billy goat that Wenz had seen. We split up the party, and I was alone with one hunter high on the face of the mountain, when we heard a strange noise coming from away below on the edge of the timber beside a little lake in an open basin. It sounded exactly like someone knocking on rocks with a geologist's hammer. When it came again from the same spot, I was sure this was what it was, for we had heard that some geologists were in the area.

I was muttering something smoky to indicate my disgust at this intrusion when the sound came a third time, and to my amazement a big sow grizzly walked out of the timber with two cubs at her heels. It was undoubtedly the same bear Wenz had encountered previously, and there was even less doubt that she was still in a very bad temper. When she came to our horse tracks in the snow, she put her nose down to smell them and then lifted her head and popped her jaws loudly together. Although she was a good thousand yards away, the sound carried loud and clear up to us. She continued to show her anger at our presence in her territory by stalking back and forth and periodically clacking her teeth.

Shortly afterward we found the goat, whereupon my hunter proceeded to miss it completely with half a dozen shots that rolled and rattled off the surrounding mountains in all directions. Having thus shot up the vicinity so effectively, it never occurred to me that we might run into the grizzly on our return through the basin. But she was waiting for us beneath a big tree close to the horse trail. When she saw us coming, she got up onto her feet and came quartering down toward us, obviously very angry but still in nothing resembling a charge. I had never seen a grizzly acting like this one, and the fact that we would be going through this canyon almost every day made her presence appear to be a threat. When she was still a hundred yards away, the hunter shot her on my request.

This would have been an unremarkable incident easily

forgotten, had it not been for the cubs. While we were skinning out the big grizzly, they hung around in the timber close by. Here and there we saw them sneaking furtively along and then standing erect as they tried to see what was happening to their mother. Every once in a while one or the other would give a soft bawling sound, obviously a call to her. They were old enough to have a good chance to survive, but before the skinning job was done, we were wishing we had given the old bear another chance. A man would have had to have a heart of cold stone to ignore those cubs. By the time we left that place, we were feeling low in our minds and not admiring ourselves very much.

In the flickering light of many a campfire to follow I saw those cubs. They truly haunted me. I came to the conclusion that very little was really known of the true character of the grizzly. I began to see them as they really are, an admirable big animal with remarkable intelligence, harried and hunted, cursed and killed too often in senseless misunderstanding. Then there was the wilderness country that the bear calls home, melting away under the pressure of greed and waste.

Even the born hunter with a deep, abiding love of pursuit can know too well the emptiness of killing and share the grizzly's dismay at the loss of the wilderness to the bulldozer. He can join the grizzly in retreat, but there comes an end to running and time to turn and fight, for the need for wilderness in a way of life is felt by more than bears. Maybe the skill of the stalker could be used to help the animals instead of killing them, thus preserving the need for hunting them in the first place. In so doing, a man could even come to a better understanding of himself.

When this thought resolved itself, a whole new hunting ground suddenly opened, unexplored, bigger than anything I had ever dreamed about, with no limits to its use all the year round. It was so huge and deep that I regretted the shortness of the years ahead and the time already past. There was a keen challenge involved that made the smell of powder smoke flat and unattractive. And so I hung up my rifle, and in its place I reached for camera and notebook.

III

Hunting with the Camera

10. Prologue to Peace

He can take one sniff of you half a mile downwind and tell you the color of your grandmother's wedding dress.
—F. H. RIGGALL

Backtracking through history along grizzly trails of the past, it is interesting to note that as early as the middle of the nineteenth century the seemingly endless and often senseless bloodletting of the frontier hunter was somewhat relieved by a few men who considered the grizzly of some certain use and interest beyond killing.

John Capen "Grizzly" Adams was likely the earliest of these. As has been described by Theodore Hittell, quoted in an earlier chapter, Adams fed his appetite for adventure and made a good part of his living by capturing grizzly bears alive and taming them on occasion for beasts of burden. Probably "Grizzly" Adams knew the character of the grizzly as well or perhaps better than any man who ever lived, and obviously he liked and admired the big animals with which he worked.

A keen curiosity and appreciation of the beauties of nature was being expressed at this time by the art of the immortal wildlife painter, John James Audubon. He had something of a nodding acquaintance with the grizzly, which he observed and mentioned in letters home to his family while on a paddle-wheel steamer trip up the Missouri River into the western plains country in 1853:

The audacity of these bears around Fort Union was remarkable. The waiter, Jean Baptiste, who had been in the company's employ for upwards of twenty years, was picking peas in the garden one day. As he neared the end of the rows he saw a large Grizzly Bear gathering that excellent vegetable also, whereupon he himself dropped his bucket, peas and all, and fled to the Fort. Immediately the hunters turned out on their best horses and by riding in a circle formed a line which enabled them to approach the bear from all sides. Finding the animal still greedily feeding on peas, they shot him without his apparently knowing of their approach. We need hardly say the bucket was empty. . . .

Audubon's enthusiasm for everything that went on around him in the colorful and adventurous plains country was apparently not dampened by the somewhat ignominious and out-of-character picture of this great grizzly being assassinated in the white man's pea patch. Where was the great, roaring, meat-hungry beast usually portrayed by the frontier chronicler? This noted naturalist quite unconsciously gave a truer picture of the grizzly than he realized, and he was likely the first man to portray the grizzly at rest and undisturbed in its native haunts; for he included a sketch of two grizzlies in his collection of mammal drawings made on this trip.

Later in the century history was made by the formation of the national parks in the western United States. These were largely set up by Theodore Roosevelt, that amazing frontier hunter who became president of his country and likely North America's most noteworthy sportsman of all time. The grizzlies at last had a haven where hunters could not go.

No man of this bloodthirsty era showed more understanding and compassion for all kinds of wildlife than is displayed in the still-popular writings of Ernest Thompson Seton. His development as a writer came at an opportune time in the late evening of the shameful massacre of the plains bison and in the midst of the decimation of the grizzly bear and other major species. It was a time when the callous approach to other forms of life was an almost universal human attribute, when very few people were aware or disturbed at the prospect of a country empty of much of its richness in wildlife. The repeating rifle and shotgun had supplanted the single-shot, breech-loading weapons, which speeded up the slaughter. Professional market hunting was at its height. Hundreds of magnificent bull elk were being killed only for their distinctive "bridle" teeth, which were in high demand for jewelry. Uncounted grizzlies were being shot for their hides. Frontier mining and lumber camps were feeding their crews on the meat of deer, elk, mountain sheep, and moose. In Seton's time the last flocks of millions of passenger pigeons was killed in an unrestrained slaughter that lasted from 1840 to 1880. Even the casual hunter who went out for wildfowl and did not come back staggering under the weight of birds was not considered much of a shot.

Seton worked long and hard to wake the public to the fact that wildlife could not stand the punishment much longer and some decent management and protection was needed. There is a strong vein of pathos running through the stories of his famous books *Wild Animals I Have Known*, *The Lives of the Hunted*, and *Biography of a Grizzly*, which shook the complacency of people far and wide. Seton was thus indirectly responsible for springboarding the initial moves toward our present-day wildlife protective legislation.

For the first time the North American white settlers had a broader awareness of the fact that other forms of life can know joy, fear, and sadness. We came to realize that the blood ran warm in the veins of other creatures just as it ran in ours. While most of us still regarded animals and birds as something put on earth for the express use of humans, at least we began to realize the necessity for some limitations of our pleasures. But in spite of this the grizzly bear still fought for existence under a cloud of popular belief aptly described by Montague Stevens, though there were other sympathetic individuals of the time taking a hand in authentic portrayal.

One of these was Charles M. Russell, the famous cowboy artist. He was most noted for his action paintings of life in the early West when the cowboy and the Texas longhorn steer were synonymous with the empires of grass. He was a sort of wilderness humanist, who loved life and living so much that he had very little use for a gun. He dearly loved to tell stories, and in these as well as in his paintings the grizzly came in for some interesting and often humorous attention. He captured on his canvases the split-second action of the frontiersmen in some close-quarter mix-ups with the big bears that today are considered among the most valuable by North American artists.

Another artist, and friend of Charlie Russell's, was Philip R. Goodwyn, whose illustrations of wilderness scenes were well known at the time and appeared in many magazines and calendar pictures. It was common to see Goodwyn calendar scenes adorning the walls of homesteaders' shacks, stores, and other public buildings throughout the West. Both he and Russell were top craftsmen, whose love of nature and wild country shone in their pictures.

At about the same time, some better knowledge and understanding of the grizzly were being generated by the observations and writings of two authors: Enos A. Mills and William H. Wright, who, for some obscure reason never achieved the recognition that was their due.

Enos Mills was a fine naturalist who spent many years of his life wandering the bear trails of the Colorado Rockies, and he made some remarkable records of grizzly habit and behavior. Although some critics branded Mills a nature faker, such criticism is sheer reluctance to recognize truth that fails to follow the path of popular belief. Nowhere in his writing does Mills "draw the long bow" as charged. What he saw, he recounted with accuracy and rare insight into the private life of the grizzly. In a great many instances his personal observations parallel my own.

In the preface of his book *The Grizzly*, Enos Mills reveals something important and interesting about his feelings for this animal. Shortly before 1910 he has this to say:

It would make exciting reading if a forty year old grizzly were to write his autobiography. Beginning with the stories of his mother, of the long and exciting journey of his ancestors from far-off Asia, and of her own struggle to bring up her family, and then telling of his own adventures and his meetings with men and with other animals, he would give us a book of dramatic quality. Just what the wise old grizzly would say while philosophizing concerning the white race would certainly be of human interest and rich in material for literature.

A vigorous, courageous adventurer himself, and a keen and constant observer, the grizzly would have clear cut views concerning the explorers, early settlers, and hunters. The arrival of the early white people aroused his extraordinary inherent curiosity. He watched them with wondering eyes. He was even inclined to walk right into camp to make their acquaintance. He had no evil intention but was greeted with yells and bullets (as was Audubon's grizzly). Relentlessly down through the years he was pursued. Dog, guns, poison and traps have swept the majority of grizzlies away. Their retreat was masterly and heroic, but the odds were overwhelming.

In the midst of this terrible hunt the Yellowstone reservation was established. Instantly the grizzly understood, years before the other big animals did, and in its protection at once came forth from hiding, eager to be friendly with men. I should like to know his wonderings about this place of refuge—why its creation, why its mysterious, invisible boundary lines, and why, outside of it, the fierce, never ending pursuit of him still goes on, until his noble species verges on extinction.

What, too, are his feelings over the increased friendly interest in his species all over the nation? How excitedly he must catch the echoes of discussions which are telling that he is misunderstood, that he is not a bad fellow! And surely, if writing, he will pause abruptly when he hears that the public, and even the hunter, is making efforts to have the hunt for him checked—learns that there may be an early closed season for grizzly bear.

The fact that the grizzly bear was the first of the big animals to recognize the protection afforded by Yellowstone Park after the banishment of hunters from within its borders reveals a superior and perceiving intelligence. It also says a good deal for the keen powers of observation and interpretive ability of Enos Mills. He was a rare man of his time, who carved a niche in Western history much more significant than has been recognized, although it is doubtful that this worried him much.

William H. Wright, whose extensive field experience as a

hunter-naturalist and professional big-game guide took him from the Bitter Roots of Montana north to the high, cool, snow-capped peaks of the Selkirk Range of central British Columbia and back to the mountains of Wyoming, was also a dedicated observer of nature and was fascinated with the grizzly bear. His adventures while photographing grizzlies in Yellowstone Park are a milestone in the history of wildlife photography. He was the first man to successfully photograph wild grizzlies in their native surroundings. His graphic description of his experiences is a source of amazement to a modern photographer, for his equipment was extremely awkward and crude in comparison to the cameras carried today.

He used cumbersome plate cameras at night. These were set close to a trail where grizzlies were expected to pass. A fine trip wire that was strung across the trail activated a fuse then triggered by the bear. This set off a pan of flash powder, thus exposing the photographic plate through the lens aperture, which had been left open. The explosion of the powder almost invariably startled the model. All kinds of complications were encountered. Sometimes the bears located the wire and avoided it. Even when one sprang it, the blinding flash and boom could cause the animal to stampede in any direction. One can easily see that a grizzly could be an unknown quantity under such circumstances in the forest darkness. Wright narrowly missed being run over several times.

He was singularly unruffled and possessed of great patience in meeting his problems. His accounts of his adventures are appreciated particularly by anyone who has worked with grizzlies for photographic models. Even in broad daylight while armed with the most modern equipment, fewer more difficult subjects can be found anywhere in the entire field of nature photography. But in spite of his handicaps, Wright obtained some excellent photos of grizzlies—probably the first ever published.

Then John M. Holzworth stepped into the arena in favor of the bear. His well-illustrated written accounts of three expeditions into Alaska between 1927 and 1930 throw considerable illumination on the big brownie of the salmon streams, and very likely he successfully exposed the first moving picture film ever taken of the bear.

A great portion of his time in Alaska was spent with Allen M. Hasselborg, a colorful wilderness adventurer who lived alone for many years with the big grizzly bears of Admiralty Island. Hasselborg liked the bears better than he did most people, and he made no bones about saying so. He was likely more familiar with the habits and character of the big northern coastal grizzlies than any other man who ever lived in that part of the country.

Holzworth not only tells a graphic and interesting story of his adventures and impressions of the big bears of the salmon streams, but he also passes along a good portion of the rich lore gathered by his friend Hasselborg—"the Old Man," as he affectionately called him. Both men were actively opposed to the slaughter of the Alaskan brown bears then being advocated by professional bear haters, who spoke in the name of making the country safe for humans but who were really a great deal more interested in lining their pockets with money from the sale of hides and the collection of bounty.

John Holzworth collected a grizzly of unusual color while hunting with Hasselborg. The skull and hide were later taken to Dr. C. Hart Merriam, and after various measurements the bear was classified as a new species, *Ursus holzworthi*. Holzworth was one of the "splitters," but he was not one of those who killed extensively merely for the sake of getting his name set down in official classification. He much preferred collecting trophies on film.

The researcher into the recorded history of the grizzly will find few enough protagonists of the animal, but when he extends his search into grizzly bear photography, there is a veritable dearth. Since wildlife photography is a recent form of recording, this is understandable enough; but even so, very few men were or are inclined to shoot their grizzly bears on film. Largely speaking, photographers have lost no grizzlies and therefore have no wish to find any. Among the personal acquaintances of my years as a hunting, fishing, and photography guide, I met several very good wildlife photographers, but none had any ambition to film grizzlies and flatly said so. Some had filmed the bear briefly here and there—and at a distance—as more or less an accidental contact. Usually these films showed evidence of extreme nervousness on the part of the photographer.

Only once do I recall seeing a good film sequence of a grizzly, and this was taken by an internationally famous lecturer. It showed a Yukon grizzly coming slowly across the tundra toward the photographer, obviously aware of him and just as obviously more curious than alarmed. Finally the bear came close enough to fill about a quarter of the screen, whereupon it reared in typical fashion to peer curiously at the cameraman. Here the sequence came to an abrupt end, and just previous to the cut there was the flashing glimpse of two or three frames showing dust and hair spurting from between the bear's eyes where a high-powered rifle bullet struck. Undoubtedly most of this man's audience missed seeing this telltale evidence of cold-blooded murder. It spoiled my evening. To kill an animal that has stood for pictures is more than unjustified: it is the mark of ignorance, lack of appreciation, and a most unforgivable breech of ethics. It is only justified in the very rare instance of self-protection, and that does not include anticipation of it.

I have spent many years following grizzly trails and have come to know a few sympathetic men who have discovered the thrills of hunting with the camera. When I return to Alaska, seeing and photographing the wildlife there will be only a part of the anticipated pleasure; for our rambling through that magnificent country has brought many contacts with people who have discovered the thrill of hunting with cameras. When I read something written about the uncompromisingly bad temper of the fierce grizzly, who is just as likely to chew a man up as look at him, I enjoy recalling pleasant hours spent with this small fraternity of wildlife camera bugs who really know the grizzly and have no need to justify their killing.

Standing out in quiet, good-natured prominence among these is my good friend Charlie Ott, whose photographs of

The upper two photos show a young male (top) and a female with her last winter's cub.

At bottom is Casper, about to justify his name by bolting for distant parts.

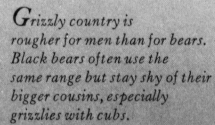

*Grizzly country is
rougher for men than for bears.
Black bears often use the
same range but stay shy of their
bigger cousins, especially
grizzlies with cubs.*

Alaskan game are famous around the world and in great demand for magazine and book illustration. Charlie lives in Mount
McKinley National Park and loves that grand wilderness country and its wildlife with a real passion. How long ago it was that
Charlie last picked up a gun with the idea of killing something I
have no idea, but it has been many years. To Charlie nothing
could be more depressing and useless than a dead animal; for he
delights in filming their live, warm-blooded presence. For this he
goes armed with a Hasselblad camera; he owns three, along
with an interchangeable battery of lenses. Sometimes he uses
bigger cameras, and he has been known to carry a huge 8 x 10
view camera for some special assignments. Not only is a man
doing this kind of thing a dedicated artist; he is also as tough as
a boot, for such equipment is awkward, heavy as lead, and not
given to floating around through the Alaskan peaks by itself.

Perhaps not so well known, but highly skilled, is Bill
Bacon, an Alaska-born professional who has spent most of his
life as a wildlife photographer for such sticklers for quality as
Walt Disney. Bill has traveled the world shooting nature subjects with his movie cameras, and he has spent a good deal of
time working with grizzlies throughout their range.

There is Glen McClane and his good wife, Steve Hatch of
Anchorage, and Cecil Rhode, all highly skilled nature photographers with more than a passing acquaintance with grizzlies; these also have wandered for years through the Alaska
wilderness armed with nothing more lethal than cameras.

There is diminutive Ruth Travers, who can carry twenty-
five pounds of camera and tripod all day in the mountains and
who often films grizzlies at close range. Along with her husband, Charlie, she has spent considerable time shooting film in
the grizzly country around the Toklat River Ranger Station and
Wonder Lake in McKinley Park, where he is employed as a
ranger.

Synonymous with Alaskan wildlife and known to thousands is Adolph Murie, for many years chief biologist at McKinley Park and now retired from the park service. He and his
brother, the late Olaus Murie, have carved a permanent corner

for themselves in the history of wilderness conservation and wildlife management through their unselfish and dedicated work. Both are famous authors, and neither are strangers to cameras. Olaus Murie was a towering personality, one of the most lovable men I ever knew, gentle and soft-spoken, yet endowed with cool, iron courage. I once saw him face the rush of an angry she-grizzly without even bothering to get up from his knees or to take his eye from the viewfinder of his camera. "Never run from a bear!" was his watchword with the grizzlies, along with a monumental knowledge of their ways.

All these have hunted the grizzly with the camera—an advanced breed of specializing explorers bent on fuller understanding. While my sons and I made upwards of two hundred grizzly contacts in three years, our experience is but a small fraction of the total made by these others. All of them know the thrill of sharing a mountain with a grizzly on amiable terms. I salute these people, for they are true friends of the grizzly.

Having spent many years following bear trails with the rifle before joining the brotherhood of photographers, but not being entirely ignorant of their ways, I suppose it was not strange that I should wake up one morning suddenly realizing that I was missing something important. Added to this was a strong feeling that something had to be done to expose a great danger.

The grizzly was being no longer threatened over the large part of his remaining range by unrestricted hunting. Now there was an even more frightening menace: that clanking, stinking, noisy invention of the devil known as a bulldozer. Every year saw the wilderness so familiar to me being chewed and torn to ribbons by these mechanical monsters, until there was no place left in which to operate our wilderness pack train. It was shocking to realize that the cold-blooded exploitation of natural resources threatened to wipe out a way of life that had been a hallmark of our family for over half a century and also threatened the grizzly by removing a very necessary element of habitat. For the first time I came really to know something of the feeling of the hunted when pressed by overwhelming odds against survival.

Apart from the development of his weapons, no invention of man equals the bulldozer in sheer destructive power. The use of no other tool has changed the face of the land so much for good or bad. No other device requires more careful administration of its use for the development of natural resources. No other device has received so precious little of this kind of care. There is something evil about this powerful earth mover that infects men and turns otherwise reasonably sensible human beings into blind, power-mad zombies with no more regard for the future of the land than its bitterest enemy.

Even Waterton Lakes National Park bordering our ranch here in southwest Alberta has been seriously stricken. One day not long ago we heard the powerful roar of diesel motors from a direction never heard before. From our lodge veranda we were horrified to see bulldozers ripping a road along the park boundary across a pristinely beautiful mountain slope that had stood unchanged for ten thousand years. This road was going nowhere. It potential use was almost nil. Following the boundary with no deviation for contours, it could not help but be impassable to any kind of vehicle for about nine months of the year. So the administration's excuse that it was needed to mark the boundary and allow more efficient patrol is not true. It has been proved that patrol by horseback is much more efficient. Certainly the Warden's Service was then a good deal more colorful.

This road has proved an abuse, for it has given access to a sort of "strip mine" for topsoil to supply a replacement need in a badly planned central campground and townsite. Gullying and erosion has further scarred a beautiful stretch of country. As is too often true, the very men charged with the responsibility of preservation from such abuse have been the ones to waste it.

Apart from their discomfiture in having heavy machinery roaring through their wilderness range, the bears have felt the direct sting of this sad lack of principle in the administration of what is at least partly intended to be their haven of refuge. Since the parks were originally formed, and according to the most up-to-date declaration of policy, feeding or interference with the lives of the bears by visitors is a misdemeanor punishable under law. I have seen posters threatening the visiting tourist with a $300 fine for feeding bears or otherwise molesting them. Yet the parks administration has been and still is, in some areas, the worst offender; for open garbage dumps are still in use. These rapidly condition the bears to becoming panhandlers, which has indirectly caused the injury of many people and the death of countless black bears and grizzlies.

But it is the insidious effect of opening the country with all kinds of bulldozed trails and roads that is so basically wasteful. This is a part of a wasteful and horridly ugly pattern threatening our wilderness areas, including our parks, and reaching almost continuously from my door north to the top of the Peel Plateau in the Ogilvie Mountains in the high Arctic of the Yukon Territory. It is a pattern of destruction more than progress, where for every acre of ground found productive, hundreds have been wasted. To be sure, if given time this grid pattern of bulldozer tracks will heal; but where the ecology of the country is delicately balanced, as it is on the tundra, the healing may take centuries, and by that time certain species may be lost forever.

The present trend is part of a much-lauded "multiple use" program enthusiastically sold to a gullible public by the pork-barrel politicos, whereby the supposed meaning is the use by many, but in reality it is the giveaway of valuable, publicly owned resources to the first private interest arriving with the required folding money in hand. It means the destruction of much valuable wildlife habitat. This will result in the loss of recreational potential, a need so rapidly developing in this country that it will be vitally important in our generation.

The threat of more and more wilderness being opened without plan or thought for the future is the greatest danger yet encountered by wildlife in its bloody history on this continent. It is a threat particularly dangerous to the grizzly, for this animal definitely requires wilderness living space. It is an unnecessary threat brought about by sheer greed of the most immediate and short-sighted nature.

When one considers a world containing civilizations of men, regardless of political creed or religious belief, where the weight of profit can tip the scale in spite of law, principle, and moral code, then it is a temptation to throw up one's hands in despair and abandon any thought of trying to maintain a decent balance. When one considers that man, of all living creatures, is largely motivated in his recent history by the plunder of natural resources, sometimes without even the motive of decent profit, then it is a sad thing. When one contemplates the fact that man is the one creature that goes against nature and is the only living animal that threatens to breed and blast himself out of existence, then it is frightening and discouraging. But liking people in general and also wilderness country in particular, I am bound to try.

In the black, threatening face of facts there is still a light of optimism. Certainly one can appreciate the insight and enlightenment of the man who placed a full-length mirror in the London zoo and beside it placed a sign reading: YOU ARE NOW LOOKING AT THE MOST DANGEROUS ANIMAL ON EARTH. It is true, but one also likes to believe that there is a wellspring of goodness in man that will overbalance his tendencies toward general bankruptcy—a blossoming of intelligence that will reveal to him the dangers and unnecessary sordidness of the path he walks. For as surely as the sun rises tomorrow morning, the dangers do not all center about the grizzly bear.

The world can likely proceed without a cataclysm in face of the permanent absence of guides and outfitters and grizzly bears, but it is the principles involved in the engineering of their passing that will create the permanent scars and the great waste. The possible argument that this is all a part of an inevitable and natural evolution, which we must be prepared to accept, is not a reasonable one; for man is involved deeply, and man insists on going against nature. Therefore it is reasonable to expect him to be bound by the dominance of his position and intelligence to manage his intrusions with gentleness and care and less concern for immediate profit.

Many questions arise. We can be very sure that the larger part of the answers will not be found in popular belief. There will be bitter medicine involved, which, though the taste be temporarily bad, may provide the means for healthy continuance. Through the many hours spent thinking about this problem under the sun and stars in many lovely places across the wilderness of this land, it has occurred to me that the grizzly could provide at least a portion of the answers if given the chance and an informed interpreter. For man, though by far the most intelligent of all life on earth and with a wonderful understanding of many things, including the means of his own permanent demise, has as yet gone practically nowhere in truly understanding himself or his relationship to other forms of life. He has long been a victim of his own common error.

Sir Thomas Brown was a doctor who lived and wrote in the seventeenth century. One of his works is a book called *Pseudodoxia: Inquiries into Vulgar and Common Errors*, which turned the searching light of criticism upon many superstitions prevalent at that time. John Holzworth has suggested that someone has long needed to write a "pseudodoxia" on the grizzly bear. Since then several other well-informed people have suggested the same thing.

No longer having a place left to wander with the pack train as an outfitter and guide because of some vulgar and common errors of this day and age, I found myself in a proper frame of mind to try. The challenge appealed somehow; and besides, what an opportunity to conduct a great hunt through country we had not seen before.

So in 1961, along with the able assistance of my two oldest sons, Dick, a zoology student from the University of British Columbia, and Charlie, a graduate of the Institute of Photography in New York, I headed a series of expeditions. With our notebooks and cameras we undertook the greatest hunt ever experienced—a hunt that was to use up most of four years of our lives, involve nearly every scrap of resources at our command, and cover about twenty thousand miles of wilderness, traveling by about every means possible through some of the wildest country left in the world.

II. *A Time of Frustration*

Of what avail are forty freedoms
without a blank spot on the map?
—ALDO LEOPOLD

When a man plans to join the fraternity of grizzly bears as late in the game as 1961, he goes with two strikes against him; for not only are grizzlies a lot less numerous than they were in the days of Lewis and Clark, but they have developed a very decided antipathy to any kind of close social contact with the two-legged ones. The plan must be wrapped in a strategy to work in widely diversified types of country and climate. Of necessity it must allow plenty of time, for this kind of thing can stretch from months into years. Grizzlies know nothing of modern man's compulsion to hang his hope for success on a close-determined schedule. The camera hunter must hang his hope on being able to adjust to the grizzly's world, and there time means nothing. Matters of equipment and supply must be worked out to the last small detail, for sometimes the corner store is a long way off in grizzly country. Territories for field operation must be chosen with great care to afford the best possible opportunity of finding a maximum of bears; and because we are particularly anxious to obtain a varied cross section of habit as well as habitat, this choice must cover all the various aspects of their remaining range.

Grizzly range throughout the regions of British Columbia,

Yukon Territory, and Alaska is almost universally mountainous, although it includes vast differences in climate and cover. This is something of great importance to the camera hunter; for if he wishes to record all of the main choices of habitat, he must be prepared to work betimes under adverse conditions. Hunting with cameras is infinitely more difficult than hunting with the rifle; not only does one work with light as his chief medium for ultimate success, but also practical operating ranges must be very close by comparison. There is nothing like a camera to teach a man the unknown quantities involved in shooting at "magnum ranges." Such a shot on film almost invariably shows the subject as an indistinct dot in the distance—a photograph more remarkable perhaps in its record of scenery than of anatomical features. Not only must shooting ranges for cameras be kept close so that detail is clearly recorded, but the presence of the photographer and his equipment should not disturb the natural action of the "model." When grizzlies are a man's choice of subject, he has the additional problem of arriving and working in the near vicinity without precipitating flight or promoting a charge. Neither result is very productive. One rapidly becomes bored with views of grizzlies leaving the country at high speed, and even more is one disinclined to accumulate a collection of photographs showing irate bears coming the other way! Neither view reveals anything of how grizzlies behave when living undisturbed, and only in records of this does one gain some knowledge of their real character.

Experience with other animals, particularly mountain sheep and deer, had taught us that humans can fraternize with so-called "wild animals" without causing them much concern, providing one learns the necessary attitude and protocol. Perhaps the most important thing a man has to learn is that while he may consider all other animals wild, the only really wild animal in nature's picture is man himself. On realizing this truth and adjusting himself to a less overbearing frame of mind, excluding all thoughts of violence and killing, he can then begin to make friends with associated life.

Wild sheep are considered the world over to be one of the

wariest creatures pursued by hunters, yet we had found them unusually gentle and trusting once they realized we meant them no harm. On one particular occasion we had practically lived with bighorn sheep among the Rockies of southwest Alberta for seventeen months, and they had accepted us into their world. We found that we could film at very short range if we moved properly in their presence. This means moving smoothly, without any jerks, an art not ordinarily practiced by people but by nearly all wild animals. It is also, strangely enough, a technique practiced in the open, for nothing makes an animal more suspicious than gumshoe flitting from one bit of cover to the next. The secret to this fraternal mingling of man with wild animals is a sincere and genuine friendliness of spirit on the man's part; for I am convinced that the wild ones have a sixth sense, an extrasensory perception that tells them what the intruder has in mind. Because of this, no hunter pursuing game can successfully make this kind of approach, for he has killing in his mind and the animals know it. We have one photo of a bighorn's eye taken at a range of three feet. Many times we climbed up among them without alarming them in the least, and more than once I have eaten my noon lunch seated among a bunch of bedded rams placidly chewing their cuds.

The grizzly offered a much different problem. We knew exactly how unpredictable they can be, but we felt confident that some means of association could successfully be worked out that would allow the gathering of pictures necessary to illustrate at least a portion of their lives. It would be a straightforward approach; for the nature of grizzlies, their choice of habitat, and their way of living made the use of such a deception as blinds completely impractical.

Our proposed hunting territory was about two thousand miles long and one thousand miles wide, so we were bound at least to try to make the best selection of it to meet our requirements. While we had to plan our campaign in the greatest possible detail, it was very necessary to keep it sufficiently flexible that we would not fall victim of our organization and thus miss important opportunities that might show themselves.

Many people at one time or another have photographed grizzly bears. Almost always their efforts were confined to a small area. Few had any definite objective in mind other than obtaining some grizzly pictures. Wright had persisted in his efforts, but he had been severely handicapped by the primitive equipment of his time. Holzworth had enjoyed improved cameras, but he had confined his efforts almost exclusively to the salmon streams of Admiralty Island. Thanks to the reputation of grizzlies and the obvious difficulties of working with them, the field of photographic recording was practically wide open and unexplored. This added zest to our adventure, even if it gave us no precedents for reference. We were largely dependent on our own judgment.

We proposed to film the big bears in both still pictures and movies, for the most part in full color. Because we would have to carry our equipment on our backs a large part of the time and would be far from service facilities, the equipment would have to be light and rugged. We chose two identical 16 mm. Bolex movie cameras with matching batteries of lenses, from wide angle to 150 mm. focal length and fitted with reflex viewing systems. These cameras are light and dependable if given reasonable care. They are spring-wound, which has the advantage of allowing operation in any place, but the disadvantage of a shorter film run than those cameras operated by battery power. We later added a 500 mm. telephoto lens complete with cradle—a tremendously powerful combination for some specialized kinds of study, but very heavy and awkward. This combination was so sensitive to vibration that even when used with a heavy tripod, heartbeats would be recorded on the film if the camera or tripod handle was gripped too tightly in the hand. Two Pro-Junior tripods with ball sockets and friction heads and a pair of General Electric light meters completed our moving picture equipment.

As a supplement to this cinema equipment we carried two 35 mm. still cameras, a pair of Exakta reflex cameras with interchangeable lenses up to 400 mm. telephoto, although we did not use the latter very much. The most effective telephoto for this camera is the 200 mm., which allows considerably more focusing latitude and additional speed. Charlie later acquired a magnificent 4 x 5 Linhof press camera, which he used for very specialized studies of an environmental nature.

All of the late winter and early spring of 1961 was spent in detailed planning for the coming expeditions. This was not new to me, for my years as an outfitter and guide required the same kind of planning, although it dealt with nothing like the scope of country.

My old hunting territory was merely an almost invisible speck on the map by comparison—a speck lost in the midst of an immensity. We were now looking at a hunting territory covering hundreds of thousands of square miles, where we could easily go astray and waste much time in fruitless search. I wrote dozens of letters to friends and connections, including government game officials and guides and hunters with experience in various areas. Details of information thus collected were checked and cross-checked until finally a pattern began to emerge revealing definite concentrations of grizzly population on the maps. We had the huge advantage of all camera hunters, for there were no closed seasons, bag limits, or any kind of restriction to hamper our operations, even in the National Parks.

As we planned to make use of the rivers to reach some suitable country in the Yukon, it was necessary to have a boat and motor for this kind of wilderness travel. Here we had to use care in our choice; for not only were boats on the fringe of our experience, but our demands were specialized. Thanks to a good friend in Winnipeg, we found a suitable craft—an aluminum fourteen-footer of excellent design with built-in plastic foam to keep it afloat in the event of a spill. We purchased a twelve-horsepower outboard to go with this boat and thoroughly tested the combination in waters near our home. It proved even better than we hoped and was virtually impossible to upset.

Finally we were ready to go.

Mid June found us in the Roger's Pass country of Glacier-Revelstoke National Park, in the heart of the Selkirk Mountains of central British Columbia. At this time the Trans-Canada

Highway was under construction, and we hoped to film some of the heavy grizzly population in this mountainous area before the flood of tourists introduced the usual complications. We also wished to record, if possible, the effect of the intrusion of heavy industry.

Leaving our car at Golden, on the western foot of Kicking Horse Pass, we loaded our gear on the train. It snaked us down the Columbia valley between the feet of the green-mantled mountains to cross a bridge and wind upgrade alongside the turbulent Beaver River. Up and up we climbed until it seemed the train would defy all laws of gravity in its last pitch to top Rogers Pass. But then it was swallowed by a mountain, and we rumbled in stygian darkness through the bowel of the five-mile-long Connaught Tunnel. We came out into brilliant sunshine at the other end to come to a stop at Glacier Station, a stone's throw from the tunnel's mouth.

Here we were met by Dale Morino, a keen young man of the Warden's Service who kindly offered to move us and our gear to our campsite. As we made the short drive, we could see that this deep-snow country was just recently out of its winter blanket. This is rain-forest country with a heavy annual snowfall of over five hundred inches in some places. Winter snows accumulate to such a depth that big game population is largely confined to mountain goats and grizzlies, with only a few, scattered pockets of deer and moose in the lower reaches.

We set up our tent on a little bench on the edge of the roaring Illecillowaet River not far from the ruins of the old hotel, Glacier House, that had been the mecca of North American and European climbers forty years before. The cottonwoods were just bursting into leaf. Here and there dirty remnants of snow still lingered in the shady places, flanked by natural gardens of glacier lilies and spring beauties. A robin sang his heart out, proclaiming his nesting territory in a tall cottonwood over our tent. A hundred yards away on a snowdrift were the great, muddy, clawed tracks of a grizzly.

In every direction sharp peaks cleaved the sky, their towers reaching from four to ten and twelve thousand feet above sea level—sharp fangs so steep that the ever-present ice cannot cling to their higher slopes except in pockets. These hanging glaciers spill off cliffs to fall in glittering chunks into the rough moraines below. The shoulders of the mountains were draped in great masses of snow—some permanent, some melting every year. Viewing them from a distance, we could see the falling streams glistening silver in the sun.

Our first days were spent exploring the country, for we had to find not only where the grizzlies were ranging in the greatest numbers but also the most suitable locations for our cameras. To be successful where big timber and brush fills the lower valleys, it was necessary to find a spot where the bears feed in the open. The most logical places were the permanent avalanche tracks down which every year millions of tons of snow come roaring, sweeping everything away except the stubborn, clinging clumps of alder brush. Because such places are open to the sun, they green up first in the spring and are favorite grazing grounds of the big bears.

So we picked up our packboards and tripods every morning and headed up along trails following the valley bottoms toward high ice and snow. The weather was unusually hot, and the whole country was running with water. Tiny rivulets tinkled merrily over the moss between the trees and down the trails. Roaring cascades and beautiful bridal-veil falls plunged and played on the cliffs below the ice and snow fields, weaving and braiding themselves into thundering rivers. Many of these could be crossed in the early hours of the morning but by afternoon were savagely impassable. We treated them with the greatest respect; for they were so swift and precipitous that if a man lost his footing while fording, he would be instantly smashed and drowned among jagged rocks and snags.

The Illacillowaet was in full flood. In the mornings it was impressive, but in the afternoons and evenings it was awe-inspiring. Not only were its waters going downhill about as fast as water can go, in wild, unbroken, frothing leaps, but it was also moving thousands of tons of rocks. From mid-afternoon till the small hours of morning the constant grind and rumble of boulders rolling down its bed was the deep bass accompaniment to the rushing roar of the flood.

There was bear sign everywhere, but the hot breathless weather drove them into the deep timber in the daytime.

The unaccustomed noisy activity of the road construction was having inevitable effect on the lives of the grizzlies. One morning at sunrise we found the tracks of a big sow with a two-year-old cub not far from our tent. They led up the Illacillowaet Trail, where we followed in hopes of finding them on the open slides farther up the valley. But the she-grizzly never deviated a step from the trail or paused. Their tracks led on past the Asulkan Forks toward high country. We trailed them high onto the seemingly limitless expanses of snow until it became obvious that these grizzlies were quitting the country completely and were heading for new range across the mountains.

Dick and Charlie were like hounds on a hot scent. Hating to quit, they climbed high onto a naked rocky comb sticking up out of the snowfield, hoping to spot the bears lying up somewhere on the cool snow. But there was no sign of them other than tracks leading over the horizon; so the boys reluctantly came down to where I was waiting in a long, sizzling glissade with the slush flying in showers off their climbing boots.

That night Dale Morino visited us in our camp, and while we cooked supper, he laughingly told us of an adventure of the kind that keeps a warden's life from getting boring.

Six or seven miles up the broken scar that was to be the Trans-Canada Highway there was a big construction camp just over the summit of the pass. This camp obtained its water supply from a stream dropping down off the mountain behind it. A small catch basin had been constructed and a large part of the stream diverted into a pipe made from sections of road culverting bolted together, which pitched steeply down about 150 feet into camp. There sufficient water was bled off to supply the needs of the men, and the rest ran off into the steambed below. The pressures generated were considerable.

One morning the plumbing in the camp suddenly went dry. The bull cook reported the condition to the camp superintendent, and together they climbed up to investigate the intake. They were amazed to find a roly-poly black bear sitting on the top end of the pipe yelling his head off as he thrashed and squirmed. Seeking relief from the heat, the bear had apparently been using the catch basin for a bathtub, and the suction grabbed him by the rear and firmly buttoned him tail first into the pipe. He was a very embarrassed and frightened bear, obviously most displeased with the advent of modern plumbing.

The superintendent radioed Dale: there was a bear stuck in their water system, and would he please come and do something about it? Hardly able to credit his ears and wondering if his leg was being pulled by some kind of practical joker, Dale piled into his truck and went to investigate.

When he saw the bear acting as a somewhat unwilling though effective cut-off valve, he could not help but laugh. The backed-up water was spilling over the dam, and from the middle of the pool the bear's head stuck up, twisting and weaving as the animal frantically struggled to escape. Wondering just how best to go about removing a bear from a pipe, Dale went closer. The bear became truly inspired in his efforts to get away. Digging and clawing for a grip, he must have got his claws hooked into something solid; for he suddenly popped out of the pipe like a cork coming out of a champagne bottle and went streaking away into the timber at high speed.

Watching him go, the superintendent marveled, "Now, ain't that something to tell your grandchildren!"

Dale agreed that it was, and knowing a little about excited bears, further suggested that it would not be a bad idea to open the taps down in camp and let them run awhile.

The bears' experience with this noisy intrusion of man into their mountains was not all one-sided. There were a score of bulldozers working the length of construction in the pass. These monstrous yellow mechanical beasts were the most modern of their kind. But strangely enough every one we saw had no upholstery on seat or arm rests except that improvised from old clothes and scraps of canvas. Somewhat mystified, I asked the company's purchasing agent for an explanation.

Laughing a bit ruefully, he told me that the grizzlies tore up the seats of the tractors as fast as they were replaced. With the cost running to about $80 per seat, the company had given up; for every time a tractor was parked for a few hours unattended, the bears seemed to delight in tearing out the upholstery.

Apparently either they were attracted by the salt from the drivers' sweat that soaked into the cushions, or this is another example of the bears' great curiosity. A bear examining a cat by the light of the moon would find only one portion of it vulnerable to claws and teeth. Likely the upholstery gave off a satisfactory ripping noise to further engage the bear's curiosity. Maybe the grizzlies were just expressing their displeasure with these great, noisy, stinking iron monsters by leaving tooth and claw marks in the only soft place they could find. In any event, tractor seats were a strange taste for bears to develop.

Speaking of strange tastes, this was only a part of the story. The previous fall, when initial construction had been stopped by bad weather, several hundred pounds of dynamite was cached in a roof-covered dugout. Attracted by the smell of the explosive, the grizzlies had broken into the cache and eaten a large portion of the dynamite with no visible ill effects.

Avalanche experts experimenting with control measures in the same area had planted several charges wired and fitted with detonators in strategic spots high on the slopes. These were to be blown later in the winter, with the idea of bringing down the accumulated snow before it achieved damaging proportions, but all the charges failed to explode. Subsequent investigation showed that the bears had also eaten these.

One often hears grizzly bears being described as "pure dynamite," and it was a bit disquieting to think of meeting one literally loaded with the stuff.

It was tantalizing to wander the trails among these towering mountains and see fresh bear sign in quantity almost every day but no bears. How many saw us is a question, but likely far more than we supposed. We read track stories of fascinating content. We gathered excellent environmental records with our cameras, but this did little to satisfy our appetite to shoot some good grizzly film. The snow was going fast, and in hopes of finding a grizzly or two above timberline, we climbed high to hunt the alplands.

Leaving camp at sunrise one morning, we hiked up the pass to the mouth of Connaught Creek. There we took the trail up a side valley through deep timber toward high country. A mile or so along our way we suddenly cut into the fresh tracks of a huge grizzly heading our way. Perhaps he had got a sniff of us and had gone into the timber to let us pass. Finding him in the thick stuff was out of the question, so without comment I continued on in the lead. Scattered snowdrifts straddling the trail showed the deep indents of bear tracks here and there. The snow made the going harder and harder, and I found myself wishing that the tracks led in the opposite direction so that there might have been some hope of reward for the hard work.

Charlie's thoughts must have been going the same way. Scrambling from a waist-deep drift, he drily remarked, "Either this bear has his feet screwed on backwards, or we are going the wrong way."

At noon we came out at timberline on the lower edge of a great, tilted alpine basin couched at the foot of rugged, snow-draped mountains. Strung out in full view to the north and west was an impressive line of peaks: Ursus Major, Ursus Minor, Grizzly Mountain, and ahead Bruin's Pass. The names were suggestive of what early cartographers had seen here and highly encouraging to three weary grizzly photographers; but the only bear sign visible was the smear on the snow, where the grizzly had come tobogganing down off the pass earlier in the day.

We ate lunch in the cool green of a moraine sticking up out of the snow before climbing to the top of the pass. Rank on rank of high, ice- and snow-hung fangs stuck up in the crystal air as far as we could see under a cloudless sky in every direction. Mile upon mile of sprawling snowfields and glaciers glittered and shone under a brilliant sun.

The snow- and ice-choked upper reaches of Cougar Creek valley were below us to the west. Flanking it to the north were a series of great steps—an ancient moraine now greening up in early summer. Here our glasses picked up bunch after bunch of goats lying indolently in the hot sun. From their lazy, carefree attitude it looked as though they had been undisturbed for a long time. No big dirty tracks in the snowdrifts indicated the presence of grizzlies.

The sun was beginning to throw long shadows when we finally tore ourselves loose from this vast mountain panorama and slid down the steep western approach to the pass. For a while we lost the trail completely under the snow and then encountered a mess of freshly avalanched timber and dangerously hidden cliffs. Packs that were not light in the morning now grew heavier. We were bone tired when we finally came down into the topsy-turvy creek botton far below the pass.

Here the creek rushes from snow caves into the open and dances briefly in the sun before going to ground in a hole in the solid rock on the side of a ridge. Behaving as no stream ordinarily conducts itself, it shortcuts under the ridge by natural tunnel, reappears for a short distance on the far side in a canyon bottom, and plunges underground again into the mile-wide Nakimu Caves. As we walked past a couple of portals of this cavern, its blackness was absolute after the vistas of shining mountains.

After twelve hours of hard hunting we had seen nothing except the tracks of the grizzly "with his feet screwed on backwards." Even here in the middle of a great national park there was no doubt that the grizzlies' normal activities were being upset by human intrusion. At every camp there were open garbage pits upon which the bears were learning to feed. Consequently they were not using the avalanche tracks.

Two weeks of continuous hunting had produced only footage and photographs of habitat. Reluctantly we were forced to concede defeat. With the weather becoming warmer as summer progressed, there was no choice. Next morning we boarded the train for home.

Upon arrival at the ranch immediate preparations for an extensive pack train trip went into action. Horses were rounded up, packs made up, and everything moved over the summit of the Divide at Akamina Pass, twenty miles to the southwest, to our old Sage Brush Camp—the jumping off point for many previous hunts with guests. The cook tent was pitched with one end of the ridgepole tied to a big pine—a grizzly's rubbing tree. From this primitive backscratcher there was a set of big tracks pressed into the grass and pine needles which led right through the tent.

My good friend Clarence Tillenius, one of the world's foremost wildlife artists, joined us at this camp. He was working on a commission to paint the dioramas for the big-game groups being set up in a new wing of the National Museum in Ottawa. Among these he was planning the background for a grizzly group and was most anxious to obtain a suitable setting close to the Alberta–British Columbia border in these colorful mountains.

Kay was with us as official cook, a most welcome addition to the crew. Naturally daughter Anne was with us, too, vibrating with the excitement of joining in our grizzly hunt. Our third son, John, joined us to guide two fourteen-year-old boys, Tom Rankin and Del Marting, from Cleveland, Ohio. I planned to use this active trio for scouts to cover the high country and also to provide fresh trout for our camp.

Almost immediately more grizzly sign was found. About a mile downvalley from camp there was a mineral spring at the site of the old oil prospect hole drilled in 1908. The strong-smelling sulphur water is a great attractor of all kinds of big game—so desirable that I have seen moose wade Akamina Creek to drink from it. Our horses were attracted to it, too, and the morning following our arrival Dick found them near this spring. On the way back to camp he spotted the place where a grizzly had ambushed sheep and goats, described in an earlier chapter.

Traveling high country by pack train successfully requires some important features of terrain. Each camp location must above all have plenty of feed for the horses plus shelter, wood, and water for the tents. Because the timberline country was just emerging from the winter snow, our initial reconnaissance was concerned with finding these in good bear country.

My journal for July 7, 1961, reads:

Clarence, Dick, Charlie, and I rode up Grizzly Gulch this morning toward Starvation Pass. The trail through the heavy timber of the lower valley was wet and boggy. Although fallen trees had to be chopped out of the way in several places, we managed to get though to the foot of the pass without undue difficulty. Fresh grizzly tracks were seen in several places along the trail. The open face of the pass was still deep in snow in many places, but the drifts were hard enough to carry our horses. We topped out on the summit about noon to find the basin on the southern exposure almost free of snow with a good cover of new grass on the meadows. The alpine parks were a vivid green and just coming into bloom. There were the tracks of a big bull moose crossing the pass. While we ate lunch, we located seven goats feeding on the shelves below the glacier on the face of Sawtooth. The Starvation Lakes were free of ice. Investigation of my old hunting campsite revealed our tent poles in good shape where they had been stacked on end under the big trees. Arrived back in camp at 8:30 p.m. to sit down to a wonderful dinner: soup, baked ham, boiled potatoes, carrots and peas, canned peaches and cream, along with plenty of hot tea. Although at home on the ranch this would be ordinary, here in the mountains it was a delicious feast.

We moved camp the following day. From the tents we could look out on the north face of Sawtooth Peak, dropping an almost sheer four thousand feet to the emerald-blue jewels that were the Starvation Lakes far below. Our hanging basin was surrounded by jagged peaks. A clear stream ran merrily past the cook tent. Grassy, terraced benches afforded plenty of feed for the horses, and by throwing a couple of logs across a narrow place in the trail on the pass, we had them effectively fenced into the basin.

Next morning we shouldered camera packs and tripods to set out toward the razorback ridge rimming the basin to the south. We went along a broad shelf among feathery larches, past pocketed meadows unfolding to some of the most rugged mountain country in the world.

These mountains are very colorful, shades from brilliant yellow and ochre to rich, deep rose. Some of this color comes from rock lichen painting the stones brilliant Indian yellow and orange in curious, maplike formations. The softer shades are in the rock itself—sedimentary rock laid down as silt in the bottom of a great ocean when the world was young. After these waters receded, the crust of the earth buckled in a great upheaval of overthrusts, anticlines, sinclines, and faults, and thus the mountain ranges were born. Resulting pressures and great heat brought about metamorphic changes shown in great variation of color. As proof of its origin, we often found the stone matrix of ripple marks made by the lapping wavelets of silty beaches. Collectively it was a color photographers' dream come true.

At every step our boots crushed brilliant alpine blooms. Glacier lilies, spring beauty, Indian paintbrush, alpine gentian, saxafrage, heliotrope, rosewort, and forget-me-nots blended with a host of others into natural rock gardens through which fountains of clear water played. Our trail led us up over rocky ledges, past a roaring waterfall, into a high basin just beginning to clear of winter snow. Here we nearly stepped on a mother rock ptarmigan almost invisible against her background in summer plumage. She was sitting on two fluffy, newly hatched chicks. We promptly named this place Ptarmigan Valley.

The face under the rim back of this basin was s semicircular wall fifteen hundred feet high broken only by a narrow ledge like a slightly winding staircase without a hand rail. A heavy goat trail led us up onto the foot of this. The ledge was littered with goat sign, and in one spot we found the week-old track of a grizzly. This was a regular thoroughfare used by these high climbers to cross the ridge. At the top of the rim we squeezed through a narrow crack in the rock and came out on another broad ledge overlooking a vast sweep of country beyond.

Not wishing to clutter this place with our scent, we sat down with our glasses to watch. Below us in the middle of the valley stood the Nunnatuk, a spectacular monument of rock standing like a giant tombstone a thousand feet high where it was carved by a passing glacier long ago. Across from us loomed the great square bulk of the Ball Park. At our level near its flat top, we could see the natural amphitheater lined with short alpine herbage looking like a well-kept lawn. This natural bowl, from which the mountain got its name, is big enough to seat thousands of spectators overlooking the flat bottom, where a ball game could be played. At our feet and a bit to the right we looked out through the great open gate of an unnamed pass at the majestic Kintla and Kinnerly Peaks of northern Glacier National Park across the International Border in Montana.

All this is wild and beautiful country full of big game in the high alplands at this time of year. Almost immediately we saw seven large mule deer bucks lying placidly chewing their cuds among gardens trapped between lingering snowdrifts directly below. Farther down the valley by the Nunnatuk five bull elk loafed on a green meadow under the spreading limbs of alpine larches. Looking over my shoulder, I found myself gazing into the whiskery features of a mountain billy goat. He was sprawled indolently on a narrow ledge under an overhang to one side of the notch in which we sat, and he was not sufficiently alarmed by the sight of us to bother getting to his feet. If we were to find grizzlies in the Rockies of southeast British Columbia, this was the place. While Clarence sketched, the boys and I combed the country with our glasses looking for bear, but none appeared.

Toward evening the giant stage of the mountains to the west was obscured by a lowering curtain of black clouds, which was our cue to come down off the rim in a hurry as thunder growled along the ridges. We made the shelter of camp barely in time to escape a downpour of rain and sleet accompanied by terrific explosions of thunder with lightning leaping and crackling overhead. John, Tom, and Del had come up from the lakes just minutes ahead of us with a fine catch of trout. We sat down to a feed fit for kings while rain drummed and roared on the cook tent roof.

All night long the thunderheads marched across the mountains. Sometimes the tents were lit for minutes on end by flickering blue-white lightning flashes in a crazy dance among the peaks. Kay and I watched the pyrotechnical display of nature gone wild through the open flaps of our tent. It was like trying to sleep during an intensive artillery barrage. It was a mountain show to put a man in his proper perspective. Sometimes the concussion of giant explosions shook the solid rock beneath camp. There would be a simultaneous flash and a sharp snap followed instantly by an earsplitting explosion, and then the long, heavy, rolling echoes cannonading through cliffs and canyons—a mad symphony of fire and giant drums. It was the beginning of a long stretch of such weather that was to harass us for the entire trip.

But next morning the sun broke through the clouds, bright and clear, to light up a bejewelled world glistening with dripping water. Across the canyon below the glacier twenty-one goats fed placidly on the hanging meadows among the cliffs. The stream draining the glacier ice was swollen, and after a short precipitous gambol down over the ledges it plunged over the lip of a cliff. There it played gracefully, a natural veil of crystal drops lifting and blowing in the wind, undulating, sometimes almost disappearing and then steadying to form a shining curtain falling into the depths far below. It was hard even to imagine the conditions those goats had endured during the night on that exposed face, but these phlegmatic animals showed no effect other than being washed snow white.

While John and his friends scouted the mountain ridges, we went back repeatedly to our lookout point above the alplands by the Nunnatuk to watch for a grizzly. Sometimes we froze on our lofty perch in chilly winds. More than once thunderstorms drove us half-drowned for cover. We luxuriated in the sunny spells when the mountains slept peacefully under sailing clouds.

We used every opportunity to film various sidelights to the story, for the grizzly has many associates. There were tiny, fast-moving pikas busily scurrying among the rocks, busily putting up hay for the winter months. We caught the beautifully marked, golden mantled ground squirrels in our lenses and recorded the rock ptarmigan. For a full day and a half we were in the midst of a great migrating river of monarch butterflies—millions upon uncounted millions of these handsome insects all flying in a southwesterly direction along the face of the mountain. We could not help wondering how far they had come and where they were going.

Day after day went by with our watching unrewarded by the sight of a grizzly. Clarence sketched continuously. We envied him a bit, for he could capture the changing moods of the mountains on his canvas, and when a scene particularly appealed to him, he could quickly create a burly grizzly standing in spectacular pose. Our films would not respond to things we had seen in the past.

Then one morning our luck began to change. Upon climbing up onto our ledge, we immediately spotted a buck deer lying dead on the edge of a snowdrift below. Two well-fed coyotes moved around the carcass. We guessed that they had either made the kill or had hijacked it from a cougar. If the smell of venison rapidly getting high in the warm sun caught the nose of a grizzly, we were due to see our jinx broken.

Two more full days went by, and still no grizzly appeared. We were beginning to feel a bit edgy, for time was running out. Almost two months had passed since we had started our hunt, and as yet we still had to shoot a single picture of a grizzly. Our supplies were running low.

The third morning following our discovery of the kill dawned clear as crystal. The air was sharp and cool, heralding an ideal day in the high country. As we checked the camera packs after an early breakfast, I had a strong hunch that something was about to break for us, and I led out along our trail feeling lighthearted.

My premonition was a good one, for when we looked down off the rim, the buck carcass was gone. Our binoculars revealed big dirty grizzly tracks crisscrossing the snowdrifts. Then I spotted a velvet-covered antler sticking up out of a familiar-looking pile of fresh-dug rubble.

Dick hissed softly through his teeth and pointed just as a fine, big, dark-colored silvertip grizzly appeared directly below coming out from under an intervening bulge of the mountain.

He stood at the top of a drift swinging his big snout into the wind, and then he sat down on his broad rump and slid happily down the steep-pitched snow. Our cameras fairly leaped from the packs onto the big tripods.

The bear went down almost to the jagged rocks at the foot of the drift, then he stood up and set his claws and turned in a shower of slush. By the time I got my lens on him, he was climbing back up the coarse talus slope. The sun was slightly in front of us, and its reflections off the snow patches made for tricky exposures. The wind was eddying, so we dared not try to get closer.

While the grizzly veered across a strip of talus, I followed him with my telephoto lens out onto another snowdrift. We kept both cameras trained on him, hoping for another slide, but instead he climbed up to a hole just under the cliffs where the snow had melted away from the rock and began to roll in it. The heat was bothering him, for he subsided into this cool niche on his back with all four feet sticking up. He presented a ludicrous contrast to the usual picture of a grizzly, and apart from his paws and nose we saw little to record.

Meanwhile the sun climbed higher to beat directly against the face of the mountain until it was like a reflector oven. Then the two coyotes showed up, coming across the pass at a business-like trot toward their hijacked booty. When they came under the grizzly's cache in a patch of shintangle brush, they set up a terrific yapping and yowling that sounded more like six coyotes than two. The grizzly jerked himself into a sitting position with his ears cocked. Perhaps this noisy addition to discomfort from the heat was a bit too much to stand, for he suddenly erupted from his snow bath and tore diagonally down the patchwork of snowdrifts at a long angle toward the Nunnatuk. Taking jumps yards long, with the snow leaping in showers over his back every time his feet came down, he covered at least a mile in short minutes and finally disappeared into the heavy timber far down the valley. Even though the buck carcass was buried beyond their reach, the coyotes were apparently delighted at this precipitous exodus of the robber baron, for they proceeded to celebrate his departure by gamboling like pups, chasing their tails and each other, rolling and romping in the snow.

Although we waited until sundown, the bear failed to reappear. The remains of the deer could not last long under this combined attention, so I planned to come back very early the following morning. Our camp grub supplies were almost gone, and it was necessary to move out next day.

Before dawn I was back on the mountain, climbing fast, and I reached the rim just as the sun was tinting a few high puffs of cloud over the peaks a pale pink. There was no sign of the grizzly, but as usual the magic of this moment was irresistible, and I stood entranced. Like the soft playing of distant strings the sky lit to a pale blue and the clouds to pink and rose. Then the tempo picked up as the waking light softly fingered the tops of the tallest mountains, turning them to deep rose and gold. One by one the lesser peaks joined in, until the sun leaped over the horizon in a great crashing climax. I stood, very small, in the royal box overlooking the great stage. The hush was broken by the long howl of a coyote from somewhere away down the far side of the pass. Then from the black shadow in the lee of an old moraine stepped the grizzly.

Quickly screwing the camera down solid on the head of the tripod, I shouldered it and began climbing down an inclining ledge toward the bear. Meanwhile the grizzly climbed up and began digging out his cache. The morning thermals were blowing up and with a minimum of luck would allow me within easy range. Then my ledge began giving trouble by dividing into a series of shallow, rubble-strewn steps, and it was only with the utmost care not to dislodge loose stuff that I was able to reach a buttress at the foot of the cliffs directly above the bear. A look through the long lens showed him feeding hungrily.

The camera had just begun to hum softly when the coyotes came drifting like gray ghosts through the rocks. The instant they came upwind, the grizzly picked up their scent and was alert. When one of the pair came over a rise of ground about twenty-five yards in front of him, the grizzly left off feeding and stalked toward the coyote at a slow walk. The coyote edged away, keeping just out of rushing range and leading the grizzly into a patch of tangled scrub firs. While the bear was thus being tolled from his cache, the other coyote slipped around behind him to steal a feed. It was a fine example of intelligent teamwork.

But this grizzly was far from stupid and seemed to realize that he was being outsmarted. He swung away from the decoy and circled back against the wind toward the kill. The feeding coyote took no chances and drifted away to join its mate. The bear was using his nose and not his eyes, for he apparently thought the coyote was still at the kill. Pussyfooting up to within twenty yards, he suddenly charged in a flash of movement to pounce on it, ready to annihilate the cheeky thief. For a few moments he stood on top of his plunder like a carving in stone, while the coyotes edged closer and closer, trying to toll him away again. But the bear was now wise to their trick and would not be moved. He went back to his feeding finally, as though coyotes no longer existed on the face of the earth.

Finishing his breakfast while the coyotes sat forlornly on a nearby drift like two disconsolate dogs, the grizzly proceeded to rebury the carcass. This was a drawn-out and very thorough process that entailed heaping hundreds of pounds of earth and rock over the remains of the deer. Using his front paws like shovels, the bear built a mound over it until the whole cache was surrounded by a sort of mote.

Then as though satisfied with a job well done, the grizzly walked out on a snowdrift to lay down and roll, scrub his face and head in the snow with obvious enjoyment. While doing this, he suddenly began to slide and went several yards on his back before rolling back up on his feet. Without another glance at the pestering coyotes, he strode off downvalley in the grand manner—proud and very dignified—toward the cool timber.

As he left, the last of four hundred feet of film ran through the camera. Knowing a charged and prolonged excitement like nothing ever experienced while hunting with the rifle, I shouldered the tripod and camera to start the long climb back to camp and breakfast. Elation made my feet light, for the first episode of grizzly life was "in the can."

Then the scene of our activity rapidly shifted.

We had driven fast far north into the wilds of the Yukon Territory, a thousand odd miles down the Alaska Highway from Mile 1 at Dawson Creek in northern British Columbia. Trailed by our own private plume of glacial dust, we came into the western Yukon, where the lesser peaks of the St. Elias Range slope off toward rolling, pine-clad hills.

It was hot and very dry—unusually so even in this semi-arid land where rainfall is sparse. One who has not traveled the north in summer will find it hard to visualize as mostly semi-desert country. The same annual precipitation a thousand miles to the south produces sagebrush, prickly pear, and rattlesnakes. Here it produces no particular feature except, on occasion, devastating forest fires from lightning.

We were driving down the long valley toward Haines Junction, a hundred miles west of the city of Whitehorse, through the hot afternoon haze when miles ahead in the midst of a vast sweep of timbered country there appeared a tall column of smoke standing straight up against the blueness of the distance like an Apache signal fire. Had it not been so ominous, it would have been pretty. Without a word all three of us knew what it meant. This expedition was due to degenerate into fighting a forest fire.

We had arranged to visit Joe Langevin and his wife, Marian, at their Forestry cabin in Haines Junction. When we arrived in mid-afternoon, it was just in time to see a Government truck coming wide open up the road from the opposite direction. It turned into the driveway of the Forestry Station, slid with wheels locked to a stop before the door, and erupted Joe. Without a backward glance he dashed into the building.

Turning to Dick and Charlie, I suggested, "Let's dig out our boots. We're going to work. Some day you can tell your grandchildren you once drove eighteen hundred miles to fight a forest fire in the Yukon."

We were lacing our boots when Marian Langevin came out

to greet us. She told us that Joe was radioing Whitehorse for help to fight the fire. Then Joe appeared, and his face lit up with a smile to temper the hard lines of concern.

Grinning at him, I said, "We volunteer! How bad is it?"

"Bad enough," Joe replied. "But if the wind behaves, there is a good chance to hold it. Most everybody around here able to fight fire is gone for the day, so you're plenty welcome. An Army 'cat' off the road is heading for the fire right now. Headquarters is sending out a tanker truck and a crew, but they won't be here till after dark."

Joe informed us that the fire had been set by a careless camper. No matter how it starts, a forest fire is cruel and devastating. Nature sets them with lightning bolts and thus cleans up old forest—a natural means of rotation. Quite likely man got his first taste of roasted meat in such a way, and very likely he learned to use fire by the same means; but now combined with his pressures, such fires are no longer beneficial. Human population has raised the incidence of fire too high.

It is one of the cruelest forces encountered in the wilds, for it kills everything unlucky enough to be caught in its path, not only by burning but also by suffocation.

I once rode up a canyon in the mountains after a forest fire had passed. The ground was still hot in places, and here and there old snags still smoked. All along the narrow valley I found the scorched husks of small animals and birds. In a couple of places there were the remains of fawns that had been unable to keep up with their mothers in the wild rush ahead of the flames.

A smoke column towering on the horizon is never an impersonal thing to an experienced wilderness wanderer. No matter which way it is heading, it carries a certain threat and air of menace even though it may look harmlessly ineffectual. Viewed at close range, even a baby fire burning out of control is the hot, crackling promise of desolation and death. So when we trailed the "cat" down onto a little blackened flat in the Dezadeash valley, we looked at this fire as grimly as we would an adversary that we intended to kill.

When Joe first saw it earlier in the afternoon, the fire was burning in the grass and scrub brush on the open flat, creeping along with its little red tongues licking up the ground cover. Now it was in the timber rimming a small swampy slough, and the tongues of flame were no longer little. It was roaring among half-dead, beetle-killed spruce, and unless we could hold it in the hollow, it could build up into a bellowing monster creating its own draft and stampeding across country for a hundred miles.

Two years previously a similar fire had almost wiped out the city of Whitehorse after coming that far on a wide front. Men who fought it told me of the futility of trying to stop it, once it began to rampage. Only a shift in the wind had saved the city. The fire came so far and so fast that even mature big-game animals had been run to earth and destroyed. Black bears were seen climbing trees ahead of it in panicked effort to escape, only to flame like torches and fall smoking into the inferno.

We did not waste a moment in attacking this fire. Joe led off through the spruces, blazing a trail for the "cat" in a sweeping arc around the front of the fire. We trailed behind with shovels, burying any spot fires from sparks that blew across the fire lane. The big tractor snorted and growled as it pushed over trees and scraped away forest debris down to the bare earth. Without water our only hope was to clear an open path through the timber and try to hold the fire inside of it.

It was hot, merciless work with no let-up. Fifty acres of ground had been blackened when we started. When we finally got a line bulldozed around in front of it, the fire had burned about three times that area.

Twice the flames, when stirred by a breeze, crowned into a sudden, roaring blast in the tree tops. Both times we thought we had lost the battle, and there seemed to be a good chance that we would get burned to a crisp ourselves. But the flames subsided without doing more than throwing some sparks across our fire line that we searched out and smothered. I found one ember that had sailed two hundred yards, where it had flared temporarily and then subsided into a mass of glowing sticks that were rapidly building up enough heat for another jump. It was too big to handle with a shovel, so I ran for the bulldozer. It arrived barely in time to avert another crown fire and buried the entire spot under two feet of earth.

For the first time in my life I looked on a bulldozer with real appreciation in wilderness country. The great, snorting monster was tireless as it did the work of a hundred men. The driver handled it with great skill as he attacked big trees and plowed them under as though they were so much grass. Had it not been for the "cat," this fire would likely have blackened thousands of square miles and burned the hamlet of Haines Junction.

But even with its help, the long hot hours passed without our knowing for sure if we could hold the line. Sweat and fresh ashes scalded our faces. We choked in the smoke and cursed people who drop live cigarettes. Finally it began to cool as sunset flared over the mountains, and the flames began to dampen down in the rising humidity. We had won. Now the fire-fighting crew could mop up.

Luck had smiled on us all around; for when we woke in the morning, it was spitting rain. We were free to move out into grizzly country; and as soon as it could be arranged, our entire outfit was loaded into a four-wheel-drive truck to be taken seventeen miles over a little-used trail to the head of Mush Lake. Here we began to relay our gear down the lake to the top of a portage on a short stretch of river pouring down a falls into Bates Lake.

The day was clear and bright with a brisk breeze stirring the lake into white caps, but we landed everything at the portage without incident. The old trail was untracked except for the marks of a big wolf, a black bear, and a huge grizzly. The latest sign of man was about two years old. We cooked supper in the open and then sat around the cheerful fire sipping hot tea while listening to the wild crying of loons. Then we rolled out our beds and stretched out under the stars.

The sound of ripping paper woke me shortly after sunrise. A black bear was busy trying to pull a side of bacon loose from the side of a grub box to which it was tied. He left when I sat up and yelled at him; but when he smelled bacon sizzling in the pan later, he came back.

Coming out of the timber at a walk, the bear approached to within twenty feet of the fire. From behind the screening branches of a little spruce he put on a most comical display of whuffing, snorting, and stamping, obviously trying to bluff me away from the grub pile. Because his hair was standing up, he looked bigger than he really was. I noticed that one of his eyes was blind, with a milky cast over it, but otherwise he was in good condition.

Then his springs ran down, for he suddenly quieted and headed into the timber again in a comical, self-conscious, somewhat shame-faced fashion, like a small boy caught with his fingers in the jam pot. While we finished preparing breakfast, the bear circled around through the timber, peeking out at us from behind bushes and trees.

We had not made any warlike gestures, and he must have come to the conclusion that we were friendly types, for a most surprising thing then happened. The bear came out of the timber toward us with head up, alertly watching. When we still made no hostile moves, he seemed to come to some conclusion, and he lay down in some low bushes only a few feet from the fire. We had an unexpected guest for breakfast.

Charlie quietly reached for his fly rod and slipped down to the river's edge. He came back in a few moments with two arctic grayling, which he threw to the bear. He was quietly appreciative and plainly asked for more. We threw him scraps, which were accepted with decorum. He licked out an empty butter tin with great relish.

While thus occupied, Charlie took his picture at a range of about six feet, and I shot both of them with the movie camera. Panhandling bears do not usually intrigue me, but this bear was no ordinary bum. He was more of a self-invited guest who had paid us the compliment of trusting us. We were convinced by this time that he had grown up in the wilds and had never seen a man before. Certainly he was not starving, for there were berries in abundance.

Clarence welcomes a quiet rest from the vicissitudes of grizzly photography (below, left). *Aggressive jaegers (attacking Dick, right) and unexpected log jams* (above) *keep things interesting between bears.*

A view from the Bates River camp in the western Yukon. In the insert is a picture of a three-year-old Alaskan grizzly.

However interesting and unusual, I know of few more embarrassing complications on a portage than a friendly bear with an exotic taste for bacon, jam, and butter. We solved the puzzle by relaying our equipment across with one man close to each end while another was traveling between. Perhaps our precautions were unnecessary, for the bear spent most of the time lying on a rise of ground midway along the trail, watching our proceedings like a friendly dog.

The last we saw of him, he was standing on a low headland watching the boat slip away down the river. We never saw him again. We sometimes wonder if he still lives near the portage, or if, trusting others as he trusted us, he came to a sudden end.

Bates Lake is about eight miles long and a mile and a half wide, a blue jewel set in magnificent mountains. Because the peaks stand back a bit from its shores, they are not overbearing, which gives the lake a charm all its own. As Charlie and I ferried the first load down its length, we were cast under its spell.

The early morning mist had burned away to leave the surface of the lake like a mirror reflecting the bordering spruce forest and mountains in sharpest detail. Our boat slid across this giant looking glass, and suddenly we had the astonishing sensation of having left the solid face of the earth to go sailing through a wonderland of sun and sky and mountains of which there was no beginning and no end.

When we finally shut off the motor and slipped the boat up onto a sandy beach down at the outlet of the Bates River, we found ourselves in the midst of a quiet wilderness where the only sounds were these of the river and a gentle breeze playing softly in the trees. The shingle along the water's edge was heavily tracked by moose, a wolf, a wolverine, a fox, a lynx, otters, and mink; and among these tracks were the great paw marks of a grizzly. Overhead the graceful arctic terns swooped and circled on brilliant wings to the plaintive accompaniment of several immature Bonaparte gulls.

We pitched camp on a little grassy flat beside the broken remnants of an old prospect camp a few yards back from the edge of the river. Here we would stay to hunt through the surrounding valleys and mountains.

This was a deep snow pocket in winter, and consequently there were no sheep and few caribou. A few miles down the Bates River, on the front of a spectacular unnamed peak at the head of Iron Creek, there was a herd of goats. Moose were everywhere in the alder and willow thickets on the lower slopes and valley bottoms. The freshest grizzly sign was found below timberline where blueberries hung on every bush growing among the alders.

Hoping to find some of the big bears out on the open alplands above timberline, we climbed onto the wide plateau southwest of the lake. Up on this great table land we found ourselves in a different world, where within an hour we could bask in warm sun or solidify in freezing winds. It was a high arctic prairie studded with rock outcrops and small glacial tarns. The ground was carpeted with dwarf willow and birch along with a host of alpine blooms, many of them similar to those found at higher altitude away south in the Rockies of our back yard. Everywhere there were legions of parka squirrels barking shrilly at us as we passed. Now and again we heard the piercing whistle of a watchful marmot from the broken boulders of the old moraines.

Mile upon mile the whole region was pocked with grizzly diggings of all ages, old and new, where the bears had excavated for the ground squirrels. Here and there all over the country were small gravel knolls and ridges—eskars of old glaciers, the favorite denning grounds of the squirrels because they were well drained, warm, and dry. These were thus also favorite digging grounds of the grizzlies. It was apparent that each fall the bears turned these gravel deposits inside out in their enthusiastic search for fat, hibernating squirrels. Each spring the small rodents repopulated these select homestead sites, not in unshakable optimism but in ignorance of the fate of former tenants.

That first day in the high country of the subarctic Yukon we sat down to eat lunch and glass the surrounding country in the midst of a great city of parka squirrels. Close to us nervous, vociferous individuals were fairly leaping in paroxysms of worry and consternation mixed with sufficient curiosity to keep them above ground. In widening rings around us the uproar faded until we were able to see squirrels going about their daily activity undisturbed. A peregrine falcon suddenly shot across the top of the plateau, shutting off the noise by driving every squirrel within eyeshot underground. The temporary lull was short-lived, and soon they were out again.

The air was like crystal without the slightest tinge of haze or smoke. In front of us the rolling tundra stretched away over the folds of ground toward the hidden reaches of the Alsek River. Across it the high frozen towers of the St. Elias Range bounding the eastern rim of Alaska glistened against the clear blue of the sky. Coming down from among these was the dirty gray flowage of the great Kuskawalsh Glacier, the biggest of all North American valley glaciers, winding down 174 miles from its source among the high mountains to its foot, sometimes damming the Alsek River. We were small dots of life wandering through this immensity—insignificant in the midst of one of the greatest remaining wilderness strongholds of the grizzly.

For this is part of the great Kluane (pronounced Kloo-waw-nee) Game Preserve, some eleven thousand square miles of rugged mountain wilderness lying between the Alaska Highway and the British Columbia boundary, bounded on the west by Alaska and on the east by the Haines Highway. It is a tribute to the far-sighted planning in years past; but it is not very carefully maintained as a preserve in the present. We found one abandoned prospector's camp with a grizzly paw bearing knife marks lying among the debris, evidence that a curious grizzly had met with bullets. Prospectors have a general inclination to shoot all bears on sight, a distressing fact with which present administration seems unable to deal. Sometimes it would appear that we still operate under the old, wasteful system where game management problems are solved by the deliberate elimination of the game.

In spite of our persistent hunting we found no bears out on the high tundra. The grizzlies were all in the thick stuff at timberline eating blueberries. Farther up all the berries had frozen.

We were plagued with bad weather, for the drought broke and the rains came down. Below camp the creek draining Wolverine Glacier went wild and washed so much gravel and loose rock down its bed that it partially dammed the Bates River. We woke one morning to find our tent awash in the flood, and we hastily moved to higher ground, muttering under our breaths while a young Bonaparte gull that had adopted us as benefactors sat huddled in the rain, watching us with bright eyes.

We wandered far when the sun gave us light. The bears were elusive, and we caught only fleeting glimpses of them at a distance. We drooled at the thought of things that might have been captured on film. We left early, full of optimism, and returned late on tired legs. We became as gaunt and hungry-looking as wolves, and we were obsessed with our hunting. Our world was one of distances, snow- and ice-hung peaks, alder hells, sunshine and storm. We endured, but still no grizzly was stalked within range of our cameras. We photographed only places where grizzlies had been.

Finally our somewhat meager grub supply began to show signs of running out completely. We were down to a diet of bannock and lake trout, and it was hardly enough to keep us going in the steady climbing with packs. Much as we hated the bitter taste of more defeat, we headed back toward the thin ribbon of civilization along the Alaska Highway.

As we went up the long trail southeast from Whitehorse, there was little to cheer us. In the late afternoon we saw a pall of smoke hanging in the distance over the Liard River valley in British Columbia's Cassiar country. In the distance the smoke cloud looked like a huge thunderhead towering on the horizon, like carved yellow ivory with its rounded cap lifting to more than thirty thousand feet. But a blue streamer blowing off its dome gave away its identity even at forty miles.

As we came in under it, the smoke became thicker till the sun was only a blood-red disk dimly lighting the gloom before going out altogether. We were driving slowly on an almost deserted road when ahead there appeared the glare of fire. The road was wide enough to afford protection from falling timber, so we went through it with the trees flaring like torches on either side. Beyond the burning perimeter there was a band where the timber still smoked and then mile upon mile of blackened, dead forest. It was an abomination of waste and ruin, stark and lifeless, a cheerless place whose streams were choked with ash and charcoal, a fantastic graveyard with black spikes of dead trees standing in mourning.

No one knew how this fire got started. No one tried to stop it. When it finally burned itself out, almost a half million acres of green, forested mountain country was charred and dead.

But we had seen only a prelude to destruction, for when we turned right at Fort St. John to go down the Hart Highway to Williams Lake in British Columbia, we found the whole country smoking fiercely. A huge blaze completely out of control was gulping timber southeast of Prince George. Twenty-eight other fires were running wild in the Williams Lake and Kamloops area. Some of these were no accident, for they had been deliberately set—some by Indians to create new second-growth willow moose pastures, others by the radical Sons of Freedom, a crackpot splinter group of the Doukabor religious sect trying to achieve recognition through arson.

We came down to Williams Lake expecting at any moment to be inducted into a fire-fighting crew by the Mounted Police, but somehow they missed us. We did not volunteer, and our consciences bothered us not at all, for it was perfectly obvious that nothing short of a change in the weather would bring these fires under control.

At Williams Lake Dick left us to return to the university, while Charlie and I turned west out along the long, winding, somewhat primitive Chilcotin Road snaking its way through the vast, remote cattle country some three hundred miles to Bella Coola at the coast. It was late afternoon when we topped the

Coast Range and looked out across the wild reaches of mountains toward the Pacific.

Consider, if you will, a broken land where the mountains leap straight up from the sea to stand with their lower flanks clad in somber green breechclouts of heavy timber, their feet warm in the backwash from the Japanese current, and their heads lost in swirling vestments of cold mist—proud, austere, and capped with ice and snow. Contemplate forests planted for giants, where the crowns of the great trees tower sometimes three hundred feet from the forest floor. Picture rivers—big, fierce rivers, some long, some short, but all with very few placid stretches and swarming with fish in the late summer and fall. Imagine jungle along the river banks as thick as anything found in the tropics, lush and lying in wait with thorns—a green tangle all sprouting and growing and dying where an annual rainfall is from a hundred to three hundred inches. Lastly conjure in your mind a river vista framed by peaks and flanked by tall timber, all looking out toward the sea, where the great bears go fishing. Then you will have some idea of the rain-forest grizzly country of coastal British Columbia.

We met Al Elsey and his guides, Dick Blewitt and Ken Stranrahan, as they were stowing a season's supplies and the gear necessary for the operation of their hunting camp up on the Owikeno Lakes beyond the head of Rivers Inlet, 180 miles by ocean to the southeast. At the same time we were again joined by Clarence Tillenius, who had flown from Winnipeg to accompany us on this phase of our hunt. It was long after midnight by the time the fifty-foot gill-netter chartered for the trip was loaded, and we pulled away from the docks towing four river boats down the sound.

Camp at the head of the Owikeno Lakes was a cabin, old and weathered, roofed with hand-split cedar shakes and thickly grown with moss. It looked like something out of Al Capp's Dogpatch, but it was dry and comfortable.

The morning after our arrival we looked out over a strip of sandy beach across the mirror surface of the lake, broken here and there by the splash of broaching salmon and the heads of swimming seals. The sun was breaking through rolling billows of mist on the mountains and lighting up a fantastic scene where the wilds stood paramount.

A quick run by boat across the lake to the mouth of the Walkwash River put us on foot up along the banks of this gin-clear stream, where the sockeye salmon were running so thick their backs were sticking out of the water in the shallower riffles. Every gravel bed had its milling host of salmon fighting for position. Grizzly tracks showed on the bars. A bear could catch all he could eat here in a few minutes. In a couple of places we found grizzlies' private dining rooms, each with its neat pile of picked and partially picked skeletons. This was our introduction to the rain-forest jungle.

The enormous trees—cedars, spruces, firs, and hemlocks—contest for place in the sun. All the mature timber is huge in scale, but certain individual spruces and firs outdo the others by growing to diameters of over seven feet. Even the lowly alder, never more than snow-twisted scrub in the Rockies, grows here to a height of at least one hundred feet, with trunks sometimes two feet in diameter.

The big timber is loaded with small epiphytic plants. A big fir can play host to a dozen varieties. A dry branch six feet long and not much bigger than one's thumb will be completely encased in a sheath of bulky moss six to eight inches thick. Mixed with the moss will be various lichens, and down the top of the gracefully bowed branch a neat row of ferns may grow. Such lush green growth covers the branches clear to the top of the trees, all adding its obstruction to the sun, so that even on very clear days very little direct sunlight filters through to the ground at high noon. One moves in a soft green light playing on the forest floor in the beautiful, weird way of fantasy wherein elves and fairies are. And everything is huge—even the woodpeckers. When one first sees one of the big pilliated woodpeckers hammering on a snag and throwing chips big enough to do credit to a carpenter, he is startled, for these glossy black birds are almost as big as crows.

In the lower reaches along the rivers the undergrowth

grows thick and rank to a depth of ten or twelve feet. To travel through it without cutting trail is next to impossible. There is a kind of thorny buck brush that grows as thick as the hair on a grizzly's back. There are high-bush cranberry, willows, birches, and cottonwoods. There is a kind of showy bracken that grows as high as a man's head with great fans like elephant ears. There are strange, exotic shelf fungi of brilliant colors and many varieties. We found one, arranged in delicate and intricate tiers two feet high and four feet wide, that was a brilliant Indian orange. Even wild rose brush grows on the grand scale; and there is also devil's club.

Devil's club is a botanical nightmare that looks like something constructed by a mad artist for some kind of animated fantasia. To the uninitiate it looks harmless enough when viewed from a distance. It has big handsome leaves that screen its weapons and give it a lush, soft look—about as misleading as a cushion stuffed with pins. Seen at close range, its stem shoots off at odd angles and is loaded with small, brittle thorns like tiny, half-straightened fishhooks, all pointing downward. There are even thorns on the backs of the leaves. All are as sharp as needles and bury themselves readily in any animal that brushes against them, whereupon the sheer genius of their design allows them to break off. They are also poisonous, and a small boil rises in two or three days around each puncture. Sometimes we could have sworn the devil's club actually maneuvered to stick us with its tiny spikes.

One does not blithely set forth and hike through the rain forest. One carries a razor-sharp machete and cuts his way through, foot by foot and yard by sweating yard. Even in the more open stretches one goes with care. I remember one particularly rank stand of devil's club encountered one morning after several hard hours of steady cutting. The plants were about twelve feet tall and spaced wide enough so that there was room to walk between, which I proceeded to do. But then I found out something new about the utter devilishness of devil's club; for when I put my weight down on a running stem between two plants, suspended between logs all artfully hidden in moss, the plant on either side suddenly snapped in to club me on both sides of the head, leaving a generous amount of thorns in my scalp.

Only in the higher reaches of the valleys does one emerge from the jungle undergrowth into open forest with its floor richly carpeted in deep moss. It covers everything—stumps, fallen logs, and rocks—and in the shadier places it harbors huge slugs.

To facilitate our travel between the open gravel bars along the rivers we sometimes used the grizzly trails. In their original form these could more aptly be called tunnels, where the big animals had forced passage through the undergrowth. As such, a man could travel them only on hands and knees, but we chopped the tops out of the tunnels with our machetes and walked them. To be sure, these trails were one-way affairs, and well I remember meeting a big grizzly on a blind corner at the mouth of a side creek one morning. It was raining, and everything was damply quiet so that neither of us heard the other. We could not have been more than fifteen feet apart when the bear caught my scent and I heard a coughing snort that froze me in my tracks. The bear exploded out of there, sounding like a boulder rolling down a mountainside. It would have been no fun to have been in his way.

Most of our travel from point to point was by boat. Besides two large freight boats used to bring in supplies from the head of the inlet, we had two river craft. One was an open design specially made for navigating fast water, with a twenty-two-foot hull and fitted with a thirty-five horse outboard slung on a steel frame fitted to the stern transom. When activated by a hand lever, this frame lifted the motor over underwater obstructions—a very excellent mechanical arrangement in white water.

Our guides' favorite boat was a posh-looking, streamlined open cruiser with a powerful six-cylinder inboard motor and jet propulsion. The big motor ran a pump that picked up water through a grid set into the forward bottom of the hull and ejected it with great force out a six-inch tailpipe. It could turn in its own length at top speed and had a very shallow draft of only five or six inches. It had two speeds—a dead stop and forty-five miles an hour—the former being particularly appreciated after a run on the river and the latter guaranteed to make the hair of the most phlegmatic stand straight on end. It sounded like a low-flying airplane when traveling, and I suspect that it scared every grizzly off the rivers upon approach, for we never saw one from it. But if you had a strong heart and a definite bent toward believing that your end would not come about in the use of boats, it was a most effective and swift way to get from one place to another on these wild waters. As I suggested to the guides, they would have needed pilot's licenses if the splash guard had been a little wider; as it was, it *almost* flew.

Traveling these rivers with this boat injected a certain aura of excitement and suspense—suspense of not knowing at break-fast time if you would still be alive to enjoy supper and excitement that started with the motor.

There was the time Dick Blewitt was tooling it upriver, going like the proverbial bat out of hell. Side-slipping around a bend and throwing water twenty feet into the air, we were suddenly confronted by two huge spruces that had fallen in the river with their heads overlapping in midstream. I expected Dick to cut the throttle or turn, but instead he hopped up on the seat, stood up for a better look with only his finger tips holding the wheel, dropped back down, booted the throttle to the floor-boards, and went roaring through a narrow gap in a sizzling S curve, just grazing a log on either side.

We were howling up another river one day heavily loaded. Three of us—Dick Blewitt, a hunter from Pennsylvania, and myself—were in the cockpit, while Charlie and Ken Stranrahan were sitting on the decked-in bow. We had been up this river a day or two previously and were not running completely blind, but when we came around a right-angle bend, we found the entire river blocked by a sweeper. A sweeper is a big tree that has fallen off the bank and spans the river, and it is well named. This one was a good eighty feet long and just awash. Dick cut the throttle, turned the boat, and slammed head on into a hidden sand bank, all in the same motion. Charlie and Ken went sailing off the bow high and dry onto the shore; I stuck my knee clear through a fancy tachometer on the dash, and the hunter painfully banged a leg. Had the windshield not been removed by a similar occurrence sometime before, we could have bitten a chunk out of it. However, the boat had a strong, double fiberglas hull and suffered no damage of any consequence.

We had not brought a saw, and I mentally wrote this day off as a loss. But Dick and Ken requested us to get on shore, and they proceeded to make a short swing downstream. Gathering speed and some room to maneuver, they came back up gunning hard for the log. Just feet short of it Dick cut the motor, and they literally slid the boat up over the log. They almost cleared it, but the powerful current grabbed the boat and hung it up by the stern. The intake grid was clear of the water, and the power was lost. The river almost rolled the boat back under the log, but in a flash both men jumped out to hold the boat bow-on into the stream. Standing on the log, they fought to push it off into the water. From where I stood, it looked like a losing battle, so I headed out to lend a hand.

I was about halfway to them, when all in the same moment they managed to wiggle the boat ahead a bit, the pump caught the water, and a rifle slipped off the front seat and slammed the throttle down. I looked up from some fancy footwork just in time to hear a roar and see half a ton of motor boat hurtling straight at me. There was just time to straight arm it and let its force throw me as far downriver as it could. I was thinking of the boat coming over the log on top of me all the way to the bottom of the river, where I arrived in good time, waders, rain parka, light meter, and all, and proceeded to head for shore. Anyone who entertains the silly notion that waders are impossible to swim with has just not been properly inspired. Try it some time in glacier water that would be frozen solid if it were not running downhill so fast. Waders do not slow a man up very much!

When I came ashore, I found everyone standing with wide grins across their faces and yelling whoops of encouragement. The boat was still on the high side of the log with its motor idling, ready to take off. After wringing some excess river water out of my clothes, we got back aboard and went on.

We made these runs up one or another of twelve major rivers feeding into the Owikeno Lakes in the early afternoons, sometimes for ten or twelve miles. There we unloaded a four-man lift-raft, inflated it, and after waiting for an hour or so to let the disturbance of the jet subside, two or three of us would float downstream in the evening.

As a contrast to the high-powered roar of the jet boat, the raft slid downstream in absolute silence. It allowed us to slip up unnoticed on animals and birds feeding along the bars, and it was about as effective a way to approach grizzlies in that kind of country as I have seen.

We got close-up glimpses of otters, seals, and deer. One evening we came floating around a bend under some overhanging alders, and from my seat on the bow I found myself looking squarely at the broad rump of a grizzly standing in the river. The swift water was carrying the boat squarely to the bear, when the big animal suddenly became aware of us and exploded straight up the bank in a shower of spray. A bit farther downriver a big grizzly stepped up on a log beside the river and looked down at us as we passed—a monstrous black silhouette against the gray, late evening sky.

Camera hunting in competition with guns was not very rewarding, for the bears were not coming down off the mountains in any great abundance to feed on the salmon. Those that did come were extremely wary and did their feeding mostly at night. Perhaps the annual hunting pressure along the bars had educated the bears. Although my experience there did not allow me any opportunity for annual comparison, I suspect that a great many more bears had been killed than the population and annual increase would support. Perhaps the hunger for profits was, as usual, inclined to kill "the goose that laid the golden egg."

In an effort to obtain some good records on film of the grizzlies feeding on salmon, we took a jack camp by boat away up into the wild and little-hunted reaches of the Neschamps River. There we pitched a silk tent under a giant spruce and proceeded to hunt on foot.

This was absolutely trackless wilderness. We carved our

own trails with machetes from our camp along the wooded banks of the river to various open gravel bars. The river was stiff with salmon and alive with birds. Hundreds of herring gulls flew up and down the open slot carved through the big timber by the river and fed on dying salmon. We saw the big fish swimming in slow, blind circles in the slack water behind logs and gravel bars with their eyes picked out, still reluctant to give up that last spark of life. It was not uncommon to put fifteen or twenty bald eagles up off a single bar within a hundred yards, where, like everything else, they fed on salmon. (If some reasonably accurate count of bald eagles were to be taken between Vancouver and the southern tip of the Alaska Panhandle, there would likely be some upping of present population estimates. It is a mistake to assume that all American eagles live in the United States.) In the slack water of pools and shallows great blue herons stalked, beaks sloped at three-quarter mast, solemn in their blue-gray garb like feathered undertakers.

The shining horde of salmon was a pulsating spectacle, permeating everything and throbbing along the river day and night. We saw them fighting their way upstream, digging their redds and mating. We smelled them dying and dead. We heard them splashing in the driving urge of procreation blindly destroying itself in the needs of their kind. It was a trading of life for the need of life, stark and cruel. Through it all, the fisheaters stuffed themselves.

Here, too, we found the grizzlies very wary of our intrusion. We had carved our way miles up into the topmost reaches of the river, beyond anything but very ancient sign of humans, yet we saw very few bears. Those that we did see we could not photograph for lack of sufficient light.

We were plagued with bad weather, for it rained almost without let-up for days. We grew accustomed to being damp, and just when we had unconsciously conceded that we had known too much rain, the sky broke open like a dirty, sagging tarpaulin ripped with a knife, and it deluged. For three days and nights it poured—sometimes an inch every hour.

Rain in a rain forest is not like rain anywhere else. For

quite a long time after it begins to rain, one is not altogether aware of it under the moss- and fern-hung trees. Tons and tons of water are soaked up by the vast arboreal canopy overhead until it can hold no more. Then it begins to rain down on the forest floor—not just drops of rain but great gobs of water that hit with a clearly audible splat—an unrythmic dirge of sound that promises to go through most any kind of rain gear sooner or later.

The river came up and up, until our boat, that had originally been tied about eight feet below the tent, now rode almost level with it, and there was only a foot of ground between staying and being flooded out.

We waited and endured. Our clothing molded onto our backs in the dampness. To dry it we built a reluctant fire against a great dead log in front of our tent. We not only dried it but also smoked it to kill the mildew. It was only by exercise of the greatest care that we were able to keep our camera equipment working. Even then some of our films showed the signs of prolonged dampness.

It had been arranged for the guides to come back with additional supplies, but no one showed up. We did not know it, but they had flown out by chartered plane to meet some hunters, and the weather came down solid over the mountains and marooned them at Bella Coola for almost two weeks.

On top of being wet most of the time, we were getting hungry. We held a council of war and decided that we would load everything in the boat and make the run back to base camp. It was not a decision made lightly; for the river channel had changed, and we knew not what hazard would be in the stretches of fast water between camp and the lake. Moreover, we were using one of the freight boats, an unwieldy twenty-eight-footer.

The morning following our decision to move out broke bright and clear. I cooked the last of our grub for breakfast, and we struck camp. With everything stowed in the boat, I took a long pole and stood in the bow. Clarence took another and stood in the stern, while Charlie cranked the motor and sat down at the controls amidship. We cast off, and in two minutes we were roaring downriver with the outboard howling to keep headway in the current. Our boat, which went under the improbable name of "Grizzly King," was wide of beam and placid of character. It was like urging a fat boy into taking up position in a marathon. Occasionally inspired, it leaped like a canoe. But then it would revert to character and wallow as reluctantly as a cast-iron bathtub.

Finding himself in trouble at the top of a steep rapids, when the Grizzly King insisted on trying to turn around, Charlie swung the wheel hard to bring its bow up into the current, gunned the motor wide open to hold it, and proceeded to run the white water backwards. Clarence and I were too busy to be scared. We pushed and pried to hold the boat off innumerable snags. We swore at it under our breaths, and salty sweat ran into our eyes. The big combers shook us, and the waiting snags showed their teeth. The sun shone, and the spray flew. Then almost magically we shot out of the river's mouth onto the mirror surface of the lake. A bit more water was sloshing on the floorboards, and we had lost some paint in a couple of spots, but the river was behind us.

Shortly before dusk we came to the camp at the head of the lakes. It was almost awash. The lake had risen almost nine feet in about three days and nights. Tired and ravenously hungry, we prepared a big supper and then fell into bed dead beat but glad to be under a roof again.

It was winter in the Yukon and late fall in the southern Alberta Rockies. Here the leaves of the cottonwoods were just turning golden, and the grizzlies would not go into hibernation till late November or early December. The prelude to winter on the coast was the increasingly heavy rains. Knowing some of the bitter taste of disappointment in spite of prolonged hunting, it was time for us to pack up the cameras and leave.

It had been a season laced with frustration in many ways, but we were already looking forward to spring, when the sun would bring the grizzlies out of den again. We had tasted the thrill of hunting with the cameras. Come another season and we would put the lessons we had learned to good use.

12. A Successful Season

Never was there an animal so fond of peace—he loves to laze and loaf in the wild places, where the sky is his roof, the mountain lakes his bathtub, the wind his newspaper, and few things are too small for him to smell or taste.
—ANDY RUSSELL

Winter was barely over in the mountains the following spring when we headed up the trail toward the summit of the Great Divide, west of the ranch. What we found on the pass was enough to make anyone pull up his horse and think about his geography. The snow was still seven feet deep in places and much too soft for pack-train travel. Twice we tried it, and both times we were forced to turn back. On the third attempt we rammed our way through and made a mid-June camp a dozen miles down the west slope along the Kishaneena.

It was a bit like falling out of the frying pan into the fire, for the snow was now melting so fast in the high country that the creeks were all roaring full. Fording the river even with horses was something to be tackled with care in the mornings and sometimes out of reason in the afternoon—if the day was warm.

The grass was lush and green down along the lower reaches of the valleys. Deer and elk grazed the park meadows in the evening and at night, sleek as fine new leather in their reddish summer coats. Moose dipped their heads into the beaver ponds and fed on the new growing shoots in the willow and birch groves. The bucks and bulls went carefully, for their heads were tender, the blunt stubs of new antlers marking the growth of their weapons for that year.

The whole valley was one vast wilderness aviary ringing with bird song. Golden- and ruby-crowned kinglets sang from top twigs of the big spruces and firs. Townsend's solitaires, robins, hermit thrushes, willow thrushes, wrens, and many others were nesting in the trees and banks along the stream. A pair of rufous hummingbirds had their tiny nest built on top of a dropping spruce bough overhanging the turbulent rapids twenty yards from the tent.

We traveled far on our horses looking for grizzly sign. We not only searched for grizzlies but also some place occupied by them where the cameras could be successfully operated. No fleeting glimpses in the timber would do for us. We had to have them in the open. Sometimes we went separately, and sometimes we hunted together. For a couple of weeks, largely due to snow and flood conditions, all we found was tracks, and these were in the heavy timber.

One day I rode several miles downriver and climbed on foot high up along a ridge separating two huge hanging basins. The only fresh signs I found were of goats and black bear, and these were all holed up on the deep shade, for the slopes faced the sun and were as hot as reflector ovens. I came down to my horse in mid-afternoon, tired, discouraged, and suffering from a splitting headache. A plunge in the ice-cold Kishaneena did considerable for my morale, but upon reaching camp I forgot all about my discomfort. Dick and Charlie had good news.

They had ridden several miles back toward the Divide and then away up onto the top of Lost Cabin Plateau, a part of a height of land dividing the Kishaneena and Sage Creek watersheds. There they had found the high country barely passable for horses, and they were forced to detour around various stretches of deep snow as they crossed the parklands heading northwest. On reaching Broken Castle—a badly rifted limestone mountain standing out by itself—they tied up their horses and climbed to its craggy top to eat lunch and glass the surrounding country.

Apart from some tracks showing up on the snowdrifts down on a saddle at the head of Sage Creek, there were no other signs of grizzlies. When they finished lunch, for want of something better to do, they pushed a big boulder over the brink of the cliff; it plummeted a thousand feet or more and then went leaping and crashing on down a long avalanche track through second growth toward the bottom of the valley.

To their astonishment the noise of its passing had barely subsided when a grizzly hidden in the timber to one side of the track opened up with some roaring and grumbling at the disturbance. Perhaps this bear blamed another for kicking the rock loose and chose to let him know what he thought of such carelessness. Or maybe he was just startled by the sudden commotion of the falling boulder. The boys did not linger to investigate further but promptly returned to camp.

We rode back up onto the Plateau the following day to look over more of the country and find a good location for a bait. It was obvious that some kind of attractor was needed to pull the bears up out of the timber into opener country, where we had a better chance to use the cameras. A mile or so beyond the slide where the boys had startled the grizzly with the rock, we found an ideal spot along a little valley in the midst of a strip of old burn. There by the small stream among scattered clumps of second growth I shot an old horse brought along for this purpose.

There was not enough horse feed on the plateau where we wished to camp; so when we moved up to a suitable site just under a big boulder field at the foot of Broken Castle, we drove all the horses out to the ranch. Loading some necessary odds and ends of food on our packboards the following morning, we headed back across the mountains on foot. When we reached the tent after a long day on the trail, Dick dropped his pack and climbed the half mile to the lookout back of the camp to look at the bait with his binoculars. He came back on the run just as I was taking supper from the fire and jubilantly announced that a grizzly bear was on the bait.

Next morning after a showery night we hiked over the ridge to the north and down into the valley. A look at the bait through the glasses from an open slope a half mile away revealed, not one, but four grizzlies loafing in its near vicinity—a sight to cheer the heart of the weary hunter.

I remember a childhood experience, when I was suddenly confronted with something dreamed about and wanted for a long time. There it was actually within reach—mine at last—but I just stood there enthralled by the sight of it, a little afraid even to move, let alone touch it, for fear the whole thing was just a dream. I felt something the same now as we looked at those grizzlies. Only one who has traveled, frozen, gone hungry, fought fire and flood, and hunted for months on end over thousands of miles of mountains with small success can fully appreciate my feeling. Would they be there when we came within camera range? Or would they vanish?

We slipped like shadows down along the slope through timber and scrub. We tested the wind and found it good. We finally edged up to a low rim of rock on the edge of the little valley for a look. The place seemed full of bears.

A medium-sized, brownish-colored boar was feeding on the bait, while fifty yards above him along the creek a sow and two yearling cubs waited their turn. They were obviously afraid to go anywhere close to the one feeding on the carcass, and they edged around a little meadow looking longingly in its direction. We slipped down under the rim, where some rocks would break our outlines, and proceeded to expose some good footage.

A roaring thunderstorm drove us to cover in the big timber a bit below and behind us about noon; and when we returned to location, it was just in time to see a fifth grizzly coming straight up the slope toward us. He swung past us as he climbed, and when he hit our tracks, he literally exploded into a galloping retreat as though booted in the tail. Another thunderstorm forced us back into cover; and when this one passed, the wind gave our scent to the only bear left in the valley. We returned to camp wet through from a third thunderstorm, but nothing could dampen our feeling of jubilation.

There are camps in wilderness country where things happen so fast that one is hard pressed to find time for sleep. This proved to be one of them. About one o'clock the following morning something invaded the tent. It was not the gum-shoeing kind of intrusion wherein one hears a little and imagines a lot. The racket would have done justice to a bull elephant, and when I came straight up in bed clutching a flashlight and reaching for my six-shooter, I was ready to defend the place. But then I remembered the boys asleep by a log out in front of the tent and left the gun lay. When I rose to investigate with a piece of stove wood, the flash revealed the satanic countenance of a trader rat leering out from between two pack boxes; whereupon I stubbed my toe, barked my knuckles on the edge of the stove, and came nowhere near killing the rat. The wily little robber finally left for the outdoors, and I went back to bed feeling the battle had ended in a somewhat less than satisfactory manner. Next to an invading porcupine, nothing is quite so destructive as a trader rat. What they do not chew to rags, they delight in stealing. When one gets into a collection of pots and pans, the resulting uproar would wake the dead.

This one was no exception. I had scarcely slipped back to sleep when again I was jolted awake by the same racket. Again we fought a short, noisy engagement, and again the rat retreated safely to the rock slide. This went on intermittently for about two hours. By the time the rat finally left for good, the eastern sky was getting bright.

I had hardly closed my eyes when Charlie woke me as he rattled the stove and frying pan making breakfast. After we had eaten, we headed back over the ridge toward the bait under a clear sunny sky.

Immediately upon arrival at our shooting location, we spotted the she-grizzly with her cubs up on a ledge on the steep slope directly across from us. She was standing motionless, gazing out across the country. Directly behind her one cub sat on the edge of the drop-off with a hind foot hanging down off the ledge. The other cub was sitting behind him looking innocent and benign. The sow then turned to look at her cubs as though inspecting them. One must have struck her as needing attention, for she went over and gave him a vigorous washing with her tongue. We were fairly drooling, for although we could see plenty of detail through our glasses, this action was far out of camera range.

When they went out to graze on a long, almost perpendicular, open meadow of lush, spring-fed growth, a fourth grizzly—a small male—showed up on the same meadow above them. It was some time before either he or the female became aware of each other, and when they finally did discover that they had company, the smaller one beat a hasty retreat. Circling wide of the sow and coming down the mountain toward us, this grizzly went into a small clump of shintangle and apparently almost fell over the big brown male we had seen the previous day. The big bear immediately gave chase across the mountain slope through alder brush and deadfalls at top speed, but finally he left off the pursuit without coming within striking distance of the intruder.

By this time the smaller bear's nerves were showing signs of fraying; as he turned back toward the bait by a very round-about route, he shied at imaginary devils all the way down into our little valley. Although he obviously wanted very badly to go to the bait, he could not at first screw up his courage. Charlie and I relayed on him with the cameras while he sashayed back and forth in a welter of indecision before he finally went in to take a fast feed. Something spooked him, and again he came toward us, walking up a series of logs. We held the cameras on him to a range of seventy feet, where his ears caught the sound of them, and almost simultaneously he got our wind. His expression of sheer, bug-eyed terror was comical. With a great sniff he swapped ends and went tearing away, ripping a hole through the scrub as he went.

Although we waited in the blazing heat all day, there was no further action till evening, when the big boar came back. But he got our wind and left again.

We arrived back at camp just in time to see a big black

bear standing in front of the tent as though undecided whether to knock or tear it down. We contrived to give him a frightful scare and saw nothing more of him.

With the coming of darkness my hopes for a good sleep were shattered by the return of the pack rat. This whiskery, sharp-nosed denizen of the boulder field had apparently come to know that I had cold-blooded murder in mind; for this time he made a real running fight of it. Every time he heard a noise from my direction, he left at top speed. Nevertheless it was an action-packed night, and by morning I felt as though I had traveled for miles. A general inventory of kitchen equipment in daylight revealed the loss of a pot scraper and a bar of soap. The rat had won the battle if not the war, and he was apparently satisfied with the spoils; for he returned no more.

It was shortly after noon before anything showed up on the bait, as we watched in turns from the lookout back of camp. When I spotted the sow and cubs, I headed out alone in a shortcut across the rock slide just under the face of the mountain to try for some pictures. On the way my foot slipped on a round rock, and I took a most spectacular spill with the great good luck of not even getting a scratch.

I arrived in time to get some shots of the two cubs playing on the edge of an elk wallow full of water. Then the sow roused herself from a nap to lead them down the creek toward the bait. They disappeared behind some scrub, and then one cub shot into view on the dead run to be followed a moment later by the other two bears. I was startled by the sudden action and thought they had got my wind. But obviously the sow did not know what to make of it either, for she reared and sniffed and looked all around. Then it was mutually discovered that the first cub was chasing a coyote.

Flying in pursuit of the little gray wolf at astonishing speed, the cub had crossed the creek up onto a flat meadow on a bench beyond. The coyote was surprised and hard pressed. He scampered like a streak up the steep slope at the foot of the mountain, swung around the top of a clump of shintangle, and headed back down for the meadow. Meanwhile the second cub had joined in the game. As the coyote shot around a corner of the brush patch, they almost collided. The little grizzly jumped straight at him and missed by a whisker with a lightning-fast swing of his paw. But in the blink of an eye the coyote leaped up and sideways about eight feet into the top of an up-tilted pan of bleached roots, where a big spruce blow-down lay.

The coyote disappeared like a puff of smoke, but the two cubs met face to face, and without pause or loss of hardly a step they piled into each other in a tail-over-teakettle free-for-all that tumbled them all over the meadow. They boxed, wrestled, tore, and scratched in every direction without let-up for several minutes while their mother sat on her broad rump contemplating their shenanigans with the greatest equanimity.

Meanwhile the coyote came sneaking around through the scrub toward the carcass to resume its feeding. Then I spotted the little grizzly of the previous day coming cautiously down across the face of the mountain. We had jokingly called him "Casper" after the comic strip character. Right now Casper was living up to the name, for he was in a fever of uncertainty; stopping, sniffing, listening, and worrying on a hair trigger of apprehension. The coyote was also a bit upset by his recent adventures, for he kept trotting out of the bushes surrounding the bait to make sure no more grizzlies surprised him. Hearing the approach of the little grizzly, he immediately ran out for a look; his sudden appearance had the most comically demoralizing effect on the bear. It was the final straw that broke the spine of what little dominance he had left. The coyote undoubtedly shared my astonishment when Casper stampeded in abject panic without another glance behind him. The coyote watched him go with sharp curiosity, then he turned and went trotting up the creek with his tongue hanging out in a doggy grin. One could almost hear him bragging to his wife and offspring about putting the run on a grizzly bear.

This grizzly's behavior was an interesting example of the psychological effect of being the lesser bear in the pecking order of the valley. Having been repeatedly run off by larger bears, and further disorganized by running head-on into us, he had lost his

self-confidence. His terrors had accumulated in his head until
now he ran from everything. In the society of grizzlies there is
some tendency toward social stratification in their dealings with
each other. We had met the lowly Casper. The following morning we met the Queen.

Following a hard rain that had continued all night into
morning, we did not get an early start. When we reached the
lookout shortly before noon, we saw a complete stranger at the
bait—a huge she-grizzly with twin cubs.

A careful approach into our shooting location revealed a
magnificent specimen in heavy winter pelage with two tiny cubs
new from the den. She was by far the biggest grizzly we had
seen—a bear with the command of royalty. She was dominant
but not obtrusive. There was a strong, quiet dignity about her
which no other bear challenged or ruffled in the slightest. She
moved through the valley around the bait with a quiet sureness.
She ignored the coyote completely and shattered Casper with a
single glance. When the big brown boar came mooching down
off the mountain, she stood up about seven and a half feet tall
and eyed him coolly. His reaction hinted at some former encounter in which he had learned the folly of argument, for he instantly retreated.

We filmed her walking down across the meandering loops
of the creek, reflected here and there with her cubs in mirror
pools. We shot the cubs playing in the water and practicing
walking a slippery, half-submerged log. To appreciate fully the
carefree atmosphere surrounding this bear family now in possession of Bear Valley, as we had named it, it was necessary to
share it. It was a revealing look into the ways of a grizzly
mother. She watched over her family with care but without
undue possessiveness. She allowed them freedom, but she obviously meant them to be obedient. There was a quiet, powerful
atmosphere of mother love around her that spoke for itself in the
very way she moved.

The cubs were small bundles of almost perpetual move-
ment. They examined everything with small inquisitive noses.
For every step their big mother took, they took many more.
While juvenile and inexperienced, it was very obvious to us that

they identified themselves as grizzlies; for they oozed the unmistakable character of their species.

With our cameras we recorded almost every move this grizzly family made. At times we were within a hundred yards of them, and we even shot them while asleep, the big mother lying on her belly with her nose on her paws and one cub sagging back against each burly shoulder.

Finally the wind spilled our scent into her nose, and she left on the gallop with the cubs at her heels.

Thereafter the big she-grizzly was extremely suspicious of the place, although she continued to come back at night for feeds of carrion. Once, while waiting, we went down into the bottom of the little valley, trying for a shot at a wolverine. Although we stayed in the open and avoided touching any bushes with our hands or clothes, she came down and immediately picked up our scent fifty yards downwind from the spot where we had waited. It was a sample of the unbelievable power of a grizzly's nose, for the day was sunny and dry, allowing a minimum of scent to linger.

In a week of continuous activity in Bear Valley we had seen and filmed eight grizzlies. The bait was almost gone. At the same time all the bears were undoubtedly aware of our continued intrusion, and they were avoiding us by coming when there was no light for photography. We had worn out our welcome here, so we left for home to get the horses, satisfied that we had at last made a start in recording grizzly life but fully aware that we still had a long way to go.

Reviewing our experiences, we had become more and more convinced that carrying arms was not only unnecessary in most grizzly country but was certainly no good for the desired atmosphere and proper protocol in obtaining good film records. If we were to obtain such film and fraternize successfully with the big bears, it would be better to go unarmed in most places. The mere fact of having a gun within reach, cached somewhere in a pack or a hidden holster, causes a man to act with unconscious arrogance and thus maybe to smell different or to transmit some kind of signal objectionable to bears. The armed man does not assume his proper role in association with the wild ones, a fact of which they seem instantly aware at some distance. He, being wilder than they, whether he likes to admit it or not, is instantly under even more suspicion than he would encounter if unarmed.

So we planned to go completely unarmed when we headed north into the wilds of the Central Range of Alaska in the region of Mount McKinley National Park a few days later. Even in the event of a charge, we theorized, a firm stand by a man who neither showed fight nor ran away would serve to throw a grizzly out of gear. Being accustomed to having most everything run from them from the time they are born, when confronted by something that does not move, it is logical to suppose that a charging bear would stop to think it over. But entertaining a good theory and putting it into practice are two vastly different things. This was particularly pertinent when dealing with angry grizzlies, for there would be small chance for second guessing. It was a kind of animal psychology that we had seen at work on occasion with other animals. For a chance to get good pictures we thought it worthwhile to try it out on the big bears.

At the far end of almost a week of dusty driving down the Alaska Highway, we turned south at Big Delta, branched off onto the Denali Highway at Paxton, and finally arrived at McKinley Park Headquarters. This national park, approximately thirty-three hundred square miles in extent, probably holds more big game than any other in the world outside those in Africa. Besides its thousands of caribou, dall sheep, moose, and smaller game, it has a heavy population of grizzlies. These bears are the mountain type, with a color trend toward the straw yellow of the tundra grizzly found in the MacKenzie Basin, sometimes known as the Toklat Grizzly after the river of the same name.

It was afternoon when we arrived, and lead-colored clouds were hanging low over the country. We could see only the great sweeps of river flats and gravel bars as we drove down the ninety miles of twisting road through the Park. Here and there were scattered small bunches of caribou sifting back from their summering grounds. Away out on the green tundra carpet of the Toklat River valley there was a big lone grizzly busily grazing.

With the clouds so low, it was something like wandering past the darkened footlights in a great theater, peaking under the lowered curtain for brief glimpses, sufficient to make one wonder what the stage setting would be like when the lights came up and the curtain lifted. We were filled with excitement and anticipation as we drove down past the park boundary below Wonder Lake and stopped at Denali Lodge to visit friends and enjoy a most memorable supper.

About 10 p.m. we drove back up the road to make camp. Coming over a rise of ground at Wonder Lake, we were treated to a sight the like of which we have never seen and most likely will never see again. Two huge Alaskan bull moose, with velvet-covered antlers that looked six feet across, were feeding in the shallows a few yards out from shore. In the arctic twilight they looked like something from the prehistoric past, huge and black, as they dipped their heads under and then lifted them to let the water cascade back into the lake. Then with dramatic suddenness Mount McKinley shrugged off the enveloping shrouds of mist and storm to emerge bathed in golden sunset—a majesty of mountain defying description.

First sight of it under any circumstance is awe-inspiring. From where we stood it was something to make a man doubt his eyes. It seemed to stand close enough to almost touch, though it was a good thirty miles away. Its huge, forty-five-mile front stood glowing in a light like the reflection of a giant mass of coals, its glittering expanses of eternal ice and snow all purple and rose. From where we stood, looking up from about eighteen hundred feet above sea level to its 20,320 foot crown, it is not only the highest on the continent but, relatively speaking, perhaps the highest in the world. Even Everest viewed from this range is seen from an elevation of fourteen-thousand feet and must lose some of its impression of height.

We stood enthralled for a few moments, then suddenly remembering why we were here, burrowed into the Land Rover for cameras. For the first time in many a year I shook with the symptoms of a case of buck fever. Grinding my teeth for control, I fought to screw a movie camera down on a tripod while Dick and Charlie wrestled with another. Somehow we got into action and captured a scene to make a photographer wonder if he were dreaming.

This was our introduction to camera hunting in the grizzly country of Alaska, something to be remembered always as having glimpsed a few moments of beauty not meant for the eyes of men.

Hunting from our camp on the Toklat River was one endless round of excitement. Never were we out of sight of game, and hardly a day went by that we did not see and photograph grizzlies. We worked in ideal surroundings, where vision was practically unlimited, the light excellent for long hours, and backgrounds illuminated like the answer to a photographer's prayer. The weather was largely good, and the atmosphere was the most brilliantly clear we had ever encountered. Mountain peaks sixty miles away showed up on the finders as sharp as the edge of a hunting blade.

Apart from the narrow, winding gravel road and its tourists the country was much as Charles Sheldon had seen it on his expeditions away back in 1905 and 1906. We were camped within a mile of his old winter cabin site, most of which had been washed away by a change in the river channel. Perhaps we saw even more game than he reported, for the pressure of meat-hungry gold seekers had long since been removed.

The days were long and full of action and interest. For August 11, 1962, my journal reads:

This morning we rose at 4 a.m. After a quick breakfast we packed some lunch and drove up the road about two miles past the Toklat crossing, where we left the Rover. Within a few minutes we spotted a big grizzly away across the valley, where he was apparently grazing in a little draw coming down the slope onto the flats. He was a long way off and nowhere between was there enough cover to hide a fox; so we headed straight for him. By watching his head and moving only when it was down, we reached a spot about fifty yards away from him, where he could be seen feeding in the bottom of the draw amongst some willows. I set my camera up and shot him just as he fed out into the open. Without pausing in his cropping of the grass, he sat down on the slope and scratched his broad bottom back and forth. Dick and

Charlie tried to cross a branch of the river a bit below me to get a closer shot, but the grizzly spotted them in the water and ran up over the top of the bank to disappear. We continued on up the valley to eat lunch on a jutting point above the river bars overlooking a vast stretch of rugged mountains. We counted seventy-two dall sheep, including twelve big rams, on the face of a pinnacle a half mile away. Shortly after we spotted a sow grizzly with a two-year-old cub, as they fed up out of a fold of ground into view. She was located on a bench in a very difficult place to stalk, so we watched and waited for her to move. While we glassed them, they began a really rough game, wherein she appeared to be punishing the cub severely but was actually very gentle. After a few minutes interval of wrestling, mouthing, and chasing back and forth, they left off to feed again. It is at times like this, when grizzlies can be observed living undisturbed in ideal habitat, that a man begins to really appreciate their most attractive characteristics. As they did not seem about to make any kind of move onto more favorable ground, we stalked them. The wind was so shifty, we dared not go closer than about a hundred and fifty yards. By this time the mother and cub were playing again, affording a chance to shoot them as they rolled and tumbled on the tundra. The wind then gave us away and sent the bears away at a tearing run straight up the mountain. She led the way up over the steepest kind of going, climbing almost perpendicular rock in two or three places, and never paused until they were briefly outlined against the sky on the summit. We returned to the car across the great gravel bars where uncounted caribou of all size and sex were running back and forth in every direction fighting flies.

This was the first of several times we observed this mother and cub. Any hint of our approach always sent her flying, for she was nervous of human intrusion into her vicinity. Observed while undisturbed, she and her cub were about the happiest, most carefree bears imaginable. Time and again over several days we saw her leave off feeding to play with the young one.

Once I saw them traveling toward some particularly desirable destination across the open flats. The irrepressible cub was feeling so good that he could not contain himself, and he ran up alongside his mother to pass her. But as he passed, he looked at her and continued to do so by twisting his head, until he overbalanced completely and fell in a tumbling heap. Immediately she pounced on him to wool and mouth him savagely, yet hardly ruffling his fur; she then left him to resume her gallop. Instantly the cub leaped up in pursuit, caught up to his big mother, disrespectfully nipped at her flying heels, and once more ran up alongside her to fix her with a stare that pulled his head around until he rolled clear over. Again she leaped on him to maul and play with him before resuming her journey. So they proceeded for about a mile, until they finally reached a huckleberry patch, where they came to a sudden stop and proceeded to fill up.

Never from one moment to the next did we know what we would see or what would happen. We were traveling up along the face of Polychrome Mountain one day when out of the blue a grizzly came barreling down onto the road right in front of us. In two jumps he was over the bank and heading straight down toward a branch of the East Fork River directly below. I pulled the car to a stop on a turn-out, and in the same motion Charlie grabbed a camera, jerked the door open, and was over the bank in hot pursuit. I started to yell a warning, but it was too late. He was gone at a tearing run down across a steep-pitched little saddle toward a pinnacle overlooking the river. The grizzly had been heading in a parallel course, but he had changed direction. The bear and Charlie met almost head-on in the saddle.

In a split second things were in a high state of tension. The bear, a small, precocious, bad-mannered three-year-old, just recently turned loose on his own in the world and afraid something or somebody would find out just how little he knew, was fighting mad. From a few short yards he took a stiff-legged plunge at Charlie with his back hair on end and his mouth wide open. Charlie stood his ground, and for a few interminable moments they argued. Then it became apparent that the grizzly wanted to find a way out of this unheard-of predicament—but without losing face, as is the inherent way of grizzlies. He solved his problem in a unique way by beginning to feed. It was a most interesting example of what might be termed "displacement activity." To cover his discomfiture and fright, he wanted us to think—and probably wanted even more himself to think—that he had come to this place to feed, and, by the little red gods, he was damned well going to feed! While we filmed him, he ate about every kind of plant that grew on that dry slope, including some unpalatable heather.

Needless to say, we were impressed and grateful, but we were also delighted when he, in a subtle sort of way, leaked out of the immediate scenery down a brush-choked chimney toward the river.

Almost immediately we spotted a big, beautiful, light-colored female with two handsome yearling cubs in a little pocket behind us. All of us were completely engrossed in shooting her when a stick popped behind us, and lo and behold! there was our erstwhile friend back again. But this time he did not linger or pass any cheeky comments; for he had apparently spotted the she-grizzly, and for some reason he wanted no further part of the vicinity. The last we saw him, he was going over the mountain the way he had come.

The country fairly teemed with game. At the same time that we were filming these bears, there were two more in sight out on the flats across the river. Thirty odd head of dall sheep ewes and lambs were feeding on a shoulder about a half mile back of us, while uncounted caribou grazed and moved for as far as we could see with our powerful glasses. A few feet away a big fat marmot looked us over from the top of his home boulder, all the while keeping an eye peeled on a lazily wheeling golden eagle. Everywhere in all directions the parka squirrels barked and chirped.

The entire region was like a vast multi-ring circus with a program that continued unbroken for twenty-four hours a day under the usually bland skies of the arctic summer. And photographers wanted to discover the reason why they were so exhausted. It was because they hated to quit long enough to sleep. Sometimes we just dropped into the green carpet of tundra to sleep awhile. We ate prodigiously, and we stopped traveling only when the weather made it impractical. We became as lean and hard as rawhide from the long hours afoot under packs. There seemed to be no beginning and no end to opportunity here, and as long as there was light and the film held out, there was always something to stalk and shoot.

Later that day, having played out the opportunities with grizzlies, Charlie and I spotted an eagle sitting on the ground high on a shoulder of Polychrome Mountain. It appeared to be dozing, so we started up to try for some pictures. This sort of thing is usually the longest kind of gambling odds in favor of getting nothing but plenty of exercise, but our luck was running gilt-edged that day. After a long climb we crept up to within twenty-five yards and got some spectacular footage of the big bird taking off and wheeling out over the darkening valley far below us.

The ever-present caribou were a constant source of interest and amusement. While traveling through the mountains we were encountering them every day in about every conceivable kind of surroundings except the sheer rock faces. At best the caribou is a somewhat pixilated beast liable to do most anything. Sometimes, especially when the nose flies are bad, they go almost insane.

Dick was watching a big old grizzly digging in a squirrel hole along the low bank of a creek one day. Suddenly out of nowhere a young bull caribou came bounding up the creek, splashing water in every direction, and passed the bear so close that he almost splashed water all over him. The bear never even lifted his head but continued with the digging as though caribou did not exist. A few minutes later the caribou came tearing back down the creek and again passed close to the bear with a great clatter. The bull was hardly out of sight before he came back again. Each time neither animal gave the slightest sign of recognizing the other. Finally whatever interest was holding the bear played out, and he moved off.

We saw and once filmed grizzlies and caribou passing within feet of each other with no reaction other than a casual glance on the part of either animal. This was long past the calving season, and the grizzlies knew that they had no chance in any kind of foot race with a caribou.

The caribous' reaction to us was ever erratic. Sometimes they would give us little more than a glance as we passed. At other times and for no apparent reason they would ogle us with utter horror, elevate their ridiculous tails, and race away as though pursued by devils. On occasion they confused their motives and made us laugh by tearing away for several hundred yards, then stopping and looking, then racing back to look at us some more at close range.

One afternoon we were coming back after a long hike, and we had stopped for a rest. Up on a peak about a mile away against the blue sky was a magnificent caribou bull with a rack of antlers like two small trees. Photographically speaking, we did not usually go out of our way to film caribou; but there was something about this one that was like grub to a hungry Indian. My ambition was dampened a bit by tired feet, but I could see that the sight of the bull standing up there against the sky was bothering Dick and Charlie. Soon they took off through a long dip to stalk him.

After several minutes, when they were well out of sight of him, the bull took off at a mad gallop straight down into a deep canyon. In a little while he came dashing up the other side and ensconced himself once more against the sky on the tiptop of a pyramid-shaped mountain. The boys spotted him there and sat down to watch.

Several minutes later the bull once more launched himself at top speed back down into the canyon. The next thing I knew, he was coming over a saddle straight at me. Caught by surprise, I barely had my camera ready when he came to a rigid stop with his head buried in a willow bush right in front of me.

I had the lens on him, watching for some movement, when I saw an ear flicker. Then the other one twitched. Gradually, bit by bit, various parts of his anatomy joined in until he was vibrating from end to end in a sort of ecstasy of discomfort—a kind of nose-fly ballet. He brought it to a sudden, jerky climax by throwing up his head, kicking up a great clod of tundra with a hind foot, and stampeding away for parts unknown.

Regardless of the numbers of hoofed game we encountered almost daily, there was no evidence of predation by grizzlies

among them. The bears did capture ground squirrels when the
opportunity afforded itself, a part of their activity which seemed
more of a lark in getting a tasty morsel than a serious part of
their feeding. We were attempting to get a shot of a grizzly with
some dall sheep in the background one morning when an unexpected eddy of wind gave us away. Immediately our film subject
took off up the mountain at a gallop. He apparently surprised a
parka squirrel away from its hole, for he veered a bit and
scooped it up in his mouth without losing a stride. The last we
saw of him on the skyline, he was still on the high run with the
squirrel dangling from his jaws.

Another afternoon I was watching a big, lone grizzly feeding out on a green island of tundra in the midst of the East Fork
River gravel bars. The bear suddenly quit his grazing and
chased after a parka squirrel. The little animal ran into a strip of
scrub brush, and when the bear plunged after the fleeing morsel,
a covey of willow ptarmigan exploded into flight all around him.
The grizzly momentarily checked his stride, and the delay probably saved the squirrel's life. To see the grizzly in action amid
flashing wings all lit brilliantly was an almost cruelly tantalizing
thing to a photographer—one of those nuggets of film material
missed due to excess range or sudden occurrence that gives no
chance to get the camera into action. But even if no record was
captured on film, I will always be able to see on my private
mental movie screen the picture of a great, straw-colored grizzly
rough-locking to a skidding stop with his head high and his ears
cocked in the midst of rocketing ptarmigan, all backdropped by
the snowy, ice-clad Alaskan peaks.

All of us had our memorable moments while wandering
among the Alaskan mountains. Charlie's twenty-first birthday
came at the Toklat River camp, a milestone he proposed to
celebrate by climbing a mountain alone. As it turned out, the
mountain climbing plan got sidetracked, but in a way that
lacked little in adventure.

He headed out early in the morning toward an impressive
set of peaks lifting their summits above the head of the river. He
left the valley on the far side and angled up the slope of a ridge

toward a high saddle. While passing a steep-sided gully, he looked down and saw a grizzly busily turning over rocks in search of bugs and grubs. It seemed that Charlie was fated to encounter precocious three-year-olds, for this was another of the uncertain-tempered youngsters.

The bear left off his rock turning upon seeing the man and headed up the slope straight toward him as though intending to treat him in the same way as the rocks. Charlie stood his ground, coolly shooting with his camera, until it was barely fifty feet away. When he yelled, the bear stopped, hesitated, and growled before turning to head back down into the gully. When Charlie resumed his climb, the young grizzly walked along parallel to him at a range of a few yards, growling and rumbling to himself. A quarter of a mile up the mountain the unpleasant animal discovered some squirrel holes that captured his attention. Charlie was not sorry to see the last of him.

From the summit of the saddle he spotted the same twelve rams we had seen before on several occasions. They were feeding and loafing on a steep slope a half mile ahead, so he took the opportunity to try for some pictures. But the rams were spooky and proceeded to lead him on a merry chase over rock slides and cliffs, always tantalizingly close but keeping just out of good camera range. Under lowering clouds with rain spitting down intermittently Charlie persisted, and finally just as a storm broke, he obtained his first good shots. As the rain came pouring down, he took shelter in a shallow cave with a sloping floor under an overhang at the top of a talus fan, where he ate lunch and then fell asleep. He woke with a great start rolling down the rock slide in the rain—a somewhat strange and unusual place to fall out of bed. Again he stalked the rams, and now they were more cooperative, allowing him to obtain some grand photos with spectacular backgrounds.

Late that night Dick and I looked out from the tent door through the stormy gloom and saw Charlie coming away out across bleak, cold flats. It was blowing and raining hard in scudding gusts of icy water that penetrated everything. By the time Charlie arrived in the cheery warmth of our tent, I had the soup pot steaming hot and fresh tea brewed. He was soaked to the hide, famished, and tired; but he was wearing a grin that spoke of rare sport and grand hunting among the crags.

The pattern of adventure is never constant. When one hunts grizzlies with a camera, it is not necessary to court it, and at the same time there is no point in being brash. We gambled a bit on occasion, but the risks were calculated; the successful gambler does not ignore the odds or step too far beyond the bounds of safety. To invite trouble was not our way, for it would have been unfair to the big animals we studied. We had no wish to cloud further their history by becoming unpleasant statistics. But careful as we were, there were times when we slipped a bit, and then things could go wrong lightning fast.

Dick had occasion one day to give our theory about charging grizzlies a really thorough testing. He and I spent part of a morning scouting up a fork of the Toklat above camp; but when a storm began rolling in over the mountains, I headed back. Dick proposed to do some exploring by climbing over a rugged spur range toward Sheldon's old winter cabin and returning from there to camp. It was a long tough climb and late afternoon when he showed up, somewhat shaken, still looking a bit grim after a hair-raising experience.

He had been coming down a long, steep tundra slope above the river, tired, hungry, and perhaps thinking more of camp than where he was heading. Ahead of him a pile of rocks stood up, and instead of swinging to look behind it, he thoughtlessly walked right up on top of it and thereby broke a rule.

Not more than twenty feet beyond, a grizzly was feeding in the midst of some berries. He was just as scared, astonished, and embarrassed as Dick; but he recovered first and charged with a bawl of anger straight up the rock pile. Dick was carrying a sheep horn he had picked up on the mountain. He stood his ground, and lifted the horn overhead, he told the grizzly in strong language that if he came one step farther, he would brain him. It was a desperate bluff, but the grizzly stopped eight feet away. Then for about thirty seconds—perhaps the longest half minute Dick will ever live—he and the bear faced each other and argued in angry tones.

The bear finally broke off the exchange by backing slowly down off the rocks, then sidling away for several yards, grumbling and growling steadily about the bad manners of those who surprise grizzly bears at close range. Finally he quieted down and began to feed again in a berry patch about two hundred yards away.

Dick sat down and shook for a while before resuming his journey to camp. It had been a frightening experience, but as is usually the case, it could not be blamed on the bear.

Right here I may as well confess that in telling of various incidents involving grizzlies, my references to their sex are largely guesswork when dealing with single bears. When speaking of a grizzly with cubs, it is correct and accurate to describe her as a sow or a female. But when speaking of a single bear, my reference to gender is more convenience than proven fact. Except for size—and this is not always a reliable way to separate the sexes—one lone grizzly bear looks just like another in general outline. Aside from feeling of them—an understandably unthinkable liberty—I know of no sure way to tell a sow from a boar in the field.

Dick's close-quarters argument with the grizzly did not deter him in his avid pursuit of good bear pictures. One morning not long afterward we were traveling up toward the summit of what we called Jaeger Pass when we spotted a big old grizzly busily feeding on berries out on the edge of the open gravel beyond some strips of willows. Dick got his camera ready first and eased down into a rocky gully to stalk the bear. I was coming about a hundred yards behind him, when he came out in the open about that same distance from the bear. The grizzly saw him, stood up briefly to look him over, and then proceeded at a fast walk straight toward the camera. Obviously the bear did not recognize what he was looking at, for curiosity stood out all over him. But the closer he got, the more uncertain and angry he became. The hair rose all along his back till it stood up like a badly trimmed hedge, and his expression became belligerent. At about forty feet he swung sideways and veered off a bit downwind. When Dick's scent struck his nose, he registered surprise and plainly did not enjoy it. With obvious intent he swung back around to the sweet side of the wind, decided the whole business was beneath further notice, and began to feed on berries again.

Meanwhile, crouched behind his camera and making no motion whatever except for a slight swing to track the bear, Dick never stopped taking footage. In this one long sequence he obtained some of the most dramatic material we collected. It was rare film in that it showed a grizzly coming at close range, displaying uncertainty and anger; but all aspects of the incident were in control, and this makes it rarer still. It is an outstanding example of the possible association between a grizzly and men, a significance of great importance that will likely be missed by most who see the film. Dick's pictures of this bear were the result of cool nerve and determination, a characteristic that I failed to emulate on this occasion.

Turning to me as I came up to him, Dick asked, "Did you get that?"

"No," I confessed. "I was paralyzed!"

For exploration of the unknown this kind of association with the big bears could not be surpassed. It was purely fascinating. Never could it become boring drudgery. No two encounters were ever alike for the simple reason that no two bears were alike, and even individuals react to their mood of the moment. Even though we had all grown up in the wilds and worked with animals all our lives, the grizzlies tossed us the greatest challenge we have ever encountered. It was not enough just to be able to get the best possible pictures with the cameras; we perforce had to study each individual to some extent in order to portray it successfully on film. We came to know some individuals by sight and, generally speaking, what reaction to expect of them at our approach.

For our convenience in identifying them we even gave them names. There was Blondie, the playful one with the two-year-old cub; and Toklat Joe, the big bear of amiable disposition that Dick filmed successfully. There was Nitchie, the big, light-colored female with the twin yearlings; and another bear we called Grumpy, with a temper like a buzz saw—a bear I did not trust as far as I could have thrown him by a hind foot.

These bears were the ones we saw most often, and likely they came to know us, a condition of minor importance, but one that may have helped create the more neutral atmosphere desired for photographic work.

One morning while Charlie was away up toward Igloo Creek investigating a wolf kill, our friend Charlie Travers, the Park Ranger located at the Toklat Station, came in from patrol and reported seeing a grizzly with cubs just a little way from camp. Dick and I loaded the movie cameras and went to investigate.

Up along the Toklat on a bench below a steep, twenty-foot terrace we found Nitchie and her cubs feeding on berries among some low willows and birches. For perhaps half an hour we moved along very slowly above her, shooting film of the family activities through various lengths of lenses. Then another big bear came out of the willows across the river straight toward Nitchie's berrypatch.

This was a definite breach of grizzly ethics, which Nitchie frowned upon decidedly. The cubs were obviously schooled not to trust other grizzlies, for they showed consternation at the approach of the outsider, none other than old Toklat Joe. The she-grizzly was in something of a dilemma, for she was caught between us and the intruder from across the river. We were somewhat surprised to see her move closer to us, until she was directly below.

We were treated to a rare opportunity to film a series of sequences recording this unusual and largely unacceptable competition for the same berrypatch. Nitchie did not at first make any hostile moves toward her ursine visitor, but she carefully kept herself between him and the cubs while she continued to feed. As he fed, he moved toward her, pushing her up closer and closer to us. The cubs were in a fever of excitement and worry. They paid us not the slightest attention but alternately reared to look at the visting bear. Once I saw one flatten out behind a bush with its nose pressed on its front paws, obviously trying to hide. Sometimes they tried to walk on their hind feet and inevitably fell to all fours.

While the mother did not appear to be watching us, Dick triggered her into a rush on two occasions by winding his camera too fast. These short charges were little but a bid for more room, for she returned instantly to the cubs.

Then, as I expected, she ran out of patience. Like a flash of light she suddenly pivoted on her heels and charged the old boar. About seventy-five yards separated them, and she covered it at top speed. Through the camera lens I could see him bracing himself and setting his hind feet in a solid toe hold to meet a horrific collision. But at the last instant the angry sow checked, and though she refrained from hitting him, she put her nose up close to his and cussed him out in tones that dripped of pending violence. It was one of those times when all living things within earshot paused to listen and feel the vibrations of tension. Toklat Joe wisely rode out the crisis by not moving a muscle or making a sound. But when she finally backed off and returned to her cubs, he turned away grumbling and mumbling to himself, as though saving face by muttering threats of murder and mayhem had she made one more sound.

We were much impressed by her obvious desire to go to almost any length to avoid a fight. She had been subjected to a most unusual and worrying situation in which she had every excuse either to tangle with the intruding grizzly or to put the run on us. But she had contrived to solve her problem without violence in consideration of the safety of her cubs—a definite tribute to her intelligence and a grizzly characteristic we came to admire more and more.

Dick and I returned to camp with some excellent film exposed. As most of our film and time was used up, it was time for us to leave on the long road home. We had enjoyed some views into the secret places of grizzly life, perhaps most impressive for what they showed that still remained to be seen. We knew by the width of the vista opened to us the great scope of exploration still to be done. We were determined to return.

13. Return to the Toklat

Just as the grizzly was in the beginning the lure that drew me to the wilderness, so now, to my mind, he remains the grandest animal our country knows.
—WILLIAM H. WRIGHT

It was early June the following spring when we pulled off the trail in the cold, blue twilight of the northern evening and rolled out our beds under some gaunt cottonwoods on the edge of the tundra hills of Alaska. Here and there new green leaves were just beginning to break from the buds of the willows and cottonwoods, as though reluctant to brave the cold winds and lowering clouds. Winter had only taken a step or two in retreat, and it still showed its gleaming teeth among the high hills ahead of us as though of half a mind to come back.

There were twenty-two hundred fifty miles and six days of dust, frost heaves, mud, and hard driving behind us. There were still three hundred miles to go before we could set our tent once more on the Toklat River, and by the look of the high country they were going to be tough miles. We were bone tired as we eased down into the warm, feathery softness of our sleeping robes.

After we broke camp early next morning, we drove straight into winter. The lakes on the high tundra were still frozen solid.

The whole country above timberline was one vast waste of deep snow. The newly plowed highway was little more than a rock- and ice-strewn track winding through freezing slush, water, and chuckholes, which slowed our sturdy Land Rover down to a grinding crawl. Sometimes we could not see a quarter mile through the blizzard of blowing snow, that felt as though it came straight from the polar icecap.

Finally dropping down into lower ground near McKinley Park headquarters, we were cheered to leave the snow behind and come into into country beginning to green up. When we reached the Toklat River campsite after ten hours of hard driv- ing, we found ourselves back on the edge of winter again; but we were happy, for it was like coming home.

While putting the finishing touches on setting up camp the following morning, I saw something dark-colored moving in the brush away out on the tundra flats across the river. The binocu- lars revealed a big female grizzly with two yearling cubs. A light-colored spot high on the shoulder of a mountain beyond was another mother grizzly with two small first-year cubs. Even at extreme range their long, luxuriant coats were evident and shone like silver in the sun.

The whole country was moving with game. The big allu- vial flats and lower slopes of the mountains were alive with caribou restlessly grazing and moving from place to place, then lying down to chew their cuds. There were hundreds of these animals in sight—the leading ranks of the coming migration, as yet not fixed in its purpose or direction. Contrasting sharply with the caribou and mixed with them here and there on the mountain slopes were bunches of snow-white dall sheep, the rams mag- nificent in their unshed winter coats. Through this gathering of the cloven-hoofed ones the grizzlies moved, a powerful, dramatic facet of life in this subarctic land.

Their relationship with the caribou was not altogether peaceful at this time of year, for the cows were just moving off the calving grounds up on the Teklanika River. The easy pick- ings among newborn calves were past, for they were growing fast and were now active enough to outrun a bear; but some of the grizzlies did not know it yet.

One morning shortly after our arrival on the dripping tail of a nightlong downpour of rain we woke to find it capped by a blizzard whose big sticky flakes threatened to flatten our tent with their weight. Permafrost was still so close to the surface that we had done little more than make slight dents in our efforts to dig drainage channels, which were now plugged with snow and running over. A two-foot-wide stream was running through the middle of the tent past our beds. We made breakfast with our boots scrunching in three inches of wet black muck. While Charlie and I set about putting the camp in some order not quite so reminiscent of a beaver lodge, Dick took advantage of a slight lifting of the storm to go up onto Jaeger Pass with the cameras.

At a point about a half mile from the summit he was standing just under a solid overcast obscuring the mountains and the top of the pass. Away down a big twisted draw toward the Toklat he suddenly spotted three caribou—a cow, a yearling, and a calf—running up toward him at top speed. Then around a bend of the creek a hundred yards behind them came a grizzly in hot pursuit. Obviously he had caribou calf in mind for breakfast but was having a hard time even getting a good smell of it.

When the caribou passed along the slope under Dick, they were running easily with a lengthening lead. Then the grizzly went by at top speed in long bounds. Every jump was punctuated by a great breath—whoosh—whoosh —whoosh—and every few jumps the bear dropped his head to scoop up a flying mouthful of cooling snow. He was persistent even though far behind and going by scent. The last Dick saw of him as he disappeared into the clouds, he was still running hard, although all he was likely to get was an even keener appetite and sore feet.

The grizzlies, as usual, were almost continuously on the move. They seemed particularly restless, probably due to the breeding season combined with sharp appetites after the long winter of fasting. They followed their noses from one interesting smell to another, spending most of their time grazing or digging roots. We recognized individuals moving from Sable Pass to Thoroughfare Pass, a distance of ten or twelve miles, in three or four days. As they moved, we also moved back and forth through this great studio, forty miles long and ten miles wide.

Although their long winter coats changed their looks a bit, we were able to recognize some bears known the previous summer. I was sitting on a bench overlooking the wide gravel bars of the East Fork River one day when out from behind the projecting snout of a bank strolled a big sow with twin two-year-old cubs. It was old Nitchie and her family. Within an hour of this spot we found Toklat Joe, looking bigger and more whiskery than ever, with his chewed-up ears now well camouflaged by fur. Blondie's cub was a three-year-old this year, and he had been turned loose to fare for himself. Several times we saw a bear closely resembling the playful one of the previous summer; but now that she had joined the fraternity of childless females and was ranging alone, it was difficult to be sure; for wheat-straw colored coats are not uncommon in that country. Dick suspected that the optimistic one seen chasing the caribou was her cub.

Wandering the country watching these and other bears was like being among old friends, although the grizzlies showed little inclination to join us in that thought. We were still intruders, tolerated in part but allowed few liberties. We conducted ourselves accordingly. However we moved with more confidence among them now, for we had learned something of their ways, as well as having acquired a smattering of the manners expected of us in grizzly society. We had come to have a real liking for the big bears, and our fascination with their ways was even keener.

It is necessary to like an animal subject if one is going to collect good picture records of it and look into its life with a true perspective. Although it is still impossible to prove or disprove at this point, I am convinced that animals have extrasensory perception—a kind of sixth sense also known to humans, but latent in us because of lack of use except in some primitives. Living season after season with grizzlies and bighorn sheep, as we have done, there were times when a certain subtle communication seemed to exist wherein we were granted certain liberties and a measure of trust far beyond ordinary human—wild animal relationship. As a result we gained opportunities to know them better and work at close range. These were the rewards for going a fumbling, uncertain step or two past the timeworn beliefs and prejudices and overcoming some fear of the grizzly.

Sometimes I stood and marveled at how I could have lived so long in wilderness country and learned so little.

For a long time it was thought that all grizzlies weaned their cubs at two years and that these did not den with their mothers again. Adolph Murie did not agree, and from evidence we encountered there was good reason to think this wrong, at least in northern latitudes. Now old Nitchie proceeded to show us the fact.

We were watching her one morning up near the foot of Polychrome Mountain as she and her family were poking around a bench meadow feeding on grass. The cubs were busy a few yards to one side when some signal seemed to pass from the mother; for they went to her immediately, and she squatted for them to nurse. The weight of their enthusiasm bowled her over flat on her back, where she looked a bit overwhelmed and out-numbered under an enthusiastic mound of young grizzlies weigh-ing close to one hundred and fifty pounds apiece. On several other occasions thereafter we saw them nurse, and although we made no record of the time lapses between feeds, she undoubt-edly fed them several times each day.

We were able to compare three different ages of cubs following their mothers and nursing regularly. There seems to be good reason to believe that the cubs suckle all winter. What else would prevent the mammary glands from drying up? How the mother succeeds in making up for the consequent dehydra-tion without drinking is truly a mystery. It will likely remain such, for grizzly bears are light sleepers and undoubtedly would take exception to anyone prying into their dens.

This was June, the mating season for grizzlies, and we were particularly keen to record as much of this little-known phase of their lives as possible. We had heard that grizzlies return periodically to the same locality for their love-making ritual, which lasts day after day for a week or more, and that we would have little difficulty seeing them if we could locate such a trysting place. Perhaps we dealt with particularly restless non-conformists, or maybe the cool weather had something to do with it, but this did not prove to be the case.

Our first sight of a mating pair was up on Sable Pass,

where we watched a light-colored female being escorted by a big, rusty-colored male for some time one afternoon. Perhaps their courtship was on one side or the other of the peak of ardor, for their activity was limited to keeping company, at least as long as we were able to watch them.

This male is worthy of mention, for he was a rarity, a cripple with a totally stiffened front leg. The bear carried this leg bowed out at the elbow with the toes turned in, and the whole lower leg below the shoulder blade seemed to be solidified in the joints. Adolph Murie told me that he had observed this lame bear for several seasons and thought that he had originally been injured by a very heavy dose of porcupine quills. Whatever caused the injury, this was a tough, unprepossessing-looking grizzly, but he did not seem to suffer much discomfort from his bad leg.

The weather was cold and wet during most of the mating season, allowing for limited observation. No doubt if it had been warm and dry, the pursuits across the valley flats would have been much shorter because of heavy winter coats and a resulting shortness of breath.

Charlie and I watched one mating pair running and walking aimlessly in great loops and tangents for over an hour one day on the naked gravel of the Toklat bottoms. In that time they must have traveled at least five miles, and when they finally disappeared away upriver, they were still going at a good clip with the female in the lead as usual, just as coy and hard to catch as she was at the beginning.

The following morning we spotted this same pair about a mile above our camp. Shortly after we focused our binoculars on them, the boar reared and coupled with the female without any preamble or ceremony. The copulation lasted for over twenty minutes, and then both bears disappeared into a wash full of willows—no doubt suffering from tender feet.

When we were trying to come within camera range of courting bears, we were very much aware of their ground-eating stride and complete disregard of the kind of country ahead. When a grizzly appears to be just strolling along, a man has to go almost at long trot to keep up unless his crotch is a long way from the ground. Even Charlie and Dick, who went like grey-hounds trying to keep the mating pairs in sight, had small success unless their quarry chose to stop. I found myself wishing for a horse.

When in top bear country looking for bears and striving for those unusual and significant shots so necessary to illustrate the beauty and drama of the subject in the film story, anything can happen and sometimes does with amazing suddenness. One evening we were standing in front of the tent after supper, and I spotted a big light-colored grizzly out on the bars.

"Here comes a bear," I announced, "and it looks like Blondie."

"Two bears," corrected Dick. "The boy friend looks like old Grumpy."

Sure enough, a big, darker-colored animal had just ap-peared from behind a stringer of brush fifty yards to the rear, and he did have the look of our erstwhile bad-tempered acquaint-ance of the previous summer.

The bears were about a half mile out on the open bars across the braided channels of the Toklat. The sky was breaking in the west after a cold, miserable day of wind and rain, and the light was strong enough for pictures. I had just finished clean-ing and checking out one of the cameras, which was mounted on a cradle supporting the big 500 mm. lens, now screwed down solidly on a tripod. So I grabbed it and headed out in the hope of getting a shot or two of this mating pair.

The big lens is a heavy, cranky combination only used on occasions like this, and it is not blithely shouldered for a day's climbing on speculation of finding use for it. Its twenty-power magnification on a 16 mm. camera has its good points, but these include no kind of magic. The most effective range is somewhere inside three hundred yards, depending on the nature of the subject involved. So I headed out at a trot for a mount of gravel at about this range from where I hoped to intercept the grizzlies.

It seemed I had barely got under way, when the bears crossed in front of me; but they pulled up to investigate some old bear diggings on the far edge of the gravel bars. Blondie was still in the lead, and when she came close to a nesting colony of short-billed gulls, they set up a great crying and began swooping and diving at her. This was just the beginning of a chain of the most maddening frustrations.

With the low sun backlighting their brilliant white wings, the gulls took turns wheeling high and then peeling off in sizzling dives ending in a zoom right over the bear's head. I was gritting my teeth at missing this tremendous shot, when Blondie chose to heap more frustration on my head by rearing and swatting at the birds with her enormous paws. Grinding my teeth in utter despair and muttering imprecations at the size of the cannon I was carrying, I plunged ahead, hoping to get some pictures before the show was over. The footing out there did not help; it was something like trying to run across a field of loose bowling balls.

In the meantime Grumpy became extremely busy with something in the low brush on the edge of the tundra, and when he picked it up in his mouth, I saw that it was a dead caribou calf. At this point Blondie apparently decided there was no future in trying to play badminton with flying sea gulls, and she began circling back toward her mate. The wind must have given his selfish activities away, for she suddenly stiffened, threw up her head, and then went straight to him. Without a bit of ceremony and notwithstanding the fact that he was bigger, she immediately challenged him for the dead calf.

Grumpy may have been in love. He might have backed off a bit, even if reluctantly. He could have at least offered to share the deadfall with her, but he did nothing of the kind. He reared up and swore at her in tones that carried clear to camp, where Dick and Charlie were watching through a spotting scope. The unimpressed Blondie also reared and roared right back and promptly clamped her teeth over the end of his lower jaw; whereupon they proceeded to flail each other unmercifully with their big front paws. Their roaring rang off the mountains, and great wads of hair flew in every direction. It was a fight to scare the little animals into hunting their holes and the big ones into attention. It was truly awful.

By sheer weight Grumpy forced his opponent over on her back, but this only multiplied his difficulties; for now he was up against four raking paws instead of two. They rolled and swore and bit and clawed, while I ran desperately trying to get into range.

Grumpy did his best to trade more than he got, but his best was not good enough. Blondie still had her hold on his lower jaw. The punishment was too much for him, and he suddenly broke free with a torn ear dripping blood, more gore running from a foot-long slash down one shoulder, and a cant to his lower jaw as though it might be broken. Throwing a glowering glance after her departing suitor, Blondie proceeded to clean up the remains of the calf.

My efforts had gone for nothing; things had happened too fast for me to get anything but a short shot of her feeding on the prize after I came into camera range. If those two grizzlies had taken lessons on how best to frustrate a photographer, they could not have done a better job.

Happily not all our efforts ended so dismally. One of the preferred shots on our list was a series of close-ups of a bear or bears. Up on the slopes of the East Fork, Dick and I got our chance one day. We spotted Nitchie and her cubs grazing on a patch of lush grass, and again we made a stalk with the Big Bertha lens rigged on camera and tripod.

Old Nitchie was in a mood to ignore us. By moving slow and easy, we came down from above across the green velvet carpet of tundra to within seventy-five feet of her and the cubs. What intrigued us was her control over the cubs. We could see their eyes roll as they watched us, yet because their mother chose to ignore us, they followed her lead.

Through the big lens Nitchie's profile more than filled the viewfinder. I could identify the herbage she was eating, and I could clearly see the flash of yellow tusks. Completely engrossed with the operation of the cameras, we failed to notice some danger signals.

At first the grizzlies were feeding on a particularly desirable patch of grass, paying us no attention as they worked around a spot about seventy-five feet away. Old Nitchie's desire to ignore us during this stage of the game went so far that she lay down with her nose on her paws and her tail toward us as though for a nap. One cub came to her and lay with its head on her side, using her for a cushion. Then they worked around us till they were about fifty feet downslope from Dick and about twenty-five yards aslant from me. Dick was swiftly and smoothly operating the still camera when Nitchie's feeding began to slow up. Several times she stood broadside and lifted her head up and gazed away off at nothing in particular. Why we failed to note these danger signals along with the almost imperceptible flattening of her ears can only be because of our complete absorption in getting some rare material.

With a snort she suddenly whirled and rushed Dick with both big cubs flanking her. We barked at her in one voice to stop, which she did, but she was of no mind to turn. For a few long moments she and Dick faced each other, and she was the picture of thinly controlled menace with fire burning in her eyes.

"Back this way slow and easy," I said softly. "Give her room to go up the mountain."

Dick eased away from in front of her, and as is usually the way, she took the opportunity to break off the argument in a face-saving manner. With no further show of belligerence she and the cubs moved up the mountain, where they again fed, paying us no more attention. We left her there, perfectly happy to let good enough alone. Later, when we viewed the films taken of this episode, we were astonished to see how obvious her danger signals had been. She had given us plenty of time to move out before she finally charged. Keen interest and concentration can be a danger in themselves when getting pictures of a grizzly mother and cubs.

There was another grizzly mother using the Toklat flats. She had two yearling cubs, beautiful little bears with fur so long and silky it could be seen blowing and rippling in the wind. She was a stranger. Because she was so typical of the color of the northern type, we called her Tananna.

One afternoon, following a hard shower, Dick and Charlie got the chance to try for some pictures of her as she and her family were digging roots on the big flat directly across from camp. Dick was busy rigging the big lens on one camera, while Charlie took the other and went ahead to try some medium-range shots with the 150 mm. telephoto.

There was a steady crosswind blowing. The bears were feeding among some waist-high willows and birches when Charlie reached a spot about 120 yards from them and shot what remained of a roll of film in the camera. Using his rain parka as an improvised shade, he proceeded to reload. While he was thus occupied, Tananna spotted a parka sleeve flapping in the wind and reared to inspect it. Her eyes told her very little except that this strange-looking apparition had not been there before; so she began to circle downwind of it for a reading with her nose.

Meanwhile Charlie finished reloading, and when he pulled the parka aside, she was striding around him with the cubs trailing at her heels. Seeing an opportunity to record her reaction when she got his scent, he lined up the lens on a spot directly downwind and waited for her to walk into the view finder.

The camera hid her from his sight as he stood hunched over it with a finger cocked on the trigger. When she failed to appear in the lens, he lifted his head to look just in time to see her coming like the wind with her mouth wide open and her ears flattened out against her head. The fishtailing wind had given his scent away sooner than expected, and instead of running, as most grizzlies do upon striking man smell, she charged.

There is no more lonely place on earth than out on a breezy tundra flat with a grizzly coming in a wide-open, flat-out charge. Charlie did what we had done on such occasions before. He anchored his feet, facing her, until she was only about twenty yards away and close enough to hear him. Then he stepped toward her.

"Ho!" he snapped out the command as though on military parade.

Tananna did not check her stride, but she swerved and led the cubs away up the slope of the mountain.

Tananna was as handsome as she was disconcerting. She wore a golden, honey-colored mantle over her shoulders and flanks that blended into the dark brown of her legs and feet. She was in magnificent condition, gleaming in the sun like pale, burnished gold. She was very possessive about her cubs and very much afraid of us—a most dangerous combination that caused her to show fight almost invariably when we approached. We respected her from the depth and profoundness of a certain fear of our own. We admired her, for she was a beautiful bear and a brave and admirable mother who put her cubs' safety before everything.

One day we caught her and the cubs in a striking sequence as they crossed the Toklat, quartering past us. To enhance the picture the bears passed a yearling caribou going the other way so close that all four animals were in the finder at once. The caribou gave them a curious look, but the bears did not spare it a glance. They came up the bank downstream a hundred yards below and headed for the broken slope of rock behind a band of cottonwoods and willows just back of us. Dick and Charlie moved fast to circle behind this screen, where they could shoot more pictures of the grizzlies climbing the rocks. While in the brush they could not see the bears, but I noticed the trio change direction toward the boys. Consequently they came out on the far side much closer to the cameras than anticipated. Immediately the hair rose over Tananna's shoulders, but for once she did not charge. One of the cubs overrode this bit of tolerance by spotting the photographers and going curiously toward them. Tananna changed her mind in a twinkling and charged. A sharp yell from one of the boys did not stop her. She kept coming until she reached the cub, whereupon she shouldered it to turn it back, slapped it on its way, and then followed—looking back over a shoulder and whuffing angrily as she went. Tananna was explosive.

It is utterly impossible to study and work with grizzlies in the wilderness without being aware of the life patterns in the intricate and often mysterious ecological tapestry.

We saw the long-tailed jaeger dive in a spectacular display of aerial acrobatics at a passing golden eagle flying over the alpine basin where the black and white predatory gulls were nesting. Like Tananna, these birds entertain a feeling of fierce possession, which they even vented on her when she chose to travel too close to their nesting site. They dived at us, too, when we moved in to film them, even going so far as to rap Dick smartly on the head with their feet.

It would be hard to find species more diametrically opposed in habit than bears, men, eagles, and long-tailed jaegers; yet the jaegers chose to tie us all together. While the association was not always one of tolerance, who could say for certain that we were not sometimes dependent on each other in some inconspicuous ways? We were all a part of the pattern in those mountains, joining at the moment in making a film record that might serve in some small way to add to men's knowledge, thus serving to bring possible mutual benefit to all.

We were being continually reminded of the throbbing power of the life surrounding us day and night. One morning we woke to find the Toklat flats swarming with caribou, all heading toward the McKinley River and the summer grounds beyond, walking, trotting, and sometimes even galloping in a steady, mile-eating gait. The great migration accompanied itself with the clicking of hooves across the gravel and tundra. This exodus was not a solid river of animals but rather a flowing chain of herds numbering from a few dozen to hundreds. They moved along the bottoms, climbed over incredibly rough summits, and traversed the slopes in between.

Away up on a shoulder of a steep mountain above Thoroughfare Pass we saw a bunch of about five hundred young bulls standing in a solid swarm on the forty-five-degree pitch of a big snowdrift fighting flies. They stood stoically enduring with their heads down close to the cool snow, and it seemed nothing could stir them from their weariness. Then over the ridge back of them came a lone bull at a wild gallop trying to escape the stinging flies. He panicked the whole herd, and they went rushing off with a great clatter of hoofs across the snow and down the serpentine spine of a ridge to the valley floor. Out on the broad flats they mingled with another herd and swept away down the Thoroughfare River to the McKinley.

On the two-mile-wide gravel bars of the upper McKinley, above the snout of the Muldrow Glacier, we caught up to them again, now joined with the main herd, and filmed acres of caribou standing so thick in places that the gravel did not show through between. On one occasion I estimated roughly over a thousand head showing in my camera viewfinder at one time.

This is one of nature's great spectacles, reminding us of historical descriptions of the great herds of buffalo on the plains in the old days. Within a few days we saw between six and nine thousand head of caribou. Through these herds, as they had among the buffalo, the grizzlies moved; but here the species were on easier terms.

Old age and accident claimed victims among the caribou, and the grizzlies laid claim to these with their usual relish for carrion. At no time did we see the smallest evidence of a grizzly killing caribou, although they often hijacked the wolf kills. With their uncanny noses they could find a wolf kill while it was still warm.

Through the long daylight hours of the northern summer, among islands of sunshine and storm, we wandered like carefree boys through this great natural circus, sometimes laughing at sheer comedy and again catching our breaths at the beauty and the stark drama that sometimes unfolded before us. We did not know from one minute to the next what we would encounter. It was a real wilderness kaleidoscope of color and action.

One bright morning we were lying prone in the warm sun looking down from a ridge crest over the broad reaches of the upper Moose Creek valley. Overhead the white clouds ran, tossing their manes, like wild horses at play in the blue pastures of sky. In front of us, scattered in bunches across the huge basin, were caribou feeding and loafing, enjoying a breeze that kept flies and mosquitoes inactive.

Suddenly I was startled to see a big, white-colored animal moving in some brush a couple of miles away across the valley. At first I thought it was an albino bull moose that we had seen lower down near the mouth of Moose Creek the previous year; but when it finally moved out into a clearing, it proved to be a grizzly. We watched this unusual animal for over an hour as it climbed and fed its way straight up and over the mountain range beyond.

For several days we prowled this part of the country trying to find this grizzly again, but apparently it had disappeared among the peaks beyond our reach.

Then one morning when I was sitting on a promontory along the banks flanking the McKinley River, a slight flicker of something on the move caught my eye about two miles downstream. I swung the binoculars to it, and there was the white grizzly coming my way along the foot of the bank on which I was sitting. But then to my chagrin the bear turned out across the river's multichanneled bed toward the snowy peaks of the Alaska Range. He practically walked through several bunches of caribou, and I could almost taste the disappointment of missing another chance to shoot him with the camera. As though reading my mind and relenting, the bear suddenly turned again and came straight toward me. Apparently he was out for an aimless stroll this morning, just following his questing nose.

He finally disappeared into the mouth of a steep ravine about halfway to the Muldrow Glacier, whereupon I picked up my camera and headed out to try for some footage of him. It was an optimistic jaunt, well larded with footwork, millions of mosquitoes, and sweat. For two hot hours that bear and I went like sin at a church warden's convention. We never quite lost each other, but somehow we never came any closer to getting acquainted. At the start the bear was about a mile ahead of me, and when I finally gave up the pursuit for want of leg muscle to keep up the fierce pace, the bear was still about a mile away— and we were both not far from where we started.

I took up a position on the breezy end of a low ridge near the mouth of a little valley emptying out onto the flats, and sat down to watch him.

If ever there was an absolutely aimless and completely carefree bear, this was the animal. He poked his nose into countless bushes without seeming to pause to investigate whatever he found. Several times he started what looked like the beginning of a nonstop marathon to the Arctic coast, but soon he turned back. He jumped nesting ptarmigan and chased ground squirrels in a most light-hearted fashion, but he caught none. Finally, as I had been hoping, he came straight toward me and turned up a little creek about one hundred fifty yards below my stand.

Through the nine-power glasses I examined him closely. The pelt was not pure white but a pale cream. This was no albino, as we first thought, for the eyes were dark. Somehow I got the impression that it was a male, although as usual I confess to more than considerable guesswork.

The camera was just trained on him with the focus screwed down to razor sharpness, when suddenly he came to a rigid stop with one front paw uplifted, like a pointer dog fastened on a covey of birds. Thinking he had located a ground squirrel, I waited with trigger finger cocked for instant action. The bear remained frozen, moving not a whisker, for an interminable half minute or so while a thousand mosquitoes took advantage of a lull in the breeze to bore into my back as I was hunched over the camera. I endured their drilling for as long as possible, and then I straightened up slightly to throw some slack into my shirt. At that instant the grizzly banged the ground smartly with his paw and whirled away in the same motion. To my utter amazement a fine, fully-grown caribou bull exploded out of the willow clump that had been just under the bear's nose and galloped up the creek. The grizzly turned to watch the caribou go, and as though delighted with his own joke, reared back against a low bank and playfully waved his paws. Meanwhile the surprised bull turned to look at the bear. Then with his ridiculous tail hoisted at a jaunty angle, he came prancing back down the creek and stopped, facing the bear at about twenty yards. There they stood for a few moments, gazing at each other in an amiable fashion, until the caribou suddenly jumped away to the side and headed for the river. Without another glance after him the grizzly came up into the draw below me to feed and loaf among some little meadows.

This was a revealing experience. Here was a grizzly, likely

weighing in the vicinity of six hundred pounds, that had spent a good half minute within ten feet of a sleeping bull caribou. He could have leaped on the animal and killed it with the same ease that a wolf would kill a rabbit, yet he had chosen deliberately to spook the caribou and let it go. More than ever I was convinced that some grizzlies never learn to kill anything bigger than a caribou calf.

Making a new grizzly acquaintance and studying its individual characteristics was always an intensely interesting experience full of unknowns; they are just as individualistic as people. One does not just walk up to a strange grizzly and introduce himself. Unless you enjoy living dangerously, the introduction is subtle and patient; and even then one is never sure what the reception will be. Unlike meeting humans, it is better and far more rewarding to be loftily ignored in grizzly society.

We will never forget Sultana. We named her after the original Indian name for Mount Foraker, a seventeen-thousand-foot peak close by Mount McKinley. Foraker was known as Sultana in the old days, meaning "The Woman" or "The Wife"—the mate to Denali, the Indian name for Mount McKinley that means "The Great One." The white man's arrogance and egotism in changing these names is not admirable; for no man, not even a president of the United States, deserves such a mountain to carry his name. It is in very bad taste, but this is apart from my story.

I first met the bear Sultana up along a little tributary of the East Fork River across from Polychrome Mountain. She was a huge, old, chocolate-colored grizzly with a tiny, almost black cub gamboling at her heels. I took plenty of time working in close enough to her for pictures, for mother grizzlies with new cubs are particularly touchy.

Keeping the wind in my favor, I eased closer and closer. I probably took at least an hour to go a hundred yards. I was encouraged, for several times when I was sure she could see me, she paid me not the slightest heed.

I was wearing a waterproof nylon rain parka and pants instead of the usual soft cotton jeans and buckskin jacket, for it had rained earlier and the brush was soaking wet. My sons inelegantly called these pants "whistle britches," and would sooner go wet than wear them. Right now I was heartily agreeing and wishing I had left them in camp, for at almost every step the brush scraped the cloth with enough noise to alert her. Finally she became so restive that she took the cub up across the bars onto a dry wash coming off the slope. It was puzzling, for she had paid practically no attention to the sight of me.

She was now in a much better position to stalk. Keeping the wind in my favor, I made a wide circle and came down the rocky wash from above. Free of the brush, it was now easy to go quietly, and I finally reached a spot about fifty yards from her when a rock rolled a bit under a boot sole. This tiny noise instantly galvanized her into hair-trigger annoyance. But even though my clothing was in sharp contrast to background, she still failed to locate me exactly. However she was angry and upset enough to go stalking away with her hair standing on end into a patch of head-high willows, where I had no inclination to follow.

The next day we located her again farther up the valley and spent considerable time watching her. Again she was sensitive to noise but failed to bristle up when we were in plain sight. We finally realized that she was almost totally blind. Once we were aware of this, it was necessary only to be very careful with the wind and equally quiet to obtain good film records of her.

Again and again we went to watch this great bear, and somehow she became one of the most fascinating grizzlies we knew. Perhaps it was her size and the fact that she was a blind mother with the responsibility of a tiny cub not much bigger than one of her massive paws. Maybe it was because she was so devoted to her offspring, around which her world revolved. To be sure, she shed more light on the admirable character of the grizzly.

Several times we saw her suckle the cub. The gentle loving motions she displayed during this procedure, the hallmark of mother love among most all warm-blooded creatures, was enough to make a man swear never to kill another grizzly. At intervals of about one and a half hours Sultana would leave off whatever she was doing and half rear and spin on her heels to go over backward on the ground. She would hardly be flattened out before the cub would land ecstatically on the vast expanse of hairy bosom and grab a tit while she caressed it with gentle muzzle and paws. The cub would move from one dug to another until all were sucked dry; and then they would play a while, with the young one galloping and bucking up and down her belly, smelling noses, and playfully swatting with paws. Sometimes she would cut this off by abruptly standing up and spilling the cub to the ground. Sometimes they would drop into a short sleep. Once I found them dead to the world, the mother lying on her back with all four paws outstretched and the cub lying on his belly sound asleep on the middle of hers.

One of the desired sequences on our preferred shot list was of a grizzly mother suckling her cubs. We recorded this scene at long range and now hoped to get a close-up. The chance came one afternoon while we were watching Sultana in some fairly heavy brush at the foot of a mountain slope. Suddenly she moved off, heading up behind a knoll. Instantly Charlie was on the move, swinging his camera up onto his shoulder.

"She's going to feed the cub up in that hollow behind that point," Charlie said. "I'm going to make a try for it."

"She might hear the camera," I cautioned, for he was going to be very close.

"There's enough wind to blank it out," he assured me as he headed out.

There are moments in a musician's life when the notes leap from his instrument as pure and perfect as music can be. The artist knows times when his brush seems to guide his hand into painting better than he knows. There are also moments in a nature photographer's life when he is at one with his subject and the whole country. The light of the sun is his magic, the film is his canvas, and the camera is his instrument—golden inspiration stirs his heart. Then he can do no wrong and is truly the artist. To watch him in action in such an enchanted moment is something to remember. This was such a time for Charlie.

He went alone. Somehow, through willows as thick as fur,

he worked his way soundlessly up the back of the knoll. It was a grand piece of stalking, and when he reached the top, I saw him spread the tripod legs and plant the camera in one smooth motion.

No sooner was the camera trained than Sultana appeared on the edge of a little marshy clearing fifty feet below. Almost immediately she sagged back and spun on her heels, going over on her back. Whereupon the cub proceeded with a single-handed riot. If bears can smile, Sultana grinned from ear to ear with pure joy—a sort of bearish beam of pleasure and indulgence. The cub pulled and tugged, leaped from one dug to another, and left wet spots in her fur to mark the trail of his passing.

Just as he finished, the wind died and the whirring of the camera caught her ears. Instantly she leaped to her feet, the picture of vibrant explosive menace. For a long, long moment it seemed as though even the mountains held their breaths. Then she was gone.

Sultana was blind, but it is doubtful that she missed her eyes very much, for her ears and nose were as sharp as razors and told her most everything she wanted to know.

Inevitably the time came when we had to tear ourselves away from these idyllic mountains. It was our last night on the Toklat, and we were sleeping under the spruces in order to get an early start in the morning. Something woke me from a deep sleep, and when I looked at my watch I saw the hands pointing to midnight. The whole country was enveloped in that great northern stillness so deeply profound.

Through a gap in the trees over the mountains to the north the Great Bear, or Big Dipper, swung with its pointers zeroed on the Pole Star. I lay there snug in my robe, caught in the spell of the quiet, contemplating this group of stars and its related constellation, the Little Bear, and wondering at these ancient ties between bears and men.